Creole Language, Democracy, and the Illegible State in Cabo Verde

Creole Language, Democracy, and the Illegible State in Cabo Verde

Abel Djassi Amado

LEXINGTON BOOKS
Lanham • Boulder • New York • London

Published by Lexington Books
An imprint of The Rowman & Littlefield Publishing Group, Inc.
4501 Forbes Boulevard, Suite 200, Lanham, Maryland 20706
www.rowman.com
86-90 Paul Street, London EC2A 4NE

British Library Cataloguing in Publication Information Available

Library of Congress Cataloging-in-Publication Data Available

ISBN 978-1-66692-267-7 (cloth : alk. paper)
ISBN 978-1-66692-268-4 (electronic)

♾™ The paper used in this publication meets the minimum requirements of American National Standard for Information Sciences—Permanence of Paper for Printed Library Materials, ANSI/NISO Z39.48-1992.

Pa nha fidja-fémia, Kenya Maria
Pa sidadons di Kabu Verdi ki ta papia só Kriolu,
silensiadu pa kes ki sta na puleru

Contents

Preface

The idea to write about the politics of language and the language of politics in Cabo Verde first originated in the late 2000s when a heated and vibrant debate on the language question occurred among Cabo Verdeans in Cabo Verde and the diaspora. Around the time, the country was going through its second constitutional revision, which eventually was agreed upon by the two dominant parties: the then ruling party, the African Party for the Independence of Cabo Verde (PAICV); and the main opposition party, the Movement for Democracy (MpD). One of the most contentious points of discussion of the constitutional revision had to do with Article 9 of the Constitution, which defined the constitutional language policy of the republic. Unlike the previous debates on the language question, which had exponentially developed since independence in 1975, the 2009–2010 language debate was characterized by high intensity and extension, as the development of social media augmented the number of arenas of the debates and the actors involved.

The language question in Cabo Verde is that of a soft diglossia. Portuguese is the official language of the republic, and its use is almost absolute in the written realms of the state. Very few families use it in private circles, but it is a language learned through formal schooling. On the other hand, the national language, the Cabo Verdean language, a Portuguese-based Creole locally known as Kriolu, is the language of informality and intimate interactions among citizens. Portuguese is not the first language of the people of Cabo Verde. There is a clear and undisputable asymmetric relationship between Portuguese and Cabo Verdean insofar as the former is the language of prestige, power, and formal education.

Notwithstanding the asymmetric relationship between the two languages, the Cabo Verdean has made some inroads into domains that a few decades earlier were reserved for Portuguese. Thus, the Cabo Verdean language can be heard in the media (chiefly television broadcasts), parliamentary debates, and religious services. Yet, the sociolinguistic situation is still that of diglossia, as the written domain in all domains is almost exclusively Portuguese.

In this book, I critically examine politics and language nexus. My key contention is that a social scientific analysis of politics must inevitably pass through an examination of the language question and the overall sociolinguistic situation of the political unity under study. As a case study of Cabo Verde, the book offers many valuable insights to grasp how politics operate in the country. Additionally, it develops ideas and theories that can extrapolate the case of Cabo Verde and can help understand politics in postcolonial African and Caribbean countries. I decided to opt for a case study of Cabo Verde since I am a native of the country and, as such, can easily navigate the complex linguistic and social milieu.

This book is a written celebration of the Cabo Verdean language, with his track record of resisting past and current deniers of its modernizing and political quality. This language is yet to be entirely accepted as the state's official language. Instead of the traditional "Cape Verde," this book uses Cabo Verde as the country's name, as instructed by the Cabo Verdean government note from 2013—unless I am citing a primary source. In the same manner, all transcriptions in Cabo Verdean are done according to the ALUPEC rule.

Acknowledgments

I incurred invaluable intellectual debts in developing my arguments and writing this book. From Boston University, Timothy Longman, Edouard Bustin, Taylor C. Boas, and Michael Woldemariam have provided valuable suggestions that found their way into the current manuscript. Many graduate school colleagues from the Department of Political Science, Department of Anthropology, and African Studies Center made my social and intellectual journey bearable; these friends spent valuable time discussing theoretical topics and themes that shaped my overall ideas: Ceren Ergenc, Jinba Tenzin, Leonardo Schiocchet, Ahmet Tekelioglu, Ariana Huhn, Mustapha Hashim Kurfi, and Joseph Robinson. I also want to acknowledge the support given by Jennifer Yanco, who I worked with for many years at West African Research Association.

I am also indebted to the late Earl N. Smith III, a companion at the University of Rhode Island Study Abroad in Cabo Verde for several years. Brother Earl's insight and insistence on what he called "indigenous knowledge" guided and structured my thoughts while I was researching and writing this book. Similarly, my colleagues at the Cabo Verdean Center for Applied Research—Ambrizeth Lima, Dawna Thomas, Marlyse Baptista, and Lourenco Garcia—provided moral and intellectual support for this project. As we worked together to develop Cabo Verdean bilingual curricula, constant and thoughtful discussions, and conversations on language, linguistics, and bilingual education have exponentially expanded my horizon. My appreciation and profound gratitude also go to Kara McArthur, who tirelessly and patiently went through the earlier version of the manuscript providing insightful and valuable editing suggestions.

This project also benefited many individuals in Cabo Verde, who took time off their busy schedules to meet and converse with me on this research topic: the late Andre Corsino Tolentino (RIP), Ulisses Correia e Silva, Victor Borges, José Luis Hopffer Almada, and Manuel Veiga. I am also thankful to the staff of the Arquivo Nacional de Cabo Verde in Praia, particularly Sandra Rosa, whose professionalism and assistance facilitated the arduous processes of data browsing and collection. I am also indebted to an anonymous reviewer of the manuscript, whose insightful comments have enhanced the overall quality of the project.

I dedicate this book to my daughter, Kenya Maria, "Keke." Her presence has been truly inspiring and allowed me to go the extra mile toward finishing this project. This work has benefited enormously from my daughter's unconditional and ever-present love. Since I embarked on this journey, I have had a battalion of people behind me, pushing me to go forward and never backward. To all my family members—and my family is huge—my particular appreciation for believing in me. My mother, Maria Felícia, has been pivotal in this reserve army of supporters. Her unconditional love, support, and absolute belief in me have been the Polaris star that has guided me over the years. I am because of you, nha kumasita. The last—but most definitely not the least—my most profound appreciation goes to my wife, Hélia Resies. I am truly indebted to your patience and backing while I was "constantly absent," even at home. This book is now completed because of your unconditional support.

Introduction

On October 13, 2011, on *Conversa em Dia*, a television talk show from Televisão de Cabo Verde, the national television channel focusing on current social and political issues, the day's topic was fisheries and their social, economic, and environmental impact. In that episode, three individuals whose livelihood and professional lives revolved around the question of fisheries were invited as guest speakers and commentators: Esperança Riviera, representing a network of artisanal fisheries' community-based organizations (the Rede das Organizações Profissionais da Pesca Artesanal); Rafael Menezes, the president of a local fishermen's association (Associação Armadores Pescadores e Peixeira Praia Santa Maria); and Oscar Melício, president of the National Institute for the Development of Fisheries (INDP), an autonomous state agency. Portuguese was the communication language between the anchorwoman and the two invited speakers, Esperança Rivera and Oscar Melício. However, the Cabo Verdean language, a Portuguese-based Creole, was the choice for communication between the reporter and Rafael Menezes. The linguistic choice is an indication, or a marker, of social status and level of formal education.

Right at the beginning of the show, when Mr. Menezes was first allowed to speak, he went on to state,

> I would like if each one of us, who could speak in [Cabo Verdean] Creole, to speak in that language, for there are fishermen, there are our colleagues who . . . do not have much formal education . . . and who want to understand the easiest words [for us to have] not a beautiful show but something that [the fishermen] understands.[1]

Responding in Portuguese, the anchorwoman stated,

1

[a]bout the language question, our show is made for not only the fishermen but all Cabo Verdeans who are watching us and those who live abroad who speak Portuguese. Thus, the rule of the show has always been Portuguese and Creole. There is no problem here.

The anchorwoman did not get the point: Mr. Menezes wanted to amplify the realm of participation in this public debate. Mr. Menezes, as the representative of fishermen, the social stratum with the highest stakes in the issue of fisheries, wanted to eliminate intermediary elements in this debate. If the debate were all in the national language, the local fishermen would more easily get the gist of what the commentators were saying about something on which their livelihood depends. Mr. Menezes, as the president of the local fishermen's association, seems to have been primarily interested in opening the content of the debate to his colleagues. In so doing, the public debate would have included ordinary citizens from different aspects of life, particularly those with only a rudimentary level of knowledge and skills in the Portuguese language.

The situation is a good illustration of the extent to which language policy, including language practice, serves as an instrument to restrict the number of participants in the public debate, curtailing ordinary citizens' chances for furthering political education. That day's show is also an interesting example of the politics of inaudibility, a concept I discuss in chapter 4. Cabo Verdean Creole is a national language spoken throughout the country and by the Cabo Verdean diaspora throughout the Atlantic world. However, the mother tongue is yet to be recognized as a respectable idiom to be used in the official public sphere. The concept of politics of inaudibility, as I see it, is linked to political exclusion insofar as citizens who use only their mother tongue are kept outside the circle of politics. The voice of ordinary citizens who are not proficient or skillful in the country's official language, the language through which power formally manifests itself, is often unheard. In Cabo Verde, the official language (Portuguese), as the language of formal communication within the state, in institutions such as public administration, the court systems, and education, is not the everyday language of the overwhelming majority of citizens.

This book studies the language-politics nexus in a Creole island state. It weaves topics of sociolinguistics and sociology of language with political science to enhance understanding of the democratic experience in Cabo Verde. One of the book's core ideas is that democracy is better realized when people fully participate in all domains of the political businesses of the polity. That is to say, better political participation breeds more and better democracy. For this reason, the book moves away from the notion of electoral democracy. If democracy is, as the etymology implies, "the rule of the people," then citizens must act in all forms and stages of government, from the debate on policies to their making and implementation. The intensity and extent of citizen participation ultimately increase the quality of democracy.

Language policy can constitute a tool for social asymmetry since it reinforces the social dominance of a language that is alien to a great majority of the people. As such, it limits the intensity and extent of political participation. When the state and the social and political elite maintain a language derived from colonialism as the main—if not the only—language of public administration, education, judicial matters, and media, the political outcome is the alienation of the people. A linguistic wall is created around the state, making it impenetrable to ordinary, vernacular language speakers. Effective political participation in public debate, policymaking, and implementation is drastically reduced. With an eye on language policy, this book explains why most people do not actively engage in or feel fully involved in politics. Understanding the processes and hindrances to full political participation is a strategy to redress the situation. Democracy is a system in which citizens are "omnipresent" and can have their interests and dislikes heard throughout policymaking and implementation. Therefore, one must look at the language situation, the starting point of any political activity.

THEORETICAL FRAMEWORK:
THE LANGUAGE-POLITICS NEXUS

Language policy includes not only the written policy itself but also the planning stage. On this point, I am indebted to Thomas Ricento, who notes that he

> deliberately use[s] 'Language policy' as a superordinate term which subsumes, "language planning." Language policy research is concerned not only with official and unofficial acts of governmental and other institutional entities but also with the historical and cultural events and processes that have influenced, and continue to influence, societal attitudes and practices concerning language use, acquisition, and status.[2]

I understand language policy as including the actions and omissions of the state institutions and the context within which the debate on language takes place. Language policy entails rules and regulations emanating from the state and other critical dimensions, such as language practice and ideology.[3] These three elements mutually support and reinforce each other.

Language policy defines not only the actors but also the arena of politics. Yet, the lack of interest by political scientists in probing the interaction between language and politics has meant a scarcity of heuristic devices that can help advance our understanding of the phenomenon. Recently, sociolinguists and other scholars have developed many analytical concepts, such as linguistic human rights or linguicism, that can be employed to fully understand the intersection between language and politics.[4] These concepts are used to describe the raw nature of political regimes, democratic and non-democratic alike. These concepts have been pushed by theorists of multiculturalism, who argue that true democracy implies recognition of minority groups' particularities, including the use and practice of their language in public spheres.[5]

Language policy and planning have been defined as "[m]aking deliberate decisions about the form of a language."[6] To better understand the concept of language policy and planning, one must break down its constitutive elements: first, it is made up of two different stages, namely that of planning and that of the policy itself—as the term indicates. In language planning, there is the source of the process, often the state itself or an organism within the state (for instance, many modern states have either a ministry or a department whose fundamental task is to devise the language policy and planning). Additionally, language is the subject or the planned element. Finally, there is the target of the project policy, which in most cases coincides with the geographical boundary of the nation-state.

B. Jernudd and J. Das Gupta argue that language planning constitutes the "political and administrative activity for solving language problems in society."[7] The approach is top-down; through administrative and legal decisions, the state seeks to modify linguistic patterns and/or behaviors of the members of a given society. The verticality of language planning in form and content leads Einar Haugen to distinguish it from what he terms as language "happening," that is, "social movement without unifying control."[8] For Joshua Fishman, language planning is a top-down directive and, at the same time, *directional* and *justificational*: not only does it prescribe the routes to be taken, but it also provides a set of elements to justify such a direction.[9]

R. de Cillia and B. Busch divide the practice of language policy and planning into three major trends: (a) a "consciously planned policy" that directly tackles the language question pertaining to a given speech community; (b) a language policy as a subsidiary of existing laws that tackle other societal issues, such as education policy, consumer law, and so on; and (c) a "laissez-faire" politics in which minimal or no intervention by the central authority is observed. Portuguese colonial language policy fits the second category; policies on language were often integral parts of laws and regulations designed to either frame the colonial policy in its totality or to tackle particular fields of colonial social life (e.g., native policy).[10]

For Bernard Spolsky, language policy is an umbrella concept that is made up of three fundamental elements:

> The habitual pattern of selecting among the varieties that make up its linguistic repertoire; its language beliefs or ideology—the beliefs about language and

language use; and any specific efforts to modify or influence that practice by any kind of language intervention, planning or management.

Only the last component corresponds to the intervention of the political authorities, such as the state, in language.[11]

Language policy and planning have two primary dimensions: description and prescription. That is to say that, on the one hand, language policy and planning *describe* the linguistic status quo by pointing out the fault lines or the areas of intervention. On the other hand, language policy and planning often include prescriptive elements as they *prescribe* a set of interventions to be done in the future.

Some scholars have probed the influence of language/language policy on political life.[12] Thus, language policy has been considered essential in nationalist politics. Language policy has also been considered part of a domination strategy by the elite in postcolonial states through the mechanism of "elite closure."[13] Furthermore, it also has been considered a critical component of some states' foreign policies, as an increasing number of states are developing and implementing language-spread policies as part of their strategies for international relations. Still, other studies identify a linkage between language policy and imperialism.[14]

The language-politics nexus implies a discussion of contemporary politics. A dominant political system in the modern world is that of liberal democracy, despite democratic regression in the past few years.[15] Democracy implies the unconstrained political presence of the people. The latter is assumed to be the foundation and the source of legitimacy for the instituted government. A democratic government, as such, is a type of political rule in which the people have a say in the political process. A question that needs to be asked is how the people have a say in the overall political process. True democracy is citizen-centered; the emphasis is placed upon full and engaging participation of the citizens in all the varied aspects of political life, ranging from partaking in elections and public and political debates, contacting and demanding accountability on the part of state agents to participating in the process of policymaking and implementation. This definition of democracy is contrasted with that of electoral democracy, a political system in which citizen participation is limited to routinely choosing the rulers.[16] This means that in between elections, the citizens are not actively part of the political system, chiefly in what concerns the debate, making, and implementation of public policies.

This book's central argument is that one must analyze the language-politics nexus thoroughly to capture the essence of the democratic experience. Language policies and practices that create linguistic hegemony of one language, mainly when most people cannot fully grasp that language, hinder the democratic experience at its core. The process of linguistic hegemony derives mainly from diglossic language, which is supported by domestic and international forces. Schematically, the argument is as follows: diglossic language policy and linguistic practices > social system in which the mother tongue is devaluated and the illegible state > curtailed political participation > decreased quality democracy (see figure 0.1).

A diglossic language policy and practice can be understood as the institutionalization of a linguistic hierarchy in which different languages are confined to different domains.[17] In such a situation, one language becomes a high language while others are relegated to a subordinate position or the status of the low language. These policies reinforce the linguistic hegemony of the chosen language, which, as the high language, becomes the medium for socially valued functions such as formal education, public bureaucracy, commerce and business, administration of justice, and mass media. On the other hand, the low language is consigned, socially and institutionally, to the private realm. It is to be used within the intimate circle of friends, family members, and neighbors. The low language is kept out of the formal public domains through social and political and formal and informal rules and norms.

Diglossic language policy assists in constructing and reproducing an "unreadable" state to most people, a phenomenon that I call the illegible state. Given that the state's operations, processes, and procedures occur almost exclusively in high language, most people cannot adequately grasp and understand the logic of the state's actions or omissions.

The social context in which the mother tongue is taken to be politically worthless, that is, without any worth in terms of being used for the performance of modern functions, limits and restrains political participation on the part of those citizens who are not proficient in the official language. Similarly, given that the state is "illegible," this situation curbs the citizens' capacity to openly supervise and oversee the actions (and omissions) of the state and/or its agents. Lastly, curtailed political participation tremendously burdens the

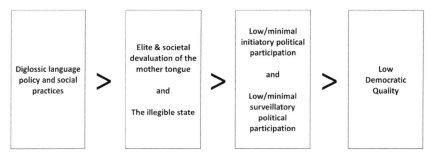

Figure 0.1   From Diglossic Language Policy to Decreased Democratic Quality. *Source:* Figure created by author.

overall quality of democracy. A good democracy is one where the general citizens do not face many informal and formal obstacles to their participation.

One of the most salient aspects of political participation is at the level of political debate. Politics, chiefly in the electoral democratic regimes, is ostensibly about communication among different actors, individual and collective, seeking a resolution of critical issues that pertain to most or all. The importance of communication in the political resolution of problems and conflicts has been highlighted by Jürgen Habermas, who developed the so-called theory of communicative action. According to this theory, cooperation among members of a polity is ultimately the consequence of a deep engagement in the dual processes of deliberation and argumentation.[18] In other words, through effective communication, actions spring up.

Political participation contrasts with other political behaviors, such as apathy and alienation. These two forms of political behaviors are the opposite of political involvement. Yet, there is a distinction between the two. Alienation is not the same as apathy. Myron Weiner defines alienation as "intense political feeling concerning the futility of political action."[19] As such, alienation can be put in the category of what Albert Hirschman called "exit."[20] I prefer the Hirschman concept of exit to Weiner's alienation—as this term suggests false consciousness and, as such, is mobilized and controlled, though by subtle and unrecognized forms, by exogenous agents (lack of agency). On the other hand, apathy suggests a total or partial absence of interest in political matters.

Victor Webb notes that political participation is fundamentally about "citizens [being] involved in one of three ways, viz. in (i) decision making (at the local levels), in (ii) being consulted about issues that concern them, and/or in (iii) simply being kept informed by politicians."[21] Effective democracy is strengthened when citizens engage in more and better forms of participation.[22] That is to say, when the quantity and quality of political participation increases, the whole democratic system significantly improves. The amount of political participation refers to the raw number of people actually and effectively partaking in politics in different forms and through various media. On the other hand, the quality of political participation indexes its intensity, the depth of participating in politics, getting involved, and following the processes and operations of power.

There are two "autonomous" arenas of politics: high politics, or politics at the level of the state institutions and the political elite, and low politics, or politics at the grassroots, at the level of the ordinary citizens, and how, whether individually or in conjunction with others, they seek to influence the composition and/or the output of the state. Political participation links the two arenas of politics, between high and low politics. While other mechanisms link the two realms of politics, such as political mobilization, the concept of political participation posits initiative and ownership of the actions on the part of the ordinary citizenry.

Non-dominant language speakers, who are most people in Cabo Verde and many other cultures, should not be taken simply as lacking linguistic agency. Instead, these citizens have developed and advanced many strategies to combat the Portuguese linguistic hegemony. In chapters 5 and 6, I discuss counter-hegemonic strategies carried out by ordinary, non-dominant language speakers through the agency in constructing the political linguistic landscape and sociolinguistic transferences by diasporized citizens.

I want to return to the current sociolinguistic situation in a postcolonial context (the first block of figure 0.1). Diglossic language policy is the result of social and historical forces. For this reason, the proper understanding of the situation of diglossia and its maintenance in a postcolonial society must consider the current politics, the historical dimension, and the influence of international politics (figure 0.2). A careful analysis of domestic politics helps us understand how powerful social forces, chiefly the elites, use language policy to maintain the situation of diglossia. The construction and maintenance of an asymmetric relationship between languages in a community are politically consequential; it crystallizes and solidifies unequal power relations among social groups with different degrees of mastery of the languages available in the polity. That is to say, the diglossic language policy reinforces the linguistic hegemony of one of the languages in the community.

Domestic politics cannot solely explain the dominance of a language in a polity. For this reason, a complete picture of the current sociolinguistic situation in a postcolonial society must also discuss the international politics of language, that is, interactions among states to advance—or even regress— the roles of different languages. In other words, one must investigate how resources, symbolic and material, developed and shared by former colonial

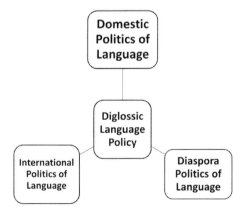

Figure 0.2   The Factors of Diglossic Language Policy. *Source*: Figure created by author.

powers ultimately result in maintaining the linguistic hegemony of their language. Through bilateral and multilateral relations, specific languages, such as English, Portuguese, and French, are propped up and maintained as a language of political officialdom and the international community.

Finally, diaspora politics of language must also be brought into the equation as it helps us to understand resistance and challenges against linguistic hegemony in the homeland. Diaspora politics, unlike international politics, centers on interactions among non-state actors—at least, one of the actors involved in the political game is a non-state actor. In this case, diaspora communities interested in maintaining and solidifying their social identity abroad inevitably develop a sense of linguistic nationalism, supporting and advancing their mother tongue. Such political behavior and stance make the diaspora a counterpower against the continuous process of linguistic hegemony of the language inherited from colonialism.

A NOTE ON THE METHODS

This book is a case study in comparative politics, as the focus was placed on one subject, of which a thorough analysis is conducted. Todd Landman notes that the case study's key objective "is the process of describing the political phenomenon and events" in one political entity (Cabo Verde islands in this case).[23] Knowledge, in this case, is built by an in-depth study. Several scholars have noted the advantage of the case study. John Gerring, for instance, has pointed out that "[w]e gain a better understanding of the whole by focusing on a key part." Attention to one particular case can be translated into a more in-depth knowledge of the current and historical relationships between the variables under study. This is because a case study analysis provides a "holistic, thick (a more or less comprehensive examination) of a phenomenon."[24]

The data collection process for the dissertation project that forms the basis of this book involved a variety of research in a period that extended intermittently from May 2010 to September 2012 in Cabo Verde. Additional trips to the field were conducted in 2015, 2017, and the summer of 2022. Given that the approach of the thesis is that of historical institutionalism, archival research was conducted at the Arquivo Nacional Histórico (National Historical Archives), the Biblioteca Nacional (National Library), and the Archives of the Assembleia Nacional (National Assembly), all in the capital city of Praia. I conducted additional archival research in Lisbon, Portugal, at the Biblioteca Nacional in the summer of 2017. My ultimate objective with the archival research was to learn about the development of language policy from a historical perspective as well as the contours of the public discourse, by the colonial and autochthone intellectuals and officials, about language practices and policies. In other words, discourse analysis is a significant component of this thesis. I first looked at colonial and postcolonial newspapers and other print documents. These newspapers are a valuable source of information about language ideologies that have developed since colonial times. Since the early twentieth century, newspapers have debated various issues, including the role of the vernacular and the sociopolitical relationships that should develop between the Cabo Verdean and Portuguese languages.

I also paid particular attention to the *Boletim Oficial*, the government official gazette, where all policies and legislation are published. A careful reading of the *Boletim Oficial*, from the colonial to the postcolonial times, describes the development of language policy from a historical perspective. Given that what is found in the *Boletim Oficial* is the "end product," I also looked at other sources, mainly newspapers and the archives of parliamentary debate. The many articles and opinion-editorial pieces published in the newspapers and the parliamentary debates are important to help fully understand the stream of the colonial language ideology, its weight, and its continuity in postcolonial times. At the National Assembly, I read the archives of parliamentary debates, chiefly the two constitutional reform debates—in which the language question was a significant and central element.

In the summer of 2011, I organized key informant interviews and focus groups. I followed a semi-structured interview approach with the key informants. I limited my interviews to ten key informant interviews—some conducted outside Cabo Verde in Portugal and the United States. The reason for this is that the research sought to stress the voices of the ordinary citizens, the main subject of study, over the opinions, however valuable, of the learned and highly trained elite. Informants were chosen in terms of their knowledge, as a result of their professional or academic experiences, of the linguistic situation in Cabo Verde. As such, I interviewed two former ministers of education and a former minister of culture, who, for many, is still the banner of the movement for the officialization of the Cabo Verdean language.

Focus group interviews were conducted in different parts of the capital city of Praia, the country's political, social, and economic hub. As such, people from all different sectors of society and various regions and islands of the country flock to the city where better economic opportunities can be found. This means that it was possible to draw quite a large representative group of people from different regions of the island of Santiago (where the city is located) and from other islands of the country. Given that the city's peripheral areas are inhabited by people from different regions of the country, a random sample of participants proved to be the mechanism that brought representativeness to the study.

A total of six focus group interviews were conducted. Each of the focus groups consisted of six people. Meetings were held at different locations, private homes, and public spaces, with the only criterion that the used space be isolated from external interferences. The focus group interviews aimed to capture political perspectives from different socioeconomic groups. I used the following criteria for the selection of the members for the focus group interviews: level of education (ranging from those with no formal education to college graduates), age (as young as nineteen years old to citizens in their sixties), origin and place of residence (from different islands and residing in major neighborhoods of the capital city), and gender (an equal representation of men and women).

To guard their privacy, participants in the focus group were identified by numbers (participant 1, participant 2, etc.). In my notes, to avoid confusion, I identified participants by combining a Roman number for the cycle of the focus group interview with the Latin number for the individual participant (e.g., participant I.1, I for the individual who participated and number 1 for the first focus group interview).

I conducted the focus group interviews with two main goals: First, I needed to understand how the average citizen constructed and perceived the current linguistic situation of the country, where one language, one that is not their everyday language, is dominant. Questions were crafted to elicit their perceptions and general feelings about the diglossic situation of the country as well as to understand the political consequences of this situation. Second, it was also my goal to know how political knowledge—the idea of the processes and operations of politics in everyday life—is constructed among the average citizens. Given that the media, the elite, and the state almost always use the Portuguese language as the medium of communication, I wanted to learn the extent to which an "enlightened understanding" of politics is possible.

In some instances, I employed the method of direct observation. I chose one state agency where much engagement with citizens could be observed— the chosen agency was the Conservatory of the Registry in the neighborhood of Txada Santu Antoni. Through an on-site observation, the goal was to capture how people behaved linguistically and how much this impacted the quality of services provided.

At different times, I also enjoyed many online and face-to-face dialogues with what can be called "language activists," individuals who write extensively, mainly in the local newspapers, to promote the national language. In this regard, I have taken advantage of social media connections and interviewed or discussed with key linguists and linguistic activists. While my original plans included interviewing several key informants, I decided to follow a bottom-up approach: focus, thenceforth, was on the ordinary citizens, the major actors of everyday politics.

THE CHOICE OF CABO VERDE AS THE CASE STUDY

Cabo Verde is a micro island state of nine inhabited islands and several unin-habited small islands and islets, with a population of about half a million. The two main languages in Cabo Verde are Portuguese and Cabo Verdean—also known as the Cabo Verdean Creole (or *Kriolu* by its speakers). The term "Creole" is also used to refer to national identity (*Kriolu* as a synonym for Cabo Verdean) or culture (as in Creole cuisine). The history of the Portu-guese language in Cabo Verde, in a way, is woven together with colonialism. Like other former colonies, the colonial state's imposition of the European language occurred mainly during modern colonialism, from after the Berlin Conference of 1884–1885 to the mid-twentieth century. Through social and political institutions, which often used physical violence, the Portuguese lan-guage became the socially and politically dominant language in the islands—the language of the elite and the educated. Since independence, the position of the Portuguese language has been reinforced by the postcolonial state reaf-firming the social and political predominance of that language. To this day, to be able to speak fluently in the Portuguese language is a marker of social distinction. With a low grasp of that language, a large population cannot critically "read" the state. Total mastery of the Portuguese language can only be accomplished by the end of secondary education or college. However, less than 40 percent of the student population finish secondary education. Consequently, most Cabo Verdeans cannot understand government directives and other written documents. Despite great investments in mass education conducted entirely in Portuguese, the number of fluent Portuguese speakers is relatively low: a fluent speaker of the Portuguese language is almost always a highly educated individual with a college degree.

The Cabo Verdean language is the national language and mother tongue of all Cabo Verdeans. It is a Creole language, that is, a language whose ori-gins and development are tied to the historical mixture of the European and African languages.[25] The Cabo Verdean language originated from the inter-connection between Portuguese with several languages from West Africa, mainly Wolof and Mandinka, dating back to the early sixteenth century.[26] In linguistic terms, the Portuguese language is the lexifier of the Cabo Verdean language, furnishing it with the lexica that form the vocabulary corpus.

The term "Cabo Verdean language" was popularized around the time of independence. Hitherto the language was often referred to as "Creole," "Dia-lect-Creole," but seldom a "language." The phrase "Cabo Verdean language" is preferred in this book as it is more precise in terms of the description, given that "Creole" is a controversial term. For instance, as noted by Louis-Jean Calvet, "the term *creole* tends to designate quite simply *something that one does not wish to call a language*."[27]

The Cabo Verdean language is not confined to the islands of Cabo Verde. Given the history of international migration, the language can be found in different parts of the Atlantic world, from Western Europe to North America, West Africa to South America.[28] Consequently, the Cabo Verdean language is the language of transnational and diasporic communication between people from the homeland and diasporic sites or among different diasporic communities.[29] Interestingly, the Cabo Verdean language gets far more attention in some countries that host immigrant Cabo Verdean communities than in the islands.

It should also be noted that language policy in Cabo Verde is an importation from the western European model, in which each state strived for official monolingualism. This idea, informed by nationalism, meant one state for one nation that speaks one language.[30] The modern state-building process in Europe, which started in the late medieval ages, was based on the principle of the dominance of a single language over the territory. The king's language (more appropriately, the king's dialect) became the state's language. Through political communication, mass mobilization, and education—or what Benedict Anderson calls "the revolutionary vernacularizing thrust"—that language became the nation's language.[31]

Four main reasons have dictated my choice of Cabo Verde as the case study for this study. The country has been hailed as an example of democratic experience in Africa and the developing world. An aerial view of political democratic experiments in the country seems to agree with the overall statement that Cabo Verde is a fully democratic nation.[32] Donor countries and major international organizations also share this assessment. Focusing on the language-politics nexus will show that the democratic situation is not as rosy as it is often portrayed.

Second, there is a line of political argument with a long history that ranges from Jean Jacques Rousseau to the most recent empirical studies of Robert Alan Dahl and Edward R. Tufte to Dag Anckar that contends that small political communities produce a more vibrant and efficient democracy than bigger units.[33] By including a linguistic dimension to the political phenomenon, I also seek to scrutinize this theory. In theory, the smallness of the political unit may be a decisive variable forcing the intensity and extensity of citizens' participation in the political business of the polity. The argument goes that living in small states should logically imply more direct contact and communication—which, as will be seen below, is not the case in Cabo Verde.

Third, studies of the quality of democracy, while having provided valuable knowledge in the subfield, are mainly characterized by superficiality. A significant disadvantage of large-N studies is that breadth takes over depth. As such, particularities are often lost in the process of analysis. That is to say that reliance on statistical data often makes analysts neglect the role of history and social ideologies in forming and developing patterns of political behavior. Political agents behave within cultural and sociological contexts; if scholars fail to examine the context, they may produce an erroneous, if not fatally flawed, understanding of political behavior.

Finally, as a native of Cabo Verde islands, I have the benefit of having an insider comprehension of the cultural and sociological context within which politics takes place. Being socialized in the culture, I can easily discern some social and political behaviors which may take an outsider some time to grasp. Moreover, as a fluent speaker of both Portuguese and Cabo Verdean, I can easily decipher general communications, speeches, and utterances produced in those languages.

This study allows one to understand the extent to which language policy and practice impact the intensity and extent of political participation—and, ipso facto, the quality of democracy. The key element of this study is uncovering the mechanisms and processes that hinder or limit ordinary citizens' political participation. By so doing, it becomes easier to understand political participation and democracy in Creole societies (particularly those from the Caribbean) and the third-wave electoral democracies in sub-Saharan Africa.

ORGANIZATION OF THE BOOK

The book consists of seven chapters. The first chapter, titled "The Language and Politics Nexus (1890–1980)," examines colonialism and linguistic knowledge, anticolonialism and the language question, and how the colonial state and the counter-elites approached the language question in their quest to maintain political order and develop new forms of political relations. The colonial system was a fertile ground for the birth and expansion of policies, ideologies, and social habitus regarding the value and worthiness of the autochthone and the imperial languages. This chapter also problematizes the relative insignificance of the language question in African anticolonial nationalism. The chapter concludes by analyzing how a postcolonial language and politics nexus grew out of colonial and anticolonial politics.

The second chapter, "Contemporary Politics of Language Policy (1991–2022)," delves into the political developments since the early 1990s, when the country experienced a democratic transition. Democratization in the 1990s has significantly shaped politics in the public sphere, facilitating, among other things, debates on the language question. The chapter discusses the current language ideological debate and how it is intimately connected to other debates, particularly about national identity and the politics of regionalization. Additionally, the chapter examines these actors' interactions and networks and the resources that shape debates and policies. Particular attention is paid to political parties, given their legal and political standing in the context of language law and policymaking.

Chapter 3, "The International Politics of the Portuguese Language," examines the role of Cabo Verde as both an agent and a target of Portuguese language-spread policy and the inexistence of a mother tongue-based linguistic diplomacy. I argue that language dominance cannot be understood solely in domestic politics; the structures of international politics, chiefly the global linguistic hierarchy, consolidate linguistic asymmetry at the domestic level. As an agent of language-spread policy, Cabo Verde is one of the founding members of the Community of the Portuguese Language States (CPLP) and its subsidiary organization, the International Portuguese Language Institute (IILP). The chapter investigates how the CPLP has globally promoted and disseminated the Portuguese language. On the other hand, the chapter also explores how Cabo Verde has been on the receiving end of Portuguese language-spread policies as constructed by Portugal and Brazil, the two dominant Portuguese-speaking states. The chapter ends by critically analyzing foreign policy—or lack thereof—designed to promote the Cabo Verdean language.

"Diaspora and the Language and Politics Nexus" is the fourth chapter, which discusses how the Cabo Verdean diaspora shapes the language question in Cabo Verde. The chapter examines the role played by diaspora organizations and groups in advancing the mother tongue in the hostland and homeland alike. Special attention is given to the cases of Portugal and the United States, the sites of the largest Cabo Verdean communities abroad. In the case of the United States, the movement for bilingual education in the 1970s and 1980s provoked great interest in the development of the Cabo Verdean language as the medium of instruction. The chapter also advances the concept of sociolinguistic remittances as an analytical device to understand the linguistic and metalinguistic transferences from the diaspora communities incorporated into social and political lives in the homeland. The chapter also argues that sociolinguistic remittances are weaved with identity politics.

Chapters 1 through 4 provide the historical and political context that helps us understand the current sociolinguistic situation in Cabo Verde. Historical factors, ranging from the colonial state and anticolonial movements, have significantly impacted contemporary language policy. In fact, the dominant ideologies that inform language debate and policy are no more than the reformation of ideas and beliefs first developed during the colonial period and by anti-colonial political ideologies. While chapters 1 and 2 discuss the historical political forces that explain language policy development in Cabo Verde, chapters 3 and 4 focus on the international and transnational dimensions of the same political phenomenon. In chapter 3, I approach the question of language from the perspective of international politics—and here, *international* is understood in stricto sensu, that is, interactions between or among sovereign states. On the other hand, chapter 4, grounded on diaspora relations, is centered on analyzing non-state actors, chiefly immigrant communities, and how they use different resources and ideas to inform and influence the sociolinguistic situation in the homeland.

In chapter 5, "The Illegible State in Cabo Verde," I argue that the postcolonial state, erected on top of the colonial state, has maintained its opaqueness and cloudiness, despite recent advances in electoral democracy. The chapter examines state–society relations and sheds light on the inability of ordinary men and women to supervise the state and its elites properly. The postcolonial state in Cabo Verde is illegible; it relies heavily on the Portuguese language for its operations, procedures, and processes. State illegibility results from language ideologies, attitudes or habitus, and policy. Language planning and policy is an essential tool at the disposal of the state elites to limit direct societal control. The overreliance on the dominant language (Portuguese in Cabo Verde) is deeper in the realm of writing. This situation provokes societal disengagement, which negatively impacts the quality of democracy. The chapter contends that the illegibility of the state is not simply a historical accident; it is also maintained as part of an "elite closure" strategy designed to limit the masses' access to the state.[34]

Chapter 6, "Language Policy and Political Participation," focuses on the consequences of current language policy and habitus on the political participation of ordinary, non-Portuguese-speaking citizens. The chapter studies language policy and habitus as a mechanism of social control. There are two mechanisms through which language is used to limit the political presence of ordinary citizens in politics: the politics of ridicule and lusophone privilege. The politics of ridicule serves to silence and restrict ordinary citizens' entry into the realm of politics. Engaging in political affairs is vocalizing ideas, passions, and interests.

Portuguese is the primary medium through which politics, the state, and policies are carried out. Consequently, there is a temptation for those seeking to enter the realm to express themselves in that language. Most people cannot correctly use the dominant language because of illiteracy or not being familiar with the internal logic of the language. This situation often results in the linguistic butchery of the Portuguese language. As a consequence, social mockery follows. The second social mechanism is a lusophone privilege. Speaking Portuguese in public is a statement of social identity (middle-class, educated, and so on) and indexes one's social ranking. Given its prestige and power, using the dominant language in social encounters is a calculated strategy to increase one's privileges. Elites often use the Portuguese language to enhance and affirm their lusophone privilege.

Chapter 7, "The Politics of Linguistic Landscape," which focuses on the triad of language, politics, and space, asks how space has been manipulated through language to accomplish political objectives. The chapter analyzes how the state and state elites control and manage the landscape in their communication with society. To this objective, the chapter critically analyzes the political linguistic landscape. A subset of linguistic landscape, political linguistic landscape refers to the written words in the public space designed to accomplish political objectives. One particular dimension of the study examines the electoral linguistic landscape. Capturing votes entails elites reducing the political and symbolic gap with the voting masses. The electoral linguistic landscape refers to the temporary deployment of the written word in the public arena to persuade and manipulate voters. The study of the electoral linguistic landscape sheds light on why one language is chosen over the other in electioneering. Elites rely on two basic linguistic strategies to capture the electorate effectively: condescension and lexical appropriation. According to the strategy of condescension, elites instrumentally adopt linguistic features of lower socioeconomic classes to accomplish previously defined political goals.[35] The other mechanism used is lexical appropriation, a subcategory of the first strategy. Political parties and candidates from different ideological backgrounds are increasingly borrowing and appropriating phrases and terms of the youth sociolect. Electoral campaigns have become a war of slogans, with political actors borrowing and appropriating extensively watchwords and other linguistic expressions created by the urban youth. Expressions such as "Uipo," an exclamation showing success, or "sen djobi pa ladu" (literally, not looking to the sides), among many others created by the urban youth, were at different times the linguistic banner of different candidates.

NOTES

1. "O Impacto Social e Económica Da Pesca," *Converça Em Dia* (Praia, Cabo Verde: Televisão de Cabo Verde, October 13, 2011), http://www.rtc.cv/index .php?paginas=47&id_cod=12881&nome_programa=Conversa%20em%20Dia&data =2011-10-13&codigo=ced.

2. Thomas Ricento, "Ideology, Politics and Language Policies: Introduction," in *Ideology, Politics and Language Policies: Focus on English*, ed. Thomas Ricento (Amsterdam: Benjamin, 2000), 23, footnote 1.

3. Elana Shohamy, *Language Policy: Hidden Agendas and New Approaches* (New York: Routledge, 2006).

4. Eduardo D. Faingold, "Language Rights and Language Justice in the Constitutions of the World," *Language Problems and Language Planning* 28, no. 1 (2004):

11–24; Paul Bruthiaux, "Language Rights in Historical and Contemporary Perspective," *Journal of Multilingual and Multicultural Development* 30, no. 1 (2009): 73–85; Tove Skutnabb-Kangas, "Human Rights and Language Wrongs: A Future for Diversity?," *Language Sciences* 20, no. 1 (1998): 5–27; Tove Skutnabb-Kangas and Robert Phillipson, "Human Rights: Perspective on Language Ecology," in *Encyclopedia of Language and Education*, ed. Angela Creese, Peter Martin and Nancy Hornberger (New York: Springer, 2008), 3–14; Tove Skutnabb-Kangas and Robert Phillipson, "'Mother Tongue': The Theoretical and Sociopolitical Construction of a Concept," in *Status and Function of Languages and Language Varieties*, ed. Ulrich Ammon (Berlin: de Gruyter, 1989), 450–77.

5. Will Kymlicka and University of Oxford, *Politics in the Vernacular: Nationalism, Multiculturalism and Citizenship* (Oxford: Oxford University Press, 2001).

6. Robert Lawrence Trask, *The Key Concepts in Language and Linguistics* (London: Routledge, 2005), 146.

7. Bjorn Jernudd and Jyotirindra Das Gupta, "Towards a Theory of Language Planning," in *Can Language Be Planned?: Sociolinguistic Theory and Practice for Developing Nations*, ed. Joan Rubin and Björn H. Jernudd (Honolulu: University Press of Hawaii, 1971), 211.

8. Einar Haugen, *Language Conflict and Language Planning: The Case of Modern Norwegian* (Cambridge, MA: Harvard University Press, 1966), 199.

9. Joshua A. Fishman, *Language and Nationalism: Two Integrative Essays* (Rowley, MA: Newbury House Publishers, 1996), ix.

10. Rudolf de Cillia and Brigitta Busch, "Language Policies: Policies on Language in Europe," in *Encyclopedia of Language and Linguistics* (Amsterdam: Elsevier, 2006), 577.

11. Bernard Spolsky, *Language Policy* (Cambridge: Cambridge University Press, 2004), 5.

12. R. D. Grillo, *Dominant Languages: Language and Hierarchy in Britain and France* (Cambridge: Cambridge University Press, 2009); Brian Weinstein, *The Civic Tongue: Political Consequences of Language Choices* (New York: Longman, 1983); Robert Leon Cooper, *Language Planning and Social Change* (Cambridge: Cambridge University Press, 1990); Fishman, *Language and Nationalism*; David D. Laitin, *Language Repertoires and State Construction in Africa* (Cambridge: Cambridge University Press, 2006).

13. Carol Myers-Scotton, "Elite Closure as a Powerful Language Strategy: The African Case," *International Journal of the Sociology of Language* 103, no. 1 (1993): 149–64.

14. Robert Phillipson, *Linguistic Imperialism* (Oxford: Oxford University Press, 2012).

15. Samuel Phillips Huntington, *The Third Wave: Democratization in the Late Twentieth Century* (Norman, OK: University of Oklahoma Press, 1993); Francis Fukuyama, *The End of History and the Last Man* (New York, NY: Free Press, 2006); Anna Lührmann and Staffan I. Lindberg, "A Third Wave of Autocratization Is Here: What Is New about It?," *Democratization* 26, no. 7 (October 3, 2019): 1095–113, https://doi.org/10.1080/13510347.2019.1582029; Svend-Erik Skaaning, "Waves of

Autocratization and Democratization: A Critical Note on Conceptualization and Measurement," *Democratization* 27, no. 8 (2020): 1533–42, https://doi.org/10.1080 /13510347.2020.1799194.

16. Joseph A. Schumpteter and Richard Swedberg, *Capitalism, Socialism and Democracy* (London: Routledge, 2005).

17. Charles A. Ferguson, "Diglossia," *Word* 15 (1959): 325–40; Joshua A. Fishman, "Bilingualism with and without Diglossia; Diglossia with and without Bilingualism," *Journal of Social Issues* 23 (1967): 29–38.

18. Jürgen Habermas and Thomas McCarthy, *The Theory of Communicative Action* (Cambridge: Polity, 2007).

19. Myron Weiner, "Political Participation: Crisis of the Political Process," in *Crises and Sequences in Political Development*, ed. Leonard Binder and Joseph LaPalombara (Princeton, NJ: Princeton University Press, 1971), 162.

20. Albert O. Hirschman, *Exit, Voice, and Loyalty: Responses to Decline in Firms, Organizations, and States* (Cambridge, MA: Harvard University Press, 2007).

21. Vic Webb, "Language Planning and Politics in South Africa," *International Journal of the Sociology of Language*, no. 118 (1996): 148.

22. Benjamin R. Barber, *Strong Democracy: Participatory Politics for a New Age* (Berkeley: University of California Press, 2009); Carole Pateman, *Participation and Democratic Theory* (Cambridge: Cambridge University Press, 2014).

23. Todd Landman, *Issues and Methods in Comparative Politics: An Introduction* (London: Routledge, 2003), 5.

24. John Gerring, *Case Study Research: Principles and Practices* (Cambridge: Cambridge University Press, 2019), 1, 17.

25. John A. Holm, *An Introduction to Pidgins and Creoles* (Cambridge: Cambridge University Press, 2000); Pieter Muysken and Norval Smith, "The Study of Pidgin and Creole Languages," in *Pidgins and Creoles: An Introduction*, ed. Jacques Arends, Pieter Muysken, and Norval Smith (Amsterdam/Philadelphia: John Benjamins Pub. Co, 1994), 3.

26. Donaldo P. Macedo, "A Linguistic Approach to the Capeverdean Language" (PhD Thesis, Boston: Boston University, 1979); António Carreira, *O Crioulo de Cabo Verde: Surto e Expansão* (Lisboa: Gráfica Europam, 1984); Baltasar Lopes da Silva, *O Dialecto Crioulo de Cabo Verde* (Lisboa: Junta de investigações do Ultramar, 1957).

27. Louis-Jean Calvet, Towards (Cambridge: Polity, 2006), 174 (emphasis added).

28. Luís Batalha and Jørgen Carling, eds., *Transnational Archipelago: Perspectives on Cape Verdean Migration and Diaspora* (Amsterdam: Amsterdam University Press, 2008).

29. Nicolas Quint, "O Cabo-Verdiano: Uma Língua Mundial," *Revista de Estudos Cabo-Verdianos* 3 (2009): 129–44.

30. Ernest Gellner, *Nationalism* (Washington Square, NY: New York University Press, 1997); Anthony David Smith, *Theories of Nationalism* (New York: Holmes & Meier Publishers, 1983); Anthony David Smith, *Nationalism and Modernism: A Critical Survey of Recent Theories of Nations and Nationalism* (London: Routledge,

2017); Benedict Anderson, *Imagined Communities: Reflections on the Origin and Spread of Nationalism* (New York: Verso, 1991).

31. Anderson, *Imagined Communities*, 39.

32. Peter Meyns, "Cap Verde: An African Exception," *Journal of Democracy (Print)* (2002): 153–65; Richard Lobban, *Cape Verve: Crioulo Colony to Independent Nation* (Boulder etc.: Westview, 1995); Bruce Baker, "Cape Verde: Marketing Good Governance," *Afrika Spectrum* 44, no. 2 (2009): 135–47; Bruce Baker, "Cape Verde: The Most Democratic Nation in Africa?," *Journal of Modern African Studies* 44, no. 4 (2006): 493–511.

33. Robert Alan Dahl and Edward Roef Tufte, *Size and Democracy* (Stanford, CA: Stanford University Press, 1975); Dag Anckar, "Small Is Democratic, But Who Is Small?," *Arts and Social Sciences Journal* 1, no. 1 (2013): 1–10.

34. Myers-Scotton, "Elite Closure."

35. Pierre Bourdieu, *Language and Symbolic Power* (Cambridge: Polity Press, 2011).

Chapter 1

The Language and Politics
Nexus (1890s–1980s)

In 1840, a Portuguese journal *O Panorama, Jornal Litterario e Instructivo,* in its 140th number, published a piece on Cabo Verde titled "Costumes Supersticiosos nas ilhas de Cabo-Verde." The unknown author starts by claiming that little is known about the Portuguese colonies, including Cabo Verde, which is defined as one of the closest colonies to Portugal. In the second paragraph of the article, the author focuses on the language question, arguing that "the indigenous people have a known antipathy towards the Portuguese language and that they communicate through a special language, that ours call *creole*."[1] The author then centers the attention on the Portuguese population on the island, stating that "many Portuguese colons that go again [to the islands] are influenced by local customs and allow their children to learn creole."[2] A similar observation was made by two Portuguese men who visited the islands in the 1840s. José Conrado Carlos de Chelmicki and Francisco Adolfo de Varnhagen's 1841 book *Corografía cabo-verdiana ou, Descrip-ção geographico-historica da província das Ilhas de Cabo-Verde e Guiné* includes an interesting observation on the language question in colonial Cabo Verde, noting that even the "children of Portugal" (*filhos de Portugal*) quickly get used to the "ridiculous language of the country."[3]

The descriptions above are relevant to understanding the language question in early nineteenth-century Cabo Verde. The following conclusions can be made regarding language use in the islands. First, while Portuguese was still the language of power and state business, used by few, the Cabo Verdean language was quite present in the public sphere. Arguably the use of Portuguese in the public sphere did not translate into absolute status and prestige. Instead, Portuguese colonists coming from Europe felt the need to learn and speak the Cabo Verdean language as part of a strategy to fit in. Second, given the public

21

conspicuousness of the Cabo Verdean language, the language served as a tool of politics, linking actors as they devised collective action.

This chapter critically describes the language question in Cabo Verde in three different moments: colonial, anticolonial, and early postcolonial. I start by critically examining the colonial language policy's development and contours. To that desideratum, I connect the language and other aspects of social life, chiefly politics. Therefore, I follow the *ecology of language* approach.[4] Einar Haugen, one of the first proponents of this approach, defines it as "the study of interactions between any given language and its environment."[5] I tackle the colonial sociopolitical structures to grasp the language question better. Only by presenting the whole picture of the colonial policies and practices can one aim to understand the impact of the colonial language in the minds of the colonized and the colonized societies.

I argue that the process that enabled the Portuguese language to become a dominant language in Cabo Verde was directly linked with the development of the modern colonial state, starting in the third quarter of the nineteenth century. I further contend that the development of the Portuguese regime of Estado Novo (1933–1974), which stood on the pillars of ultra-nationalism and imperial mysticism, reinforced the Portuguese position in its colonies through policies that combined rewards and punishments. In the second section of the chapter, I discuss the role of language in the context of the development of anticolonial politics. As in the case of other African territories, post-World War II Cabo Verde saw a surge in anticolonial ideals, ideas, and movements. Of all the Cabo Verdean anticolonial movements, the African Party for the Independence of Guinea-Bissau and Cabo Verde (PAIGC), led by Amílcar Cabral, was, by far, the most successful. As such, I discuss Cabral's political linguistics and the extent to which his ideas on language informed the liberation movement language policies, which ultimately guided the postcolonial state linguistic views. In the final section of the chapter, I discuss language policy and planning in the first postcolonial regime in Cabo Verde (1975–1990), in which I argue that these state actions reproduce the PAIGC's language policy and worldviews.

MODERN COLONIALISM AND THE
LANGUAGE-POLITICS NEXUS

Studying colonial language policy is analytically valuable as it allows learning about the formation and development of a dominant language ideology in the postcolonial context.[6] Language ideology refers to the attitudes, beliefs, and myths constructed about language(s).[7] We all espouse such attitudes and values. Often, these values and attitudes are informed by stereotypical and discriminatory views about the role and domains of a language. Yet, these belief systems influence and inform institutions' formation, development, or even change—including language policy.[8] Language policy, after all, has been defined as the "manipulative tool in the continuous battle between different ideologies."[9]

The Portuguese were the first to settle in Cabo Verde permanently in 1462 and, soon after that, began importing enslaved Africans as part of a strategy to develop a plantation economy.[10] The co-habitation of the European and African elements in the islands led to the genesis of a miscegenated society, in which a Creole language became its most noticeable expression. Attempts to set up a plantation economy were unsuccessful; thus, the re-exportation of seasoned enslaved people became a significant industry, turning the islands into the "crossroads of the Atlantic."[11] The first three centuries of Cabo Verdean history translated into the development and internal diffusion of the Cabo Verdean language, creating a sense of shared identity among the islanders while facilitating political or otherwise exchanges of views. The diffusion of the Cabo Verdean language in colonial Cabo Verde reached its peak in the first half of the nineteenth century, when the language, as noted in the chapter's introduction, was conspicuous in all different domains of public life. The Cabo Verdean language was the language of the local elites. Portuguese settlers coming to the islands had to learn to fit into social circles and avoid being ostracized.

The first half of the nineteenth century was a period of political turmoil in the islands. Several peasant and slave rebellions occurred, of which the best known are the Engenhos Rebellion (1822) and the Achada Falcão Rebellion (1841).[12] As examples of open resistance against the oppressive regime, these rebellions were led and carried out by ordinary peasants. The Cabo Verdean language played an important role as the medium through which mobilization and organization of these rebellions were carried out. At the same time, the colonial state in Cabo Verde was incipient at best, lacking state capacity (ability to advance its own goals in society) and autonomy (ability to formulate its interests independent of the interests of social groups that make up the polity).[13] As it lacked human, financial, and other resources, the colonial state was a failed state—unable to provide political order at the time.

Moreover, the colonial state experienced stiff competition from big landowners and self-titled colonels who did not recognize the state's authority.[14] It can be argued that Cabo Verde of the first half of the nineteenth century was an example of a "big society/weak state," as a social force centered on big landowners competed with and did not accept the hegemony of the state.[15] Due to a weak colonial state, the Portuguese language could not find the institutional support to sustain its social dominance. Despite the written realm being exclusively Portuguese, the Cabo Verdean language was widespread, as attested by the Portuguese commentators cited at the beginning of the chapter. It can be concluded that colonial *glottophagy* (replacement of a "minor" language with a "major" one) is about the colonial state's absolute power and cannot be accomplished simply through the enactment of laws and policies. It is precisely in the next hundred years, with the reinforcement of the colonial state, that colonial glottophagy would be implemented in force in Cabo Verde. The first step taken was to modernize the colonial state.

By the mid- to late-1800s, as imperialism and modern colonialism became the dominant political forces in European and global politics, Portuguese authorities began to pay more attention to their African possessions.[16] Institutional and social reforms were carried out to reinforce the imperial rule. To further the reach of imperial power and advance the penetration of royal authority in the colonies, Lisbon mandated the establishment of a printing press in the mid-1800s—through the in-loco publication of royal decrees and other legal norms. During that period, the processes of rationalizing the colonial state were carried out: the improvement of a modern state apparatus with a clearly defined territory and population over which it enjoys jurisdiction. The colonial power developed and sustained an industry of scientific knowledge, fundamentally focused on analyzing and understanding the non-European peoples as part of a strategy of enhancing its power. Across Western Europe, imperial development was simultaneous with expanding the industry of knowledge of non-European peoples and cultures. Portugal was not indifferent to this trend. The last quarter of the 1800s and early 1900s was the era of the development of colonial science in Portugal—or what is often called colonial knowledge.[17] It suffices here to note the creation of key institutions of colonial knowledge, such as the Lisbon Society of Geography (1875), the School of Tropical Medicine (1902), and the Higher Colonial School (1905).

Two significant developments paved the way for the social dominance of the Portuguese language in the colonial public. First, printing press technology reached Cabo Verde in 1842. In the written sphere, the Portuguese language became overwhelming. By the late nineteenth century and throughout the twentieth century, the systematic colonial policy would not only halt the language development of the vernacular but also hinder its use in the colonial public sphere. The second significant development was the formation of a public school system in the colonies. Until the late nineteenth and mid-nineteenth century, the Catholic Church led education in Portuguese African colonies. Instruction was mainly about training the locals to become or assist the priest in his religious functions. In the nineteenth century, the Portuguese authorities instituted public schools in the colonies to advance the "civilizing mission" and to train local cadres to fulfill the lowest ranks of the colonial bureaucracy. Ultimately, this situation led to the entrenchment of a dominant position of the colonizer's language vis-à-vis the local languages.

The advance of the Portuguese language in nineteenth-century Cabo Verdean public space was followed by the rise of a language ideology that debased the Cabo Verdean Creole. The native language, labeled as a corrupt version (*corruptela*) of the Portuguese language, was deemed unworthy of any serious public function—from public administration to schooling.

As it sought to entrench its power at all levels, the colonial state concomitantly adopted linguicist language policies that ultimately were put in place to establish Portuguese linguistic hegemony. Sociolinguists like Tove Skutnabb-Kangas define *linguicism* as "ideologies and structures which are used to legitimate, effectuate, and reproduce unequal division of power and resources (both material and non-material) between groups which are defined on the basis of language."[18] Similarly, Robert Phillipson understands it as a system of domination whereby language "is the crucial criterion in the beliefs and structure which result in unequal power and resource allocation."[19] Inferring from the two given definitions, one can conclude that linguicism is no more than a language-based ideology and practice of social domination. The hierarchy of languages was one of the primary mechanisms operationalized by the colonial state to classify and categorize their speakers. Informed by the assimilation ideology, in 1921, the colonial state passed a law that eliminated the use of African vernaculars as a medium of education, except for teaching religion and the Portuguese language in the first years of primary education. Eduardo Ferreira notes that such a regulation gave a comparative advantage to the Catholic missions in the last instance. They, unlike the various Protestant missions, were filled with Portuguese nationals.[20]

Changes in the metropolitan political regime, with the republic supplanting the monarchy in 1911, did not result in a change in living conditions for the colonized Africans. In 1933, another significant political change occurred in Lisbon, when the First Republic (1910–1926), which the military regime had toppled in 1926, gave way to the *Estado Novo* ("New State," from 1933 to 1974) instituted with the 1933 Constitution. The *Estado Novo*'s colonial policy essentially brought the highest levels of imperial domination. Ideologically, the new regime was an eclectic combination of traditional values, family, and the Catholic Church, blended with modern ideas and practices of right-wing dictatorships of 1930s Europe, chiefly German Nazism, and Italian Fascism.[21] Under the authoritarian command of António Oliveira Salazar, the Estado Novo reformulated and rationalized the colonial state, stretching the scope of domination and extraction of resources. Tighter and more centralized control of the colonies became the official colonial policy.[22]

Against this backdrop, the Portuguese language fostered loyalty to a plurinational and multiracial nation. Marcello Caetano, one of the regime's leading organic intellectuals, saw the Portuguese language as the link that brought together diverse peoples that made up the empire. He argued that "the principle of spiritual assimilation demands an easy communication among all members of the Portuguese community."[23] Needless to say, the instrument of communication among the members of this supposedly culturally united community was the Portuguese language. The use of other languages within the *Espaço Luso* (Luso Space) was not only an affront to the principle of unity of the nation/empire but also a powerful obstacle to supposedly eventual assimilation into Portuguese culture.

Alastair Pennycook, while focusing on the British example, suggests that the analysis of colonial language policy must pay close attention to the issues of its complexity and contextuality. The study of colonial language policy is but a piece in a web of relations and, as such, it has to be done in connection with the development of other discourses and practices of domination (e.g., the discourses of civilizing mission, white/Western superiority, colonial peace, and so on). The contextuality of language policies refers to the fact that one must carefully study the local conditions and the extent to which they produce unique situations in the promulgation and/or application of the stated language policy.[24]

Colonial institution building fed the totalitarian drive insofar as the colonial state sought to maintain control in different sectors and aspects of public life in the colonies. The colonial project aimed to create a new African man in the image of the European—thus indicating the narcissism of the colonial project. Language was one of the critical tools employed in this process of social engineering. In the case of France and Portugal, it was assumed that their respective language had value beyond facilitating communication. French and Portuguese colonizers believed their language led to behavior modification insofar as it was the language of culture and civilization. Against this backdrop, one must understand the contours of language policy in the colonies. Colonial policies and practices often change as a function of changes in the international environment, domestic changes in the colonies themselves, and changes in the domestic politics of the metropolitan power.

The native languages in the former Portuguese colonies in Africa, in contrast to many indigenous African languages in Southern and West Africa under British colonialism, were not the target of language planning (particularly corpus planning—i.e., graphization and lexical modernization), in part as the consequence of Portugal's colonial policy.[25] The British thought that the English language was too complicated for the minds of the "primitive" people. Therefore, their language was kept away from most Africans. An exception was made for the select few who would be taught the English language under the British doctrine first put into force in India—the so-called Macaulay Doctrine.[26] The indirect rule system favored developing indigenous languages and their employment in public. In British Africa, such language policy ultimately led to the development of "vernacular newspapers."[27]

For the French, on the other hand, civilization is expressed solely in the French language, the language of high culture and arts *par excellence*. The theory behind the French model was essentially to civilize the uncivilized through language and culture. The situation did not diverge much from the British colonies: training a small number of intermediaries who could mediate between the colonial authorities and the great African mass. Fluency in the French language was one of the core elements deciding the social status of the African people. As a scholar of French colonialism noted, "the use of French was crucial to leaping barbarism to civilization."[28] The Portuguese colonial system followed a similar model as the mastery of its language became one of the preconditions and prerequisites for the Africans to transition to higher social and legal status, from the condition of native to that of *assimilado*.[29] Modern Portuguese colonialism was fundamentally based on the pillars of assimilation and the central role of the Catholic Church. The assimilation policy was constructed to turn Africans into acculturated Portuguese.

Consequently, it involved a total commitment to the Portuguese culture and, concomitantly, a categorical rejection of the native culture and language. In its turn, the Catholic Church, particularly in the last half-century of Portuguese colonialism in Africa, enjoyed moral and material support from the state—making it a religious arm of Portuguese colonialism. Therefore, the Catholic Church played a central role in the diffusion of Portuguese culture and language as they pursued the evangelization of Africa.

The late colonial discourse centered on notions of lusotropicalism and assimilation, the twin colonial ideologies that posited that Portugal's encounter with the tropical peoples was based on benevolence and humanity; however, the reality was quite different. For instance, statistics of the late colonial period undoubtedly indicate the failure of the colonial assimilation policy. The Portuguese colonial system was inherently contradictory. While professing a civilizing mission and the necessity of elevating the "uncivilized" African, the system permitted a few escape valves for Africans to escape the domination trap. Rather than allowing the opening of the public sphere, the system fenced itself in. Fluency in the Portuguese language was an essential element for social and economic upward mobility. Such a thing was only attainable through schooling—public or carried out by the missions. Judging by colonial statistics (table 1.1), it is easy to conclude the poor performance of the Portuguese colonial system. The table indicates that only a minority had access to education (public or ecclesiastic): less than 5 percent of the total African population and about 22 percent in the case of Cabo Verdeans. In other words, only those 5 percent had any chance to participate in the colonial sphere—by attaining the status of *assimilados*.[30]

Colonial domination was multifarious, and diverse tactics and instruments were employed to manufacture consent among the dominated. Christian

Table 1.1   Illiteracy in Portuguese Africa (1960)

	Total Population	Illiterate Population	Percentage Illiterate
Angola	4,145,266	4,019,834	96.97
Cabo Verde	148,331	116,844	78.50
Guinea-Bissau	510,777	504,928	98.85
Mozambique	5,738,911	5,615,053	97.86

Source: *Anuário Estatístico do Ultramar*, Instituto Nacional de Estatística, Lisbon (1950), and calculations by the author (table created by author).

missions were but another tool at the disposal of the colonial state for such an objective. At the same time, they were also used in the training cadres for the lower echelons of the colonial bureaucracy. Consequently, the colonial state sought to maintain tight control and supervision of the works of the missions within its borders, particularly those coming from other states.[31] In the case of Portugal under Estado Novo, the Catholic Church was utilized as the religious wing of colonialism. This institution was charged with the diffusion of the Catholic faith and promulgating Portuguese culture and language. From the discursive and symbolic points of view, the regime insisted on its historical role of *Padroado Português* (Portuguese Patronage) and the planned use of the Cross of Christ to represent the state. The missions, therefore, were privileged agents of a language-spread policy in the colonies. Through a combination of positive and negative reinforcements, namely easing the conditions for the Portuguese Catholic missionaries who would serve as cultural and linguistic agents while making it difficult for non-Portuguese missionaries to work freely in Portuguese-controlled Africa, the regime aimed to limit the scope of other European languages in its colonies.[32]

ANTICOLONIALISM AND THE LANGUAGE QUESTION

In this section, I critically discuss the language-politics nexus among Cabo Verdean public intellectuals and anticolonial movements of the second half of the twentieth century. The past hundred years of colonial order have seen a rise of different political and language ideologies grounded on the defense of the interests of the people of Cabo Verde. Indigenous political ideas and movements that sprang up among Cabo Verdeans never questioned the role of the Portuguese language; many were interested in lifting the Cabo Verdean language, hoping that it could reach a sociopolitical status similar to that of the Portuguese language.

The earliest defense and promotion of the Cabo Verdean language can be traced back to the late nineteenth century and the first quarter of the twentieth century when the ideology of nativism grew among Cabo Verdean intellectuals.[33] Nativist liberal thinkers such as António de Paula Brito (1852–1894), Eugénio Tavares (1869–1930), and Pedro Cardoso (1890–1942) published extensively in Cabo Verdean and advocated for its use and development. Informed by the development of Creole language studies in Europe, under the leadership of scholars such as Hugo Schuchardt and Francisco Adolpho Coelho, Paula Brito organized the first proposal for the writing of Cabo Verdean.[34] Through artistic expressions such as music and poetry and other activities such as op-ed pieces published in colonial newspapers, these thinkers were zealous defenders of the native language.

Pedro Cardoso was perhaps the most vocal advocate of the Cabo Verdean language. Nonetheless, his understanding of linguistics impaired his thinking of the mother language. In his view, Cabo Verdean Creole was a simple transformation of the Portuguese language. In other words, the linguistic distance between the two is minimal and can explain the evolution of the mother tongue in the islands. For him, Cabo Verdean was a dialect of Portuguese—as it was commonly accepted then. According to Cardoso, the mother tongue is to be represented graphically as close as possible to Portuguese. The sounds that have no corresponding forms in Portuguese are written in a format as close as possible to what is found in written Portuguese.[35] He took a step further and was among the first to advocate for the inestimable value of the mother tongue as a medium of education—some thirty years before the famous UNESCO position that children's education bears better fruit when conducted in the mother tongue.[36]

The generation of *Claridade*, a journal that was the voice of the Cabo Verdean literary-cultural movement for almost fifteen years (1936–1960), also had a say in the language question. In its first number, a poem written in Cabo Verdean Creole made the cover page. The fact that the journal's cover had a poem in basilectal Creole is a sociopolitical statement. The second half of the 1930s was when the Estado Novo began to affirm itself as the new regime in Portugal and the Empire—once all the opponents were almost totally neutralized and crushed. As an ultra-colonialist, nationalist, and conservative regime, the Estado Novo was essentially about glorifying Portuguese culture and language. Accordingly, there was no room for the exhibition of the colonized languages in the public realm. The colonial public sphere, chiefly in the urban areas, was to be exorcized entirely of the native languages, leaving it open for the complete and hegemonic domination of the Portuguese language.[37]

Baltazar Lopes da Silva, one of the most prominent members of the *Claridade Movement*, took an essential step toward affirming the language. His 1957 study of the Cabo Verdean language, the first scholarly study done by a native speaker, brings much insight into the understanding of the social roles of the language.[38] Yet, Lopes da Silva could not wholly dissociate himself from the dominant colonial language ideology. Most importantly, he maintained the colonial label that insisted that the Cabo Verdean language was a *dialect*—and not a language in its own right. The employment of this label is politically consequential, as it aims to describe a certain identity point of view. In other words, the Cabo Verdean Creole was taken as a dialect of the Portuguese language, the language that provides most of its lexicon. It follows, thus, that the two languages (Portuguese and Creole) are closely and intimately related to the point that one cannot speak of an autonomous linguistic system in Cabo Verde. Subsequently, the people of Cabo Verde, like their language, were unbreakably tied to the Portuguese culture and nation.[39] As described above, Cabo Verdean public intellectuals' political linguistics was indexical to many other sociopolitical ideologies. One of these social ideologies that attracted considerable attention from these actors was the idea of adjacent islands. According to the proponents of this ideology, whose origins date to the second half of the nineteenth century, since Cabo Verde was culturally Portuguese, its political order needed to reflect that sociological reality. Accordingly, as defined in law, Cabo Verde's legal and political status needed to be changed from that of a colony to that of adjacent islands, as was the case of the two archipelagoes, Madeira and Azores.[40] This political position was crushed by the writings of the Brazilian sociologist Gilberto Freyre after he toured the Portuguese empire, financed by the Estado Novo, to legitimize Portugal's rule in Africa and Asia. Unlike Baltazar Lopes da Silva, who had written on the dilution of Africa in Cabo Verde, Freyre argued that Cabo Verde was essentially Africa—a position that left Lopes da Silva and many other public intellectuals emotionally devastated.[41] "The messiah betrayed us," Lopes da Silva would lament.[42]

The movement of people and ideas and the establishment of formal and informal alliances against Portuguese colonialism made Cabo Verde a piece of a big puzzle. As in the case of other African colonies, the 1950s was a period of blossoming for anticolonial organizations.[43] In the 1950s and early 1960s, Cabo Verdeans created many political organizations, including the PAIGC, which was the most successful. It was a binational anticolonial united front, formed by people of different social backgrounds from Guinea-Bissau and Cabo Verde and led by Amílcar Cabral up to his assassination in 1973.[44] PAIGC's primary political objectives were the national independence of Cabo Verde and Guinea-Bissau and the fusion of these two states into a federal political unit following their independence. Unlike those from previous decades who might have developed a certain degree of cultural or linguistic nationalism, the generation of the 1960s and 1970s embarked on full political nationalism, advocating for complete delinking from Portugal.

A fervent linguistic nationalism did not accompany the anticolonial political nationalism of the late 1950s through the 1970s. The nationalists of the

1960s did not pay as much attention to the language question—at least, it did not take the front seat of their political campaigns. Anticolonial activists were far more interested in the question of political independence and the issue of economic development, thus minimizing the language problem. The PAIGC, the party that led the liberation struggle, did not develop an explicit language policy. Instead, the PAIGC's language policy was built in the footsteps of the colonial language policy—that is, the predominance of Portuguese in education and public administration since a proto-state was constructed in the liberated areas.[45]

Amílcar Cabral's writing indicates the party's position on the language-politics nexus. In his *Análise de Alguns Tipos de Resistência*, Cabral lays out his thinking on language and takes an instrumentalist approach. He argues that a language is no more than "an instrument for the men to relate among each other, an instrument, a means to speak, to express the realities of life and the world."[46] In this way, Cabral is taking a position that is directly antagonistic to what was taken by other radical anticolonial nationalists such as Franz Fanon. For this leader of Algerian independence, language can never be a neutral and value-free instrument. Instead, on the contrary, the colonial language is a powerful and hidden vehicle for cultural expansion and alienation.[47]

Colonial language, as an instrument, does not in itself lead to political and social alienation. Cabral argues instead that the colonial language can be used to advance the goal of national liberation and development as it is the language of modernity. In this regard, Cabral further asserts that

> we must take advantage of the experiences of others, not only of our experiences. However, if we want to employ that experience so we can use it in our land, *we must employ the expressions of other languages. Well, if we have a language that can explain all of this, we shall use it. There is no harm in so doing.*[48]

At the same time, Cabral, like many other African nationalists of the time, was somewhat skeptical of any socioeconomic and political value of the vernaculars—at least, right away. Fears of ethno-nationalisms and what he calls "opportunism"—defense of one's ethnic language by many ethnic entrepreneurs—might have dictated his ambiguous position on the various indigenous languages. Yet, the PAIGC program and official discourse were filled with declarations in defense and support of the African indigenous languages, including the Cabo Verdean Creole.[49]

Taking the distinction made by Eric Hobsbawm between mass, civic, and ethnolinguistic nationalism, it can be argued that PAIGC's nationalism was essentially civic-territorial.[50] Unlike *ethnonationalism*, grounded on the idea that a nation is based on essentialist notions such as ethnic belonging, *civic nationalism* constructs the nation based on the already defined territory. All

those who reside within the region's limits are, ipso facto, part of the nation—
regardless of their ethnic origins. As a territorial and civic nationalist organization, PAIGC aspired to construct a new state—a federal state—comprising
the two colonies, Cabo Verde and Guinea-Bissau. The new postcolonial state
would have to be fundamentally multiethnic and multilinguistic. The two territories share two common languages: the Portuguese language, the language
inherited from colonialism, and the Portuguese-based Creole language.

Cabo Verdean Creole, chiefly the southern dialect (*Sotavento*), is mutually
intelligible with the Bissau-Guinean Creole (*Kryol*). Yet, while in the case
of the former, it is a native language of the people, Bissau-Guinean Creole
has essentially performed the role of the communicative instrument across
ethnic boundaries. In other words, Creole is nativized in Cabo Verde—which
is not the case in Guinea. This situation guarantees a comparative advantage
to Cabo Verdeans in postcolonial federalism should the Creole language be
institutionalized as the official language.

THE LANGUAGE AND POLITICS NEXUS
IN THE POSTCOLONIAL PERIOD

Following the fall of the Estado Novo in Lisbon, the second half of 1974 was
a period of complex and multifaceted political competition in Cabo Verde.
A veritable propaganda war developed among the PAIGC, the Democratic
Union of Cabo Verde (UDC), and the Union of the Peoples of the Islands of
Cabo Verde (UPICV). This propaganda war occurred mainly through various pamphlets, posters, brochures, and flyers distributed in urban areas. The
propaganda war was also about "occupying" the public space with a political
message. Political graffiti on walls throughout the country became a primary
vehicle for disseminating political messages.

By 1974, the PAIGC had subdued both the UPICV and UDC. These
circumstances, facilitated by the radical section of the Portuguese military
who maintained strong sympaties and respect for PAIGC, can be explained
by the following factors. First, the PAIGC was far more organized than the
unstructured, understaffed, disorganized UPICV and UDC. A higher level of
political organization is often correlated with political success.[51] As a political organization with more than a decade of active political experience that
included leadership in an anticolonial war, the PAIGC had clearly defined
structures and hierarchy, with its members aware of their roles and functions. Second, in structural terms, the UDC and the UPICV resembled the
elite party, detached from society.[52] The UDC was more a political gathering
or association of the members of the cultural and political elite of the late
colonial society. Third, given that PAIGC led a successful national liberation

campaign, it enjoyed wide international recognition. It suffices here to note that the United Nations General Assembly and the now-defunct Organization of African Unity considered the party the "sole and legitimate representative of the people of Guinea Bissau and Cabo Verde."[53]

Modern state builders face a fundamentally political problem: finding the equilibrium between political order and liberty. The United Kingdom is an example of a state that has simultaneously developed political order and liberty. The example of the United States is the opposite, with liberty preceding order.[54] Like most of their African counterparts, Cabo Verdean state builders focused more on political order, often at the expense of liberty. The primary political goal was to construct a state that could consolidate itself, particularly in the context of foreign and domestic destabilizing threats. Language policy grounded on the continuity of the colonial state practices and rules was an important tool in creating political order. The reliance on the language inherited from colonialism instead of the languages found in the community fulfilled many political objectives. First, it limited political participation, given that the political arena, as it was in the late colonial period, was that of the dominant language. Second, it allowed the early postcolonial state to draw on the reservoir of past practices and ideas stored in the dominant language. Finally, a radical language policy could easily spill over to other policy and political areas, leading to unmanageable political changes.

The period between the fall of the Portuguese dictatorship on April 25, 1974, and its Independence on July 5, 1975, can be said to have been the zenith of cultural and linguistic nationalism in Cabo Verde. While the official historiography has tended to show that the critical political actors of this period were, in one way or another, linked to PAIGC, spontaneous civic organizations were created, mainly in the urban areas, to bolster the Cabo Verdean language. A heated debate on the language question took place in the public sphere for the first time, mainly via the written press and civil society organizations. For instance, high school students of the capital city of Praia demanded that the national language be used as the medium of instruction in place of the Portuguese language.[55] New forms of writing Creole were put forth that would graphically augment the linguistic distance between the language and its lexifier. One of the linguistic strategies cultural entrepreneurs use to construct a linguistic distance between Portuguese and Creole in the written form is the employment of the letter "K." The Portuguese alphabet does not include such a letter.[56] Kaoberdiano Dambara, with his *Noti*, a collection of revolutionary poems written in Creole, might have been one of the earliest proponents of this trend. The use of grapheme <k> was justified as a mechanism to embrace African-ness (the idea, though wrong, was that the letter "K" was very African as it is extensively used in many African languages).[57]

The new postcolonial government, led by the revolutionary PAIGC, maintained the policy of "Portuguese-only" in education, media, and public administration. Carlos Reis, the first minister of education in the postcolony, considered "indispensable the teaching of Portuguese."[58] The Ministry of Education's decision resulted from the youth's reluctance to retain the Portuguese language as the medium of education.[59]

The fact that many high school students were at the forefront of linguistic nationalism is not purely a historical accident. The high school space, first in Mindelo (the island of São Vicente, since 1917) and later in Praia (the island of Santiago, since 1960), was a major linguistic battleground. The high school, considered the ideal-typical area of modernity and cultural advancement, was supposed to be a "Portuguese-only" site. State and high school norms and regulations outlawed using the Cabo Verdean language within the confines of high school. For this reason, Dulce Almada uses the expression "field of the linguistic exclusion" to refer to the ideologies and practices within the high school precinct.[60]

The main argument of the Ministry of Education was based on two main propositions. First, there was the influence of colonial evolutionism, according to which the Cabo Verdean language was supposedly not as highly developed as Portuguese. The gist of the argument of the Ministry of Education can be found in one of its earliest political communique: "according to the laws of linguistics, our Creole is of relatively recent formation and will have to continue its evolution, to become richer and to affirm itself, before it becomes a language, in the classical sense of the word."[61] Second, there was the idea that the Cabo Verdean language was not unified, given the plurality of dialects.

The Ministry of Education's decision to follow a "Portuguese-only" education language policy can be interpreted in terms of political motives. To submit to the pressures of the students to institute the use of the Cabo Verdean language as a medium of education corresponds to submitting to societal demands. In the view of the Ministry, this situation would have created a terrible political precedent, creating significant political problems in the future. The regime's political creed was that the party guided society—and not the other way around. At the same time, and related to the above reasoning, the "Portuguese-only" decision in education can be explained as a political strategy to undermine societal linguistic nationalism. Societal autonomy was something that the regime did neither want nor tolerate. If left unchecked, linguistic nationalism would eventually evolve into political nationalism. Despite its anticolonial nationalist record, the PAIGC was moved by political pragmatism. Uncontrolled societal nationalism—linguistic or otherwise—would eventually clash with the political pragmatism of the regime. The importance of this decision cannot be overstated. It was a path-dependence-changing moment. Ruth Collier and David Collier note that institutions endure throughout time, and it is during the periods that they call "critical junctures" that institutional reforms are made possible.[62] This political decision, however, did not deter the language debate, which was prolonged for another two to three years after independence.[63] In the end, the postcolonial government followed a formula already entrenched in most states in the region: the distinction between official and national languages, whereby Portuguese is granted the status of the former and the Cabo Verdean language the status of the second.[64] Despite this purely "declaratory" policy on the national language, it was not until the late 1990s that some attempts were made to change the political status of the mother tongue in Cabo Verde.

Political discourse in postcolonial Cabo Verde, as in other parts of Africa, was fundamentally based on the notions of economic development, relegating the language question to a secondary issue. The PAIGC's ideology of "National Reconstruction," which turned into a policy of development in Cabo Verde and Guinea-Bissau after independence, attests to this situation. Within the new postcolonial government, some linguistic nationalists wanted to see the status of the language—or the language question—brought to the fore. Despite this, there were some attempts toward language corpus development.[65]

In 1979, under the leadership of Dulce Almada Duarte and financed by UNESCO, a linguistic colloquium took place in Mindelo, Cabo Verde. The goal of the meeting was to bring Cabo Verdean and international scholars, writers, and educators to discuss the Cabo Verdean language. A chief outcome of the meeting was the establishment of a standard orthography for the language for the first time in history, based on the phonetic-phonological model.[66] The adopted model, however, makes extensive use of diacritics, particularly circumflexes, leading critics to label it as the "alfabeto de chapéu" (translatable as the "hat's alphabet").[67] In 1989, another meeting was convened, which included people engaged in literacy campaigns and education. Given the level of criticism of the model adopted in 1979, the meeting radically changed the alphabet to be proposed for writing the Cabo Verdean language. Unlike the model of 1979, fundamentally informed by linguistic theory, the new system adopted in 1989 relied on the sociolinguistic aspect of it—particularly whether it would be accepted or rejected by the community.[68]

The proposed 1979 alphabet was adopted in some activities, such as teaching the Cabo Verdean language at Secondary Teachers' College. However, the system faced many challenges since it was characterized by "sociolinguistic dysfunctionality." This situation eventually led to its demise.[69] Ten years later, under the aegis of the General Directorate of Extra-School Education, the agency in charge of adult literacy organized the "Bilingual Literacy Forum." A new orthographic system from this meeting considered the critiques against the 1979 proposal. However, in 1990/1991, the country underwent radical political changes, dismantling the one-party state and institutionalizing the liberal democratic order. Once again, the language issue was placed on the back burner, and only in the mid-1990s would the question begin to resurface (as discussed in the following chapter).

CONCLUSION

The chapter briefly described the Portuguese colonial language policy and the development of a nativist discourse on the mother tongue. Looking back to the past is a mechanism that allows us to uncover present social forces and the extent to which these forces might have gathered momentum over the years. From a historical institutionalist approach, the colonial language policy can be well characterized by path dependence: the cost (political or otherwise, for the local elite or others) of changing it may be well over the costs of maintaining it.

The study of the colonial language policy permits one to understand better how the institutions of the state and other non-state institutions, particularly the Catholic Church, embed the European language in their core. The institutional linkage between the colonial and postcolonial states implied that the former colonizer's language would maintain a privileged status. As the status of the colonial language suffers minimal or no change within the configuration of the postcolonial society, postcolonial politics resembles much of the old political structures of the colonial period: the splitting of two different realms, the state and society, defined, among other things, by the dominant language in each domain. The linguistic divide, as such, reinforces the distance and curtails the people's participation in the processes of controlling the state.

The colonial language policy still has an impact on the dominant language ideology. The postcolonial elites' beliefs and attitudes toward language have been described as biased in favor of the former colonial language (and, not infrequently, biased against the indigenous languages). The former colonizer's language is often exalted and constructed as the only viable means to progress toward social, political, and technical modernity. Subsequently, efforts are constantly made to block any attempts to promote the indigenous languages.

The Portuguese language is the sole official language of the state. The revolutionary enthusiasm of 1974 and 1975 did not translate into a higher status for the Cabo Verdean language. This situation can be explained by the fact that the PAIGC, the party that fought for independence and controlled power after independence, was more of a territorial nationalist organization and, as such, did not emphasize language as a symbol of state-building. It is also the result of the political objective of the unification of Guinea-Bissau and Cabo Verde. In the event of such a unification, making the Cabo Verdean language an official language in Cabo Verde would have given them a comparative advantage vis-à-vis the Bissau-Guineans.

In Cabo Verde, the postcolonial state-building and its emphasis on nation-building paid no serious attention to the language question. While political discourse emphasized the national language, the political practice seemed to condemn the Cabo Verdean language to its secondary status and role. During the first fifteen years, the language question was not among the key issues on the governmental agenda. It suffices to note that the government and/or party documents during the period included no design for status planning of the Cabo Verdean language. The elites' linguistic conservatism prevailed.

NOTES

1. "Costumes Supersticiosos Nas Ilhas de Cabo Verde," *O Panorama, Jornal Litterario e Instructivo*, 1840.

2. "Costumes Supersticiosos Nas Ilhas de Cabo Verde."

3. José Conrado Carlos de Chelmicki and Francisco Adolfe de Varnhagen, *Corografía Cabo-Verdiana, Ou, Descripção Geographico-Historica Da Provincia Das Ilhas de Cabo-Verde e Guiné* (Lisbon: Typ. de L.C. da Cunha, 1841), 331.

4. Einar Haugen, *The Ecology of Language* (Stanford: Stanford University Press, 1972).

5. Haugen, *The Ecology of Language*, 325.

6. Bettina Migge and Isabelle Léglise, "Language and Colonialism. Applied Linguistics in the Context of Creole Communities," in *Language and Communication: Diversity and Change. Handbook of Applied Linguistics*, ed. Marlis Hellinger and Anne Pauwels (Berlin: Mouton de Gruyter, 2007), 297–338.

7. Kathryn Woolard, "Introduction: Language Ideology as a Field of Inquiry," in *Language Ideologies: Practice and Theory*, ed. Bambi Schieffelin, Kathryn Woolard and Paul Kroskrity (New York: Oxford University Press, 1998), 3–50; Kathryn A. Woolard and Bambi B. Schieffelin, "Language Ideology," *Annual Review of Anthropology* 23 (1994): 55–82; Ricento, "Ideology, Politics and Language Policies."

8. Vivien A. Schmidt, "Discursive Institutionalism: The Explanatory Power of Ideas and Discourse," *Annual Review of Political Science* 11, no. 1 (2008): 303–26; Colin Hay, "Constructivist Institutionalism," in *The Oxford Handbook of Political Institutions*, ed. R. A. W. Rhodes, Sarah A. Binder, and Bert A. Rockman (Oxford: Oxford University Press, 2006), 56–74.

9. Shohamy, *Language Policy*, 45.

10. Georges E. Brooks, *Western Africa and Cabo Verde, 1790s–1830s: Symbiosis of Slave and Legitimate Trades* (Bloomington, IN: Authorhouse, 2010), 27; Thomas Bentley Duncan and University of Chicago, *Atlantic Islands; Madeira, the Azores,*

and the Cape Verdes in Seventeenth-Century Commerce and Navigation (Chicago: University of Chicago Press, 1972).

11. Duncan and University of Chicago, *Atlantic Islands; Madeira.*

12. Eduardo Adilson Camilo Pereira, *Política e Cultura: As Revoltas, Engenhos (1822), Achada Falcão (1841), Ribeirão Manuel (1910)* (Praia: Imprensa Nacional de Cabo Verde, 2015).

13. Peter B. Evans, Dietrich Rueschemeyer, and Theda Skocpol, *Bringing the State Back In* (New York: Cambridge University Press, 2002).

14. António Carreira, *Cabo Verde: Formação e Extinção de Uma Sociedade Escravocrata (1460–1878)* (Lisboa: A. Carreira, 1983); Brooks, *Western Africa and Cabo Verde, 1790s–1830s.*

15. Joel Samuel Migdal, *Strong Societies and Weak States: State Society Relations and State Capabilities in the Third World* (Princeton: Princeton University Press, 1988).

16. R. J. Hammond, *Portugal and Africa: A Study in Uneconomic Imperialism 1815–1910* (Stanford: Stanford University Press, 1996); Gervase Clarence-Smith, *The Third Portuguese Empire, 1825–1975: A Study in Economic Imperialism* (Manchester: University Press, 1985).

17. Didier Péclard, "Savoir Colonial, Missions, Chrétiennes et Nationalisme En Angola," *Genèses* 4, no. 45 (2001): 114–33.

18. T. Skutnabb-Kangas, "Multilingualism and the Education of Minority Children," in *Minority Education: From Shame to Struggle*, ed. T. Skutnabb-Kangas and J. Cummins (Clevedon: Multilingual Matters, 1988), 13.

19. Phillipson, *Linguistic Imperialism*, 54.

20. Eduardo de Sousa Ferreira, *Portuguese Colonialism in Africa, the End of an Era; The Effects of Portuguese Colonialism on Education, Science, Culture and Information* (Paris: Unesco Press, 1974), 62.

21. Philippe Schmitter, "The 'Régime d'Exception' That Became the Rule: Forty-Eight Years of Authoritarian Domination in Portugal," in *Contemporary Portugal: The Revolution and Its Antecedents*, ed. Lawrence S. Graham and Harry M. Makler (Austin: University of Texas Press, 1979), 15; Antonio Costa Pinto, *Salazar's Dictatorship and European Fascism: The Problems of Interpretation* (Boulder, CO: Columbia University Press, 1995).

22. Alfredo Héctor Wilensky, *Trends in Portuguese Overseas Legislation for Africa* (Braga: Editora Pax, 1971).

23. Marcelo Caetano, *Tradiçoes, Principios e Métodos da Colonizaçao Portuguesa* (Lisboa: Agencia Geral do Ultramar, 1951), 44.

24. Alastair Pennycook, "Language, Ideology and Hindsight: Lessons from Colonial Language Policies," in *Ideology, Politics, and Language Policies: Focus on English*, ed. Thomas Ricento (Amsterdam: John Benjamins Pub, 2000), 49–66.

25. William J. Samarin, "The Linguistic World of Field Colonialism," *Language in Society* 13, no. 4 (1984): 435–53.

26. Janina Brutt-Griffler, *World English: A Study of Its Development* (Clevedon: Multilingual Matters, 2004).

27. Ali Al'Amin Mazrui and Alamin M. Mazrui, *The Power of Babel: Language & Governance in the African Experience* (Oxford: Currey, 1998), 29.

28. Alice L. Conklin, *A Mission to Civilize: The Republican Idea of Empire in France and West Africa, 1895–1930* (Stanford, CA: Stanford University Press, 1997), 84.

29. David Cassels Johnson, *Language Policy* (Basingstoke: Palgrave Macmillan, 2013); Feliciano Chimbutane, "Can Sociocultural Gains Sustain Bilingual Education Programs in Postcolonial Contexts? The Case of Mozambique," in *Bilingual Education and Language Policy in the Global South,* ed. Jo Arthur Shoba and Feliciano Chimbutane (New York: Routledge, 2013).

30. Amílcar Cabral, *Our People Are Our Mountains: Amilcar Cabral on the Guinean Revolution* (London: Committee for Freedom in Mozambique, Angola and Guiné, 1973).

31. Luis B. Serapião, "The Preaching of Portuguese Colonialism and the Protest of the White Fathers," *Issue: A Journal of Opinion* 2, no. 1 (1972): 34.

32. Adriano Moreira, *O Novíssimo Príncipe: Análise da Revolução* (Braga: Intervenção, 1977).

33. José Marques Guimarães, *A Difusão Do Nativismo Em África Cabo Verde e Angola Séculos XIX e XX* (Lisbon: África Debate, 2006).

34. N. Quint, "Les Apontamentos de António de Paula Brito (1887) ou la Naissance d'une Tradition Grammaticale Capverdienne Autochtone," *Histoire Épistémologie Langage* 30, no. 1 (2008): 127–53; Holm, *An Introduction to Pidgins and Creoles.*

35. Pedro Monteiro Cardoso, *Folclore Caboverdiano* (Paris: Solidariedade Caboverdiana, 1983).

36. Manuel Brito Semedo, *A Construção da Identidade Nacional: Análise da Imprensa entre 1877 e 1975* (Praia: Instituto da Bibliotheca Nacional e do Livro, 2006), 128–29; Cardoso, *Folclore Caboverdiano.*

37. Louis-Jean Calvet, *Linguistique et Colonialisme: Petit Traité de Glottophagie* (Paris: Payot, 1974); Semedo, *A Construção da Identidade Nacional,* 270.

38. Lopes da Silva, *O Dialecto Crioulo de Cabo Verde.*

39. Manuel Ferreira, *A Aventura Crioula* (Lisboa: Plátano, 1985).

40. Baltazar Lopes da Silva, "'As Ilhas Adjacentes de Cabo Verde,'" *Notícias de Cabo Verde,* 1931.

41. Gabriel Fernandes, *A Diluição da África: Uma Interpretação da Saga Identitária Cabo-verdiana no Panorama Político (Pós)colonial* (Florianópolis: Editora da UFSC, 2002).

42. Baltazar Lopes da Silva, *Cabo Verde visto por Gilberto Freyre: Apontamentos lidos aoMicrofone de Rádio Barlavento* (Praia: Impremsa Nacional, 1956); Manuel Ferreira, "Comentarios Em Torno Do Bilinguismo Cabo-Verdiano," in *Coloquios Cabo-Verdianos* (Lisbon: Junta de Investigações do Ultramar, 1959), 51–80; Felix Monteiro, "A Margem de Uma Agenda," *Cabo Verde: Boletim Documental e de Cultura* 3, no. 26 (1951): 5–7.

43. Ronald H. Chilcote, *Emerging Nationalism in Portuguese Africa: A Bibliography of Documentary Ephemera through 1965* (Stanford, CA: Hoover Institution on War, Revolution and Peace Stanford University, 1969).

44. Patrick Chabal, *Amílcar Cabral: Revolutionary Leadership and People's War* (Trenton, NJ: Africa World Press, 2003); Mustafah Dhada, *Warriors at Work: How

Guinea Was Really Set Free (Niwot, CO: University Press of Colorado, 1993); José André Leitão da Graça, *Golpe de estado em Portugal ... : traída a descolonização de Cabo Verde!* (Praia: José André Leitão da Graça, 2004); José Vicente Lopes, *Cabo Verde: Os Bastidores da Independência* (Praia: Spleen, 2002).

45. Sónia Vaz Borges, *Militant Education, Liberation Struggle, Consciousness: The PAIGC Education in Guinea Bissau 1963–1978* (New York: Peter Lang, 2019); Chabal, *Amílcar Cabral*; Dhada, *Warriors at Work*.

46. Amílcar Cabral, *Analise De Alguns Tipos De Resistencia* (Lisboa: Seara Nova, 1975), 101.

47. Frantz Fanon, *Black Skin, White Masks* (New York: Grove Press, 2017).

48. Cabral, *Analise De Alguns Tipos De Resistencia*, 104.

49. Lars Rudebeck, *Guinea-Bissau: A Study of Political Mobilization* (Uppsala: Scandinavian Institute of African Studies, 1974).

50. Eric J. Hobsbawm, *Nations and Nationalism since 1780: Pogramme, Myth, Reality* (Cambridge: Cambridge University Press, 2012).

51. James Q. Wilson, *Bureaucracy: What Government Agencies Do and Why They Do It* (New York: Basic Books, 2000), 1.

52. Maurice Duverger, *Political Parties: Their Organization and Activity in the Modern State* (New York: Science Editions, 1993); Ruth S. Morgenthau, *Political Parties in French-speaking West Africa* (Oxford: Clarendon Press, 1967).

53. Chabal, *Amílcar Cabral*, 96.

54. Larry Diamond, Juan J. Linz, and Seymour Martin Lipset, "Introduction: Comparing Experiences with Democracy," in *Politics in Developing Countries: Comparing Experiences with Democracy*, ed. Larry Diamond, Juan J. Linz, and Seymour Martin Lipset (Boulder, CO: L. Rienner Publishers, 1990), 1–35.

55. Maria Dulce de Almada, *Bilinguismo ou Diglossia? As Relações de Força entre o Crioulo e o Português na Sociedade Cabo-Verdiana: Ensaios* (Praia, Cabo Verde: Spleen, 1998).

56. Macedo, "A Linguistic Approach to the Capeverdean Language"; Russell Hamilton, "Cape Verdean Poetry and the PAIGC," in *Critical Perspectives on Lusophone African Literature*, ed. Donald Burness (Washington, DC: Three Continents, 1981), 143–57.

57. Virgílio Pires, "'O 'Crioulo Reinventado,'" *Novo Jornal Cabo Verde*, September 5, 1974; Kaoberdiano Dambarà, *Noti* (Guinea: Edição do Departamento da Informação e Propaganda do Comite Central de Parido Africano da Independência da Guiné e Cabo Verde, 1965).

58. "Combate Ao Analfabetismo Exigência Do Nosso Partido," *Voz de Povo*, August 14, 1975.

59. Almada, *Bilinguismo ou diglossia?*, 128.

60. Almada, 128–29.

61. Almada, 130.

62. Ruth Berins Collier and David Collier, *Shaping the Political Arena: Critical Junctures, the Labor Movement, and Regime Dynamics in Latin America* (Notre Dame: University of Notre Dame Press, 2009); Giovanni Capoccia and R. Daniel

Kelemen, "The Study of Critical Junctures: Theory, Narrative, and Counterfactuals in Historical Institutionalism," *World Politics* 59, no. 3 (2007): 341–69.

63. Luis Romano, "Luta de Nôs Letrad," *Voz de Povo*, May 3, 1976; "A Distinção Entre Língua e Díalecto Tem Uma Base Política," *Voz de Povo*, May 13, 1976; Mariano Verdeano Raimundo, "O Crioulo e o Português No Futuro de Cabo Verde," *Voz de Povo*, June 26, 1976; Artur Vieira, "A Questão Do 'Crioulo'—Uma Réplica de Artur Vieira," *Voz de Povo*, August 7, 1976.

64. "'O Problema Do Bilinguismo'. Nota Oficiosa Do Ministério Da Educação e Cultura," *Voz de Povo*, November 5, 1977, 2.

65. Manuel Veiga, ed., *Primeiro Colóquio Linguístico sobre o Crioulo de Cabo Verde* (Praia: Instituto Nacional de Investigação Cultural, 2000).

66. Manuel Veiga, "Introdução: O Primeiro Colóquio Linguístico, 21 Anos Depois," in *Primeiro Colóquio Linguístico Sobre o Crioulo de Cabo Verde*, ed. Manuel Veiga (Praia: Instituto Nacional de Investigação Cultural, 2000), 9–30; Eutrópio Lima da Cruz, "No Limiar Do Bilinguismo," in *Cabo Verde 30 Anos de Cultura*, ed. Filinto Correia e Silva (Praia: Intituto da Biblioteca Nacional e do Livro, 2005), 70–76; Carlos Alberto Delgado, *Crioulos de Base Lexical Portuguesa como Factores de Identidades em África: O Caso de Cabo Verde, Subsídios para uma Abordagem Metodológica* (Praia: Instituto da Biblioteca Nacional e do Livro, 2009), 339.

67. Veiga, "Introdução," 1; Almada, *Bilinguismo ou diglossia?*, 187–205.

68. Veiga, "Introdução," 13; Cruz, "No Limiar Do Bilinguismo," 76.

69. Veiga, "Introdução," 11.

Chapter 2

Contemporary Politics of Language Policy (1991–2022)

In 1986, an exciting debate on the language question developed in *Voz di Povo,* Cabo Verde's state-owned weekly newspaper. The debate first started with an op-ed piece by Daniel Benoni, entitled "O Crioulo, Língua Oficial Porque? Par que?" ("The Creole language, official language: Why? For What?").[1] The author's key argument—and fear—is that any state-sanctioned policy of making the Cabo Verdean Creole into an official language would result in the total abandonment of the Portuguese language. The author feared the "substitution" of Portuguese by Cabo Verdean Creole. To this author and others who share his ideas, the Cabo Verdean language is not modern, so its use may lead to regression in the development path. The critical point was that there couldn't be room for true bilingualism since the outcome of any language policy is always a zero-sum game. He further argued that the key proponents of the policy were those who "express[ed] badly in Portuguese." Benoni's article provoked an avalanche of criticism, mainly from those with some inclination toward linguistic nationalism.[2]

The importance of this debate cannot be overstated. Despite the authoritarian regime, this 1986 debate on the language question took place with almost complete freedom of expression and thought. At the same time, the debate brought in significant issues about the language question in Cabo Verde, particularly the issue of the relationship between the vernacular and the Portuguese language and the question of the functional roles of the Creole language. It is also interesting to note how colonial language ideology, informed by social Darwinism, could still find adherents in the postcolony. And lastly, this was the first time an open debate on the Cabo Verdean language question occurred in the postcolonial period.

This chapter comprises four main sections. In the first section, titled "The Politics of Language Policy and Planning since 1991," I discuss political development in Cabo Verde with the institution of multiparty electoral democracy. The new political system has created fertile ground that has led to the country's first-ever language legislation. The second section of the chapter discusses the politics of constitutional revision in the context of language policy and planning development. I examine the constitution as the primary locus of the language-politics nexus and maintain that the specific characteristics of the country's political regime explain constitutional outcomes regarding language policy and planning. The third section discusses the ideological debate over language in Cabo Verde. This debate is complex, multidimensional, and indexical to other relevant issues of society, such as national identity and the politics of regionalization. Finally, I compare the case of Cabo Verde with other Creole island states in the Caribbean in terms of the language-politics nexus.

THE POLITICS OF LANGUAGE POLICY AND PLANNING SINCE 1991

By the late 1980s, the signs of "the third wave of democratization" could be discernible in Cabo Verde and other parts of the world.[3] Like elsewhere, the one-party regime faced a major political dilemma: opening the political sphere to competition or augmenting its authoritarianism. The government first tried to duck from the growing diasporic and international pressures fueled by the global rise of democracy and human rights discourse. To that end, Aristides Pereira, the president of the republic and the secretary general of the PAICV, speaking to the National Assembly in December 1987, mentioned that "the Cabo Verdean democracy is not dictated by 'fashion' [*modismo*]."[4] By "fashion," he meant the contemporary global discourse and practice of multiparty democracy. Yet, the juggernaut of democratization was too robust for a small, aid-dependent island state to duck.

Earlier divisions between soft-liners and hardliners surfaced during the Third Congress of the PAICV in 1988. Soft-liners of the regime rehearsed some political openings, however timid. It became clear that a modicum of liberalization was warranted if the regime was to survive. Against this backdrop, the regime opened the economic realms with the so-called strategy of extraversion that permitted the free flow of foreign direct investment in Cabo Verde.[5] Economic liberalization, called the policy of "extroversion of the economy," was the first step in dismantling the one-party state.[6] By the decade's end, pressures from domestic and international quarters were amounting. In 1990, the one-party state was formally dismantled, and new institutions were created to facilitate the transition toward multiparty democracy.

Democratization in Cabo Verde has been classified as a *pacted transition* insofar as the regime agreed with key political opposition groups to devise the new institutional framework and to schedule the founding elections.[7] The founding elections resulted in a humiliating defeat of the incumbent party, the PAICV, and the rise of the MpD. Cabo has since been classified as an *exemplary liberal democracy*.[8] Since the first multiparty elections in Cabo Verde, the country has been through a total of twenty-four elections: seven parliamentary, nine presidential (including two second-round run-off elections), and eight local government elections. These elections have produced a peaceful and orderly change of government, with the two dominant political parties, the PAICV and MpD, assuming control in all different layers of power. The last electoral cycle (2020–21), held during the COVID-19 pandemic, translated into the PAICV-backed candidate taking over the presidential seat, while the MpD managed to win a second term in the parliamentary elections, thus creating a divided government.[9]

Multiparty electoral democracy has given new impetus to language policy and planning politics. Though the state has been its epicenter and its leading actor, with agencies and personnel affiliated with the Ministry of Culture at the forefront in promoting changes, other sociopolitical actors, particularly political parties and public intellectuals, became involved in this political arena. Four different moments of language policy and planning can be discerned.

In the first half of the 1990s, language planning was initiated within the state by a small group affiliated with the Linguistics Department of the National Institute of Culture (INAC), part of the then Ministry of Education and Culture. In 1993, a commission was tasked with developing a new model of the writing system for the Cabo Verdean language, given the critiques against the previous model. The commission (*Grupo para a Padronização do Alfabeto*) included six different personalities from the world of linguistics, education, and literature, under the leadership of the linguist Manuel Veiga. The group's final product was a new writing system called *Alfabeto Unificado para a Escrita do Caboverdiano* (ALUPEC, in its acronym and as it is now known). The new model sought to create a consensus between the two previously adopted models (1979 and 1989).[10] In other words, the group grounded its activity in Cabo Verdean language corpus planning, centering on orthographic innovation and spelling reform. According to the classification of corpus planning proposed by Einar Haugen, the group's activities consisted of codifying the language.[11] Despite the dominant discourse of the 1990s that emphasized civil society, the Cabo Verdean language corpus planning was an internal process with close to no participation of social forces outside the state.

The second moment began with the government's approval of the ALU-
PEC system "on an experimental basis" for five years. This decree was the
first-ever language law ever passed by the postcolonial state. The law presented itself as the basis upon which all future language policy and planning
would stand, chiefly the standardization of the writing and eventually the
process of making Cabo Verdean an official language of the state.

One should note that these two moments of the Cabo Verdean language
policy and planning coincided with the development of an international Portuguese language-promoting organization, the Commonwealth of Portuguese
Speaking Countries (CPLP, in its Portuguese acronym), founded in 1996. As
will be discussed in chapter 7, the establishment of the CPLP further solidified the dominant position of the Portuguese language, as the organization
amasses material and symbolic resources in promoting this language.

In the meantime, in the elections of 2001, the PAICV returned to power.
A significant political development was the appointment of Manuel Veiga as
the minister of culture in 2004, a position he maintained until 2011. Veiga is
a well-known and strong-minded advocate of the ALUPEC system, which he
helped design in the 1990s, making the Cabo Verdean language an official
language of the country.[12] Under his leadership, two significant language
laws were approved by the Cabo Verdean government: the *Estratégia de
Afirmação e Valorização da Língua Caboverdiana* (Strategy for Affirming
and Valuing the Cabo Verdean Language, Resolução n.º 48/2005, de 14 de
Novembro) and the *Instituição do Alfabeto Caboverdiano* (Institution of the
Cabo Verdean Alphabet, Decreto-Lei n.º 8/2009). The two language laws
were seen as significant steps toward making Cabo Verdean an official language of the state, which was supposed to occur with the constitutional revision of 2010. This third moment of language policy and planning unfolded a
lively yet sensitive and emotive language ideological debate, which is yet to
end. A "war of orthography" ensued, as those opposing ALUPEC criticized
and debased it for being delinked from the Portuguese etymology. Debate
on the language question in Cabo Verde has always been situated with Portuguese as the reference for linguistic distancing or closeness. Moreover,
as those leading the project decided to choose the basilectal Cabo Verdean
Creole, this has further augmented opposition among the cultural elite, which
is still attached to the Portuguese language. Given the significance of this
language's ideological debate, I will discuss it in a separate section later in
this chapter.

The last moment, since 2010, has been characterized by the Cabo Verdean
language question being placed on the back burner of state interventions,
despite the continuous debate in society and the number of individuals who
support changes in the current language policy. In many ways, the politics
of the officialization of the Cabo Verdean language has become a sort of

third-rail politics that causes political actors to avoid taking any concrete action—despite political discourses emphasizing the language as essential to the Cabo Verdean nation. The 2020s will probably be a decade in which the language question is brought to the fore as the new government is talking about re-instituting pilot bilingual education at the primary and secondary levels. The mother tongue has now been classified as a national immaterial patrimony.[13]

There are two main pathways to *formal language policy*—the enactment of codified norms by the state. The first of these pathways is through constitutional revision, which places the parliament (the National Assembly) as the main arena of language policymaking. The next section of this chapter discusses the constitution as the primary locus of language policy and planning. The second pathway is through the executive branch, which involves actions carried out by the state bureaucracy, which are then approved by the executive and promulgated by the president of the republic. In other words, language policy could emanate from ordinary law approved by the executive (decree-law and resolutions).

Language policymaking consists of different stages. In Cabo Verde, a typical process starts with the *Instituto do Património Cultural* (IPC, Institute of Cultural Patrimony), an autonomous agency within the Ministry of Culture and Creative Industries, another key actor in language policymaking. The IPC advises the Ministry of Culture on language, among other functions. The IPC assists in drafting a bill, which is brought up to the minister of culture, who, in turn, engages in agenda-setting with their peers in the context of the Council of Ministers. Once included in the agenda, debated, and approved, the bill is sent to the president of the republic, who has the power to promulgate it and, thus, make it a law. In the case of a governmental resolution, as happened with the *Estratégia de Afirmação e Valorização da Língua Caboverdiana*, it enters into force once approved by the Council of Ministers.

THE CONSTITUTION AND THE
OFFICIAL LANGUAGE QUESTION

The process of officialization of the Cabo Verdean language has faced exogenous and endogenous forces. In chapter 3, I will discuss the exogenous forces that have worked to entrench Portuguese linguistic hegemony in Cabo Verde. In this section, I focus on the domestic politics of the official language. One of the main points of contention is the language conflict over which dialect to choose as the standard norm. Some believe that the dialect of Santiago is an ideal choice because of the island's demographic, political, and economic weight. The focus has been, for symbolic reasons, on the *basilectal Creole* of Santiago, the version that is farthest from the *lexifier*. Public intellectuals from the island of São Vicente, the second most important island of Cabo Verde, are the most vocal opposers of the idea, a topic that is further developed later in the chapter. Creolists talk about the Creole continuum to refer to the different levels of the Creole language. It ranges from the basilect, that is, the Creole dialect far removed from the lexifier (the acrolect or the European language that furnishes the lexicon) to the mesolect, the mid-range, or a variant of Creole that is made to approximate, in lexicon, phonology or even syntax, the lexifier.[14] As far as the exogenous threat that accounts for the subordinate position of the mother tongue in the formal public sphere, it can be found in the global politics of the Portuguese language, which is developed in the next chapter.

The modern state, a political construction from European political history since the end of the Middle Ages, is, by essence, multilingual. The idea of a nation-state as a political community characterized by a single ethnicity that speaks the same language is a myth. Given multilingualism—and multidialectalism—in political communities, official sanction of a single linguistic variety was assumed as a primary vehicle through which the state operates. Once chosen, the state sought to do all it could to disseminate this chosen, official variation throughout the country.[15] The selected language/linguistic variation, as such, becomes the official language of the state. It may be that the official language is also the language of the nation that people use in everyday life, but that is not necessarily the case.

Many scholars have studied the notion of an official language. The *official language* has been defined as the language chosen by state law to be used as the vehicle for official business in the domains of government communication, administration, law, education, and general public life.[16] Noted sociolinguist Joshua Fishman, building on a definition first advanced by Ralph Fasold, considers an official language to include seven main characteristics: (i) as the language of communication by government officials in carrying out their duties at the national level; (ii) for written communication between government agencies at the national level; (iii) for the keeping of government records at the national level; (iv) for the original formulation of laws and regulations that concern the nation as a whole; (v) for such forms as tax forms; (vi) in the schools, and (vii) in the law courts.[17] The state's official language is the means through which institutional memory is conserved, given its role as the language through which the state records are kept.

Robert Cooper distinguishes three main types of official language. The first category refers to a language legally classified as official by the government or its agents (*statutory official language*). The second classification, defined as *working official language*, as the name indicates, denotes a language the government uses to conduct its primary business, chiefly within itself.

Lastly, there is the *symbolic official language*, which arises when a language becomes a state symbol.[18]

In the African postcolonial context, the official language confers political identity on the state and, in many ways, informs how international diplomacy is conducted. The official language has become a defining symbol of the postcolonial state—though not of the nation. Thus, one finds *anglophone*, *francophone*, and *lusophone* states, polities where the language of conducting official state business is English, French, and Portuguese, respectively. Consequently, the defining external characteristic of the postcolonial state is conferred by its colonial history, which has resulted in the superimposition of the language of the former colonial master as the dominant language—often at the expense of local languages.[19] With the notable exception of Tanzania, the sub-Saharan African state maintained the old colonial language policy at independence.

While pressure and influence may come from civil society organizations and individuals, the official language status can only be fully accomplished through an act—or practices—at the level of public authorities. The government of a polity, through law or any other normative instrument, has the authority and legitimacy to make a language an official language. In recent decades, the question of official language has become constitutional, with an increasing number of states inscribing their official language policy on their respective political constitutions.

With states' constitutions becoming the site of official language policy, the following conclusions can be drawn. Given that the countries' political constitutions are to be taken as a holy document, something like a political-religious artifact, it follows that the purpose of including official language policy is to grant the chosen language the same level of political sacrosanctity. There is also a political dimension to the constitutional official language policy. Given the institutional and political constraints in amending and revising the constitution, including an official language policy clause is part of a strategy to create a durable, even permanent and unchangeable, linguistic order in the polity.

Official language status planning can assume two primary forms, implicit and explicit. Take, for instance, the case of the United States, where the official language is implicit. In this case, no legislation or a constitutional clause considers English the state's official language. Nonetheless, since the public's inception, this language has been used as the only language through which the operations, procedures, and processes of power are carried out. Many other states, however, have constructed explicit official language status planning, in which a given language—and, in some cases, as in the case of South Africa, many languages—is openly proclaimed to be the official language. Explicit official language status planning entails specific language legislation, that of the official language law (which can either be a constitutional clause, an ordinary law, or a decree mandated by the legislature or executive branches of the government). The norm today is for the states to inscribe the principle of official language in their respective constitutions. The official language should not be confused with the national language, a *demolect* (community language) used throughout the country by the people.[20]

In the case of Cabo Verde, the current official language status planning is overt, as it is inscribed in the country's constitution. Since its independence, Cabo Verde has seen three different political constitutions: the Law of the Political Organization of the State (LOPE, 1975–1980), the constitution of 1980 (1980–1992), and the current constitution (1992–present). LOPE, as the supreme law of the land, was put into place as an interim constitution until the legislative body could effectively draft a more comprehensive constitution. LOPE, the 1980 constitution, and the first version of the 1992 constitution were all silent on the official language question. Until the constitutional revision of 1999, Cabo Verde had an implicit official language policy, as the topic was not explicitly addressed in any legislation. Nonetheless, state business was conducted almost exclusively in Portuguese. Along with Angola, Mozambique, Guinea-Bissau, and São Tomé and Príncipe, Cabo Verde formed the informal international network called *Países Africanos de Língua Oficial Portuguesa* (PALOP, African Countries with Portuguese as the Official Language).

Since 1999, the parliament has become the epicenter of the politics of official language when a constitutional revision included the official language clause in Article 9. During the constitutional revision sessions held in the summer of 1999, two different perspectives, deriving from the two dominant parties of the Cabo Verdean political system, were debated. The position of the MpD, then the party in power, was that of a piecemeal approach, focusing on creating institutional conditions that would allow the real and effective officialization of the mother tongue. The MpD proposed a two-section article that would be incorporated in the final version of the revision. The PAICV's position was that the officialization of the language would accelerate the construction of the conditions for its implementation. The PAICV had a somewhat radical approach, with its proposal stating, "In the Republic of Cabo Verde, the Cabo Verdean and Portuguese languages are official languages."[21] While, at first glance, the proposal seems to constitute a de jure official bilingualism while placing primacy on Cabo Verdean, the first language to be listed, the PAICV proposal did not indeed maintain a true parity of the two languages. Instead, the idea was "a co-officialization, in construction," a phrase coined by the linguist and ardent advocate of the officialization of the Cabo Verdean language, Manuel Veiga.[22] It was evident that the two parties had opposing views on how the officialization of the Cabo Verdean language should occur. After much discussion, the MpD, which had political control over the National Assembly (with more than two-third of its members and thus with the capacity to approve any constitutional reform), submitted a new proposal that eventually included the third section approved by the body.

As a constitutional clause, it can only be modified or changed through a parliamentary act promulgated by the president. The official language status is found in the ninth article of the Cabo Verdean Constitution, which reads:

Article 9 (Official languages)

1. The official language shall be Portuguese.
2. The State shall promote conditions for making the Cabo Verdean mother language official, on par with the Portuguese language.
1. 3. It shall be the duty of all national citizens to know the official languages and shall have the right to use them.

This particular constitutional article has three main vectors. The first section of the article codifies, in the constitution, what has been hitherto a de facto official language policy. The second and third sections are prescriptive in that the objective is to alter the current linguistic state of affairs while being duty-bounded to the state and citizens. The second section imposes duties on the state to "promote conditions for making the Cabo Verdean mother language official, on par with the Portuguese language."

The third section of the article uses two dimensions of language policy: *language as a right* and *language as a duty*. The first dimension (language as right) has been the target of many studies and comments over the past four decades.[23] However, the constitutional article also includes the duty dimension, grounded on the principles of personal responsibility—a clear indication of the influence of conservative political philosophy on constitutional language policy. It follows thus from this principle that the state should not be liable for citizens' linguistic incapacity, who must incur their costs to "know the official languages."

The article is mainly characterized by vagueness and ambiguity. For instance, the summary header (or *epitome*) refers to "official languages" in the plural, but the article's first line spells out a single official language. In fact, this is a point that is often pointed out by those who study and analyze the official language policy of Cabo Verde.[24] Moreover, in the third section of the same article, there is a reference to "official languages" The wording of the article is quite controversial. Consequently, since the early 2000s, there have been calls to change it. Recently, a documentary on the topic brought the issue to the general public, indicating the continuing controversy regarding constitutional language policy in Cabo Verde.[25]

Despite its ambiguity and vagueness, the article re-positions and entrenches, symbolically, Portuguese as the country's dominant language, with the nation's supreme law clearly illustrating the *primus inter pares* condition of that language. In other words, the country's constitution serves as the means through which Portuguese linguistic hegemony is reconstructed and reinforced. The fact that the very first section of the article centers on the Portuguese language is a mark of the symbolic supremacy of that language. An interesting example to contrast this situation is the case of the Mozambican constitution of 2004, in which constitutional language policy is included in two articles, namely the ninth and the tenth. While the ninth article focuses on the national language, thus placing symbolic primacy on the indigenous languages, the official language policy is included in the tenth article.[26]

Late 2004 was another period in which the constitution could go through a revision, as per the supreme law. In Cabo Verdean constitutional law, the constitution can go through a process of revision if more than five years have passed from the previous one. Consequently, in 2004 and 2005, the two political parties that dominated the Cabo Verdean legislative politics developed their proposals for constitutional change. The question of the officialization of the Cabo Verdean language was a key component of these two proposals, with the PAICV proposing the Cabo Verdean language as a *de jure* official language.[27] After five years of legislative politics, the PAICV and MpD finally agreed to a constitutional revision. To resolve the differences between the two proposals, the two dominant parties entered into a political agreement in which common grounds were found, and areas of differences were not included in the next revision.

The Cabo Verdean official language question was thus left out of the formal agreement. The MpD argued that "there [was] a need for maturing the public debate on the matter and that the conditions for the officialization of the mother tongue are not yet sufficiently created."[28] As the party was quite strong in this position, no consensus could be built. Despite its ambiguity, the article was maintained unaltered.

As noted with the other pathway to formal language policy (through executive lawmaking power), constitutional language policymaking occurs without effective and actual civil society participation. Apart from a few influential public intellectuals who are, in one way or another, connected with the dominant parties, constitutional language policymaking resulted without any concrete dialogue with society. Instead, Cabo Verdean party politics, characterized by the duopoly, set the terms of the entire process and dictated the outcome. The two dominant parties, in essence, cartel parties, maintain absolute control over constitutional politics.[29] Other political parties, even those with parliamentary representation, which lack veto power because of their numerical insignificance, did not have much to contribute—despite voicing critiques.

DIMENSIONS OF THE LANGUAGE IDEOLOGICAL DEBATE IN CABO VERDE

There is not a single country—or other political community—in the modern world that is free from debates regarding what languages, or varieties of the same language, should be used for what functions—including linguistic graphization. In other words, language policy and planning are, at their core, political processes insofar as pressures to change or maintain them are linked to power relations.[30] In fact, language ideological debate, the confrontation of language ideologies and worldviews, has become a central aspect of social life, given the pervasiveness and conspicuousness of language in modern society and life. Thus, language ideological debate is fundamentally political as it is grounded in the redistribution or maintenance of actual or perceived power to speakers of different languages spoken in a given polity. A language ideological debate occurs whenever enough voices are raised to challenge and redesign the current linguistic status quo. In other words, voices within society, typically led by public intellectuals and other prominent political actors, argue about the necessity of revisiting the linguistic order. These important actors form ideological brokers, and their actions are related to the twin processes of producing and reproducing language ideologies.[31] These *ideological brokers* are not only concerned with disseminating a particular worldview about language; they also seek "authoritative contextualization," a strategy to end the debate by turning their particular views into common sense—and thus, readily accepted by all.[32]

It is necessary to unpack the concept of language ideology. Michael Silverstein defines language ideology as a "set of beliefs about language articulated by the users as a rationalization or justification of perceived language structure and use."[33] These ideas guide individuals' interpretation of a range of notions about language, from how they work to the legitimacy of their use in specific domains.[34] Language ideologies are found in three main "sites": language practices, explicit metalinguistic discourses, and implicit metapragmatic strategies.[35] Language ideologies, as such, are essential products that facilitate both the public construction of languages and the linguistic construction of the public.[36] Through language ideologies, specific languages—or varieties of a language—are deemed to possess the right qualities to carry out certain functions that others cannot. At the same time, using a specific language in a given sphere confers legitimacy and naturalizes the idea that the language is the right fit in the domains where it is used.

Language ideologies are not about language alone; connections with other areas of social life, such as identity, aesthetics, and morality, are developed, strengthened, and maintained.[37] Social actors who advance language ideologies and, in so doing, enter into the language ideological debates understand that the ultimate goal is not simply a linguistic outcome. Control of how a language is perceived by the wider society, including acceptance or rejection, are strategies to influence other socially relevant aspects that are far more difficult to address. Through language ideological debates, whether explicitly or not, a language (or a variety of it) could become accepted as a tool of oppression or resistance, depending on the views of different actors.

Language debates occur not only in terms of the linguistic corpus of one language but also in the status of one language vis-à-vis others. Linguistically homogeneous nations (with negligible linguistic minorities) experience language debate mostly over how the language is used or in terms of its proposed written reform. The examples of the Czech Republic and Germany are illustrative.[38] Globalization, international migration, and the new focus on the rights of minorities have broadened the scope of language debates, with many countries debating whether other languages could also be used in accomplishing and realizing other socially important functions, such as education, government, and the like.

In Cabo Verde, language ideological debate has been a sociopolitical fact since independence. While occurring constantly, these language ideological debates are characterized by low- and high-intensity periods. The quantity and quality of voices regarding the language question mark the periods of high intensity. In periods of high intensity, opinion editorials are written, debates are held and aired through the radio and/or television, and political officers are pressured to comment on the matter. The advent of modern information and social media technologies means that far more people are voicing their ideas and opinions about languages in Cabo Verde. However, the social media public is fragmented and delinked from one another. Periods of high intensity tend to occur at critical political moments, such as elections and constitutional reforms. Additionally, these periods of high intensity develop around certain ephemerides (annual events) and national holidays, chiefly International Mother Language Day (February 21). With the advent of social media, especially Facebook, the periods of high intensity have had far more impact, with far more people entering the debate.

Because language ideological debate as a concept can be complex, researchers have divided it into different spheres for analytical simplification. Of course, it should be stressed that the dividing line between spheres of debate is rather difficult to draw. The first sphere of debate in Cabo Verde is officializing the Cabo Verdean language. In the previous section, I note that the two dominant parties have tightly controlled constitutional language policymaking. Nonetheless, voices from society, however fragmented and disorganized, seek to influence the outcome. Though the Cabo Verdean language is widely accepted and celebrated as the maker of national identity, there is no consensus regarding official language planning. As noted above, the PAICV and MpD, the two main parties of the Cabo Verdean political system, have developed different views on the matter, with the former centering on immediatism and the latter on gradualism. In many ways, these two parties' positions are a microcosmic representation of society. However, at the societal level, there is still a third perspective, however minority, that opposes the elevation of the Cabo Verdean language as the official language.[39] Those who adhere to this latter position base their arguments on functionality and redundancy. According to the functional view, the mother tongue is not equipped to perform the duties of modernity. This position fails to accept that interventions, chiefly corpus and status planning, can allow a language to perform duties in many domains. Moreover, others argue that there is already an official language, Portuguese, which has performed the role for centuries. Consequently, making Cabo Verdean an official language would be redundant, and such a process's economic and financial costs are prohibitive.

A second dimension of the language ideological debate occurs at a more dialectal level. The debate centers on what formula should be designed and implemented if the Cabo Verdean language is made the official language. Many advocated monodialectalism, the view that one of the dialects should be chosen to form the standard Cabo Verdean.[40] This position is rarely accepted, though the most ardent supporters of the officialization of the mother tongue tend to be speakers of the Santiago dialect. For this reason, pluridialectalism, the view that different dialects that make up the Cabo Verdean language should be used in official settings, is now the formula that most seem to support.

Language ideological debate in Cabo Verde is not locked on the issue of status planning. There is also a more heated debate regarding corpus planning, chiefly the graphization of the two languages that are part of the country. The spelling reform of Portuguese codified in the 1990 international agreement involving all seven states with Portuguese as their official language (Angola, Brazil, Cabo Verde, Guinea-Bissau, Mozambique, Portugal, and São Tomé and Príncipe) has not produced an intense debate. Instead, few voices presented themselves against the reform and stuck with the old spelling system. As with the case of their counterparts in Portugal, these few agents consider the new spelling reform as resulting from Brazilian linguistic imperialism.[41]

However, the introduction of the ALUPEC, now called the Cabo Verdean Alphabet, has provoked high-intensity debates regarding the spelling of Cabo Verdean words. The terms "ALUPEC" and "AK" (Cabo Verdean Alphabet), as they are officially known, are indeed misnomers; they do not constitute alphabets. Instead, the ALUPEC and AK are writing systems comprising the conventions to implement a specific alphabet and the guiding and foundational principles used to construct those same conventions.[42] In contrast, the term alphabet more narrowly corresponds to the basic signs of any writing system.[43]

A significant characteristic of the ALUPEC/AK system is that it does not include the grapheme <c>. Sounds that in the Portuguese writing system are represented by the <c> are written in this writing system either by the <s> (*sidadi*, city) or the <k> (*kaza*, house). The fundamental principle of a single and direct link between a sound and a letter in the ALUPEC/AK system made using the <c> unnecessary. The absence of the <c> has become the main talking point among those who disapprove of the ALUPEC/AK. Their argument is constructed around the idea that with the ALUPEC, one cannot have "Vitamin C"—a strategy to deride and, thus, delegitimize the writing system.[44] Linked to this argument is the erroneous notion that the <k> is an importation from Africa to indicate a specific ideological position, Pan-Africanism.[45] Though António de Paula Brito had suggested the introduction of <k> in the writing of Cabo Verdean in the late nineteenth century, its popularity is linked with the poetry of Kaoberdiano Dambara. He believed that the <k> possessed African characteristics. Therefore, the inclusion of the <k> is part of a strategy of re-Africanizing the Cabo Verdean mind. It is improbable that Dambara was familiar with the literature of linguistic relativism, the perspective that language informs behaviors and thought. Nonetheless, this particular writing strategy was indeed employed to modify the behaviors and thoughts of Cabo Verdeans—particularly to shape their notion of Africanness. The controversy over the <k> is not peculiar to the Cabo Verdean language. A few other Creole-language societies have gone through a similar debate, namely Haiti and the ABC islands (Aruba, Bonaire, and Curaçao).[46]

Language ideological debate in Cabo Verde is not only about the Cabo Verdean language question. In fact, language debates cover more than language and are woven together with many other sociopolitical issues. The language debate in Cabo Verde is multidimensional; it is connected with debates on national identity, regionalism, and significant historical questions. As noted in chapter 1, different ideas about national identity have developed since colonial times. To this day, there are three leading schools of thought about Cabo Verdean national identity: western, African, or simply Cabo Verdean. Ideas about language reinforce these positions. The ongoing debate on the state-sanctioned writing system for the Cabo Verdean language is interwoven with the issues of postcolonial identity, with opposing sides of the argument emphasizing either an African or a European cultural legacy as the main argumentative corpus for their respective positions. Those supporting the ALUPEC/AK writing system are likely to emphasize pan-African identities as opposed to the Eurocentrism of those who support a writing system based on etymological principles.

There is additionally a division around the ALUPEC/AK based on the politics of regionalization. There is now a growing movement, particularly on the island of São Vicente, toward decentralization of power. Many public intellectuals and social activists argue that resources are overconcentrated in Santiago, where Praia, the capital city, lies.[47] "The Republic of Santiago" has become a catchphrase among those from São Vicente to describe Praia's total control by Praia of the state resources.[48] For those adhering to this perspective, Praia's control over resources includes control over language policy and planning. Consequently, introducing and promoting the ALUPEC/AK system is part of a strategy of domination of Praia over the other islands, including São Vicente. For them, the ALUPEC/AK forms a Trojan horse designed to make the Santiago variety hegemonic.[49]

CREOLE SOCIETIES AND THE LANGUAGE-POLITICS NEXUS

The islands of Cabo Verde are one of many sovereign and independent territories in which a Creole language is widely spoken. Jamaica, Haiti, and Mauritius are a few examples of independent and sovereign states where a Creole language is spoken throughout the territory. In other words, Creole, whether French-, English-, or Portuguese-based, is the national language in these polities and is used by ordinary men and women in all aspects of their everyday life. However, as noted in the case of Cabo Verde, another significant characteristic of these polities is that the European language still constitutes the dominant language. Consequently, the European language is the language of power and prestige and is used in all formal domains, from public administration to education. There is another group of non-sovereign Creole islands, such as Martinique and Guadeloupe (an integral part of the French Republic) and the so-called ABC islands, that are part of the Netherlands.

A significant similarity among Creole island states is their history. Like Cabo Verde, European powers took over the Caribbean islands and parts of Africa as part of their strategy of colonial expansion. The plantation economy soon became the dominant system, with enslaved Africans compulsorily imported to work in various cash crops, chiefly sugar, to meet the demands of European markets.[50] Despite their small size, the Caribbean islands received some 40 percent of all enslaved Africans, generating high profits for European plantocrats at the expense of the African blood. Slavery and plantocracy were the dominant political-economic system until the nineteenth century when Haiti became the first sovereign nation in the Western Hemisphere to abolish the institution of slavery with its progressive constitution of 1804.[51] Throughout the century, slavery was declared illegal in all of these Creole islands, with the Cabo Verde being among the last in 1867.[52]

As noted above, Creole island states followed two paths in terms of their political history. Some were incorporated into the metropolitan administrative system, and, as such, their de jure political status changed from a colony into an administrative unit as part of the mother country. The example of the French dependencies in the Caribbean (Martinique, Guadeloupe, and the northern part of Saint Martin) is quite illustrative of this trend. With the institution of the French IV Republic in the aftermath of World War II, these territories were incorporated into the French national system, today constituting Overseas Departments (Départements d'Outre Mer). A similar case is that of the ABC islands, which have maintained intact political links with the Netherlands.

The other group of Creole island states chose the way of independent statehood, with different modalities of sovereignty being implemented since the 1960s. Some preferred to maintain independence and symbolic links with the colonial power. In the case of Jamaica, the queen of the United Kingdom remained as its head of state. Others opted for establishing a republic (like Cabo Verde and many others). Given their political history and geography, Creole island states tend to develop similar approaches to global politics. It is possible to observe such a political stance in global environmental politics: all of the Creole island states now form the Alliance of Small Island States, an international organization created to advance the interests of these states against the threat of climate change.[53]

Another common point, which can be applied to these Creole island states, is the legacy of the colonial language ideology, in which Creole is considered all but a language. Without exception, these different Creoles were labeled as "broken," "degenerate," and "corrupt" languages. These Creoles were—and still are—thought not to have the properties to serve in official and public domains—such as education, public administration, and the like. Diglossia, the social and political superimposition of one language over another, is a sociolinguistic condition common to most Creole societies.[54] Given that a large segment of society stigmatizes its Creole language, the process of its officialization and/or use as a medium of education has often been controversial and challenging.[55] Haiti is the only Creole-speaking nation in the Caribbean that has made a de jure recognition of the Haitian Creole language as an official language of the country, along with French. Another Creole island state that has recognized Creole (Seychellois Creole) as the official language is Seychelles in East Africa.

Two main types of speech communities can be found if one considers the current "co-habitation" with the lexifier language (see table 2.1). The first situation relates to cases where the Creole language "cohabits" with its lexifier. This category can be further broken down into two distinct subcategories: (a) the cases of Cabo Verde, Jamaica, and Haiti, in which the lexifier is the official language of the state, the primary language of politics, and the main language of education; and (b) the cases of Mauritius and Seychelles where the lexifier (French in this case), while still in use, is not the language of power, a position that English holds in these countries. The second category corresponds to situations where a Creole language "cohabits" with another European language as the high language, which is not its lexifier. The ABC islands are illustrative examples of this category. As these islands are politically dependent on and an integral part of the kingdom of the Netherlands, Dutch is the primary language of power. The lexifier of their Creoles (Spanish and Portuguese) is absent in those speech communities.

With this typology in mind, it would be easier to concur with C. Jourdan's argument that when the Creole language and its lexifier share the same speech community, the former often lacks linguistic and sociocultural legitimacy.[56] In other words, making the Creole languages official and/or upgrading their social status (status planning) in their respective habitat depends on the existence of the lexifier—or the lack thereof. Social and political recognition of the Creole languages has been more forthcoming in the cases of the islands of Mauritius and Seychelles and dependent Creole islands, such as the ABC islands.

In the cases of Cabo Verde, Jamaica, and Saint Vincent and the Grenadines, the presence of the lexifier, particularly in the realm of officialdom, has made the process of turning their respective Creoles into a medium to be used in education and other formal domains extremely difficult. For one, given that the Creole lexical corpus borrows extensively from the base language, historically, there has been a social stigma attached to the Creole, which is considered a wrong way of speaking the high language.

Table 2.1 Creole Languages and Their Lexifiers

Country	Lingua Franca	Lexifier	Official and Political Language
Haiti	Haitian Creole	French	French/Haiti
Jamaica	Jamaican Patwa	English	English
Cabo Verde	C.V. Creole	Portuguese	Portuguese
ABC	Papiamentu	Portuguese/Spanish	Dutch/Papiamento
Mauritius	M. Creole	French	English/French/Creole
Seychelles	S. Creole	French	English/French/Creole

Source: Compilation by the author (table created by author).
ABC islands: Aruba, Bonaire, and Curaçao.

Moreover, language conflict has also been observed within the Creole language relative to corpus planning (standardization and graphization of creole). Several scholars have noted that the campaign for standardization and graphization of different creoles is a linguistic battleground. The choice of an orthography, more than a simple choice of which symbols should be used to write the language, is, above all, a political statement. Those proposing a pro-etymology orthography seek to strengthen the links between the Creole language and its lexifier. On the other hand, those seeking to construct a more phonological orthography consciously aim for linguistic independence by increasing the symbolic differences with the lexifier.[57] Given the situation, these postcolonial Creole islands have developed into a mandarinate system in which the defining element is the knowledge of the lexifier.[58] This is because a tiny linguistic elite has controlled the state.[59]

CONCLUSION

This chapter has critically analyzed the contemporary language-politics nexus in Cabo Verde. Given that the new era of Cabo Verdean political history started in 1991 when the political regime changed from a single-party state to multiparty electoral democracy, I analyze the most significant political developments regarding language policy and planning. Political change has created a new institutional framework within which significant developments in the language-politics nexus have occurred.

I discussed the political processes through which language policy is made in contemporary Cabo Verde. I noted two pathways to formal language policy and planning, with two different arenas: the executive and the legislative. Regarding the first arena, which has made significant language legislation since the 1990s, the key actors involved in the process are the state bureaucracy, particularly the IPC, and the Ministry of Culture and Creative Industries. Ultimately, the Council of Ministers holds the authority to pass legislation on language matters—though some of these bills require the president of the republic to sign them to make them law. I also note that language legislation tends to be locked within the structure of the state, with little to no input from civil society—apart from a few individuals, chiefly public intellectuals, who are part of the network of language workers or experts.

In the second section, I centered my analysis on the constitution of the republic as the primary site of official language policymaking. With the introduction of the official language clause in the constitutional revision of 1999, the constitution has since become the principal target of the politics of language in Cabo Verde. I argue that the ninth article is ambiguous and vague; as such, there are constant calls to modify its wording. Given the sensitivity of the language question, the article has yet to go through any real change, despite being rejected by different sections of society. The last constitutional revision, from 2010, ended with the language question not being addressed.

In order to grasp the contours of the language-politics nexus in contemporary Cabo Verde, I critically analyzed the language ideological debate that has been happening since the late 1990s. I noted that there are periods in which the language ideological debate tends to be intense and more profound, with many actors pronouncing the topic in national media and, more recently, on social media. I also emphasized that the language ideological debate in Cabo Verde is indexical to many other socially and politically relevant questions, particularly national identity and the politics of regionalization.

Finally, I compared the language-politics nexus of Cabo Verde with other Creole islands in the Caribbean and Africa. Creole island states are similar not only in terms of their political history but also in terms of their current language-politics nexus. In these territories, three languages dominate, with French, English, or Portuguese as the language of prestige and power, while the Creole language is the language of everyday interactions. Despite calls to make the mother tongue the official language of these islands, there has been tremendous resistance, primarily from the local elites.

NOTES

1. Daniel Benoni, "O Crioulo, Língua Oficial Porque? Par Que?," *Voz Di Povo*, 1986.

2. José Luis Hopffer Almada, "Ainda Sobre o Crioulo e Os Seus Apaixonados," *Voz Di Povo*, May 7, 1986; Eduardo Cardoso, "Contribuição Para o Debate Sobre o Estatuto Do Crioulo," *Voz Di Povo*, 1986; Horácio Santos, "Kiriolu?...Purtugues?... Kal d'es Dos?," *Voz Di Povo*, May 28, 1986, 9; Manuel Veiga, "Ainda a Proposito Do Crioulo," *Voz Di Povo*, June 11, 1986; Manuel Veiga, "O Diálogo de Surdos Não é Meu Estilo," *Voz Di Povo*, August 9, 1986; Arcádio Monteiro, "De Perguntas a Respostas. Um Terceiro Atingido No 'Directo' Benoni/Veiga," *Voz Di Povo*, September 10, 1986.

3. Huntington, *The Third Wave*; Roselma Évora, *Cabo Verde: A Abertura Política e a Transiçao para a Democracia* (Praia: Spleen Edições, 2004).

4. "Comentário Discurso Do Presidente Aristides Pereira Na ANP," *Voz Di Povo*, December 31, 1987.

5. Partido Africano da Independência de Cabo Verde, *III Congresso, 25-30 de Novembro de 1988: Resoluções, Moções, Discurso de Encerramento Do Secretário Geral* (Praia: O Partido, 1988).

6. Victor Andrade de Melo and Rafael Fortes, "Identidade Em Transição: Cabo Verde e a Taça Amílcar Cabral," *Afro-Ásia*, no. 50 (December 2014): 34, https://doi .org/10.1590/0002-05912014v50vic11.

7. Évora, *Cabo Verde: A abertura pol?*

8. Meyns, "Cap Verde"; Baker, "Cape Verde," 2009; Baker, "Cape Verde," 2006.

9. Abel Djassi Amado, "Parliamentary Elections under Covid-19: The Case of Cabo Verde Case Study," October 26, 2021, http://democracyinafrica.org/elections-in-a-pandemic-the-case-of-cabo-verde/.

10. Grupo para a Padronização do Alfabeto, *Proposta de Bases do Alfabeto Unificado para a Escrita do Cabo-Verdiano* (Praia: Instituto da Investigação e do Património Culturais (IIPC), 2006).

11. Einar Haugen, "The Implementation of Corpus Planning: Theory and Practice," in *Progress in Language Planning: International Perspectives*, ed. J. Cobarrubias and J. A. Fishman (Berlin: Mouton, 1983), 269–89.

12. "Novo Ministro Cultura Aposta No Crioulo," *A Semana*, Outubro 2004.

13. IPC, "Conselho de Ministros Aprova Elevação Da Língua Cabo-Verdiana e Da Tabanca a Património Cultural e Imaterial," July 29, 2019, https://www.facebook.com/patrimoniocultural.caboverde/posts/pfbid02BuKPpPNtqnKcSVDzpJAiNqaXsqsVUDBtsFein15E1FkE45B6XJKtpR1jLJN4ZgH4l.

14. Derek Bickerton, *Dynamics of a Creole System* (London: Cambridge University Press, 1975).

15. Eugen Joseph Weber, *Peasants into Frenchmen: The Modernization of Rural France, 1870–1914* (London: Chatto & Windus, 1979), http://www.gbv.de/dms/bowker/toc/9780701124397.pdf.

16. Alastair Walker cited in Nkonko Kamwangamalu, *Language Policy and Economics: The Language Question in Africa* (London: Palgrave Macmillan, 2016), ix.

17. Joshua Fishman and Ralph Fasold cited in Kamwangamalu, *Language Policy and Economics*, ix.

18. Cooper, *Language Planning and Social Change*, 100.

19. Tove Skutnabb-Kangas, *Linguistic Genocide in Education, or, Worldwide Diversity and Human Rights?* (New York: Routledge, 2000), 232.

20. Conrad M. B. Brann, "The National Language Question: Concepts and Terminologies," *Logos. Anales Del Seminario de Metafísica* 14 (1994): 125–34.

21. Assembleia Nacional de Cabo Verde, "Atas Da Assembleia Nacional de Cabo Verde," July 20, 1999; "PAICV Quer Oficialização Já, Do Crioulo," *A Semana*, July 9, 1999.

22. Manuel Veiga, "Kriolu: Dja Bu Grandi Dja," *A Semana*, May 14, 1999.

23. Skutnabb-Kangas, "Human Rights and Language Wrongs"; Skutnabb-Kangas and Phillipson, "Human Rights: Perspective on Language Ecology"; Faingold, "Language Rights and Language Justice"; Bruthiaux, "Language Rights."

24. Interview with José Luis Hopffer C. Almada, July 17, 2010.

25. *Artigo 9o: A Situação Linguística Em Cabo Verde*, 2022, https://www.youtube.com/watch?v=pevjwn2cbp4&t=1s.

26. Gregorio Firmino, "Diversidade Linguistica e Nacao-Estado Em Africa: O Caso de Mocambique," *Platô* 1, no. 1 (2012): 43–55.

27. Grupo Parlamentar do Partido Africano da Independência de Cabo Verde, "Projecto de Lei de Revisão Constitucional," n.d. http://www.parlamento.cv/downloads/projectos%20de%20revisao%20consticioanal/Projectos%20dos%20Deputados%20do%20PAICV.pdf.

28. "Memorando de Entendimento Entre o MPD e o PAICV Sobre Matérias. Essenciais Para a Segunda Revisão Ordinária Da Constituição," in *As Constituições de Cabo Verde e Textos Históricos de Direito Constitucional Cabo-Verdiano*, ed. Mário Ramos Pereira Silva (Praia: Edições ISCJS, 2014), 497–502.

29. Klaus Detterbeck, "Cartel Parties in Western Europe?," *Party Politics* 11, no. 2 (2005): 173–91; Richard S. Katz and Peter Mair, "Changing Models of Party Organization and Party Democracy: The Emergence of the Cartel Party," *Party Politics* 1, no. 1 (1995): 5–28.

30. James W. Tollefson, *Planning Language, Planning Inequality: Language Policy in the Community* (London: Longman, 1996).

31. Jan Blommaert, *Language Ideological Debates* (New York: Mouton de Gruyter, 1999).

32. Sally A. Johnson, *Spelling Trouble?: Language, Ideology and the Reform of German Orthography* (Clevedon: Multilingual Matters, 2005), 5.

33. Michael Silverstein, "Language Structure and Linguistic Ideology," in *The Elements*, ed. P. Clyne, W. Hanks, and C. Hofbauer (Chicago: Chicago Linguistic Society, 1979), 193.

34. Deborah Cameron, "Ideology and Language," *Journal of Political Ideologies* 11, no. 2 (2006): 143.

35. Darren Paffey, "Policing the Spanish Language Debate: Verbal Hygiene and the Spanish Language Academy (Real Academia Española)," *Language Policy* 6, nos. 3–4 (2007): 313.

36. Susan Gal and Kathryn A. Woolard, "Constructing Languages and Publics Authority and Representation," *Pragmatics* 5, no. 2 (1995): 129–38.

37. Woolard, "Introduction: Language Ideology as a Field of Inquiry"; Paul V. Kroskrity, "Regimenting Languages: Language Ideological Perspectives," in *Regimes of Language: Ideologies, Polities, and Identity*, ed. Paul V. Kroskrity (Sante Fe, New Mexico: School of American Research Press, 2000), 1–34.

38. Neil Bermel, *Linguistic Authority, Language Ideology, and Metaphor: The Czech Orthography Wars* (New York: Mouton de Gruyter, 2007); Johnson, *Spelling Trouble?*

39. Benoni, "O Crioulo, Língua Oficial Porque? Par Que?"; "Oficializar o Crioulo? Porque a Pressa?," *A Semana*, April 24, 2009.

40. Veiga, *Primeiro Colóquio Linguístico*.

41. Ondina Ferreira, "O Acordo Ortográfico Do Nosso Desacordo?," *Expresso Das Ilhas*, April 25, 2008, 8.

42. Florian Coulmas, *Writing Systems: An Introduction to Their Linguistic Analysis* (Cambridge: Cambridge University Press, 2003), 35; Bermel, *Linguistic Authority*, 4.

43. Coulmas, *Writing Systems*, 35.

44. Amália Maria Vera-Cruz de Melo | Lopes, "Língua Cabo-Verdiana: Desconstruindo Mitos-Mito 12/12," *Santiago Magazine*, September 24, 2020, https://santiagomagazine.cv/cultura/lingua-cabo-verdiana-desconstruindo-mitos-mito-1212; David Leite, "ALUPEC, Um Alfabeto Nos Ku Nos. E Os Nossos Emigrantes?," *A Semana*, September 19, 2009, https://www.asemana.publ.cv/spip.php?page=article&id_article=45529&ak=1#ancre_comm.

45. Macedo, "A Linguistic Approach to the Capeverdean Language," 163; Dambarà, *Noti*.

46. Bambi B. Schieffelin and Rachelle Charlier Doucet, "The 'Real' Haitian Creole: Ideology, Metalinguistics, and Orthographic Choice," *American Ethnologist* 21 (1994): 176–200.

47. Arsénio Fermino de Pina, José Fortes Lopes, and Adriano Miranda Lima, *Na Encruzilhada da Regionalização: Rumo à Descentralização* (Mindelo: Movimento para a Regionalização de Cabo Verde, Grupo de Reflexão da Diáspora, 2017).

48. "Os Recados de Onésimo Silveira Para Mário Lúcio e JMN," *Notícias Do Norte*, April 30, 2014, https://noticiasdonorte.publ.cv/990/os-recados-de-onesimo-silveira-para-mario-lucio-e-jmn/.

49. Adriano Miranda Lima, "Diálogo Sobre a Questão Da 'Língua Cabo-Verdiana': II Parte," *Notícias Do Norte*, March 10, 2015, https://noticiasdonorte.publ.cv/31751/dialogo-sobre-a-questao-da-lingua-cabo-verdiana-ii-parte/; David Leite, "Tubarões Azuis, a Diáspora e a Caboverdeanidade," *A Semana*, November 2, 2013, http://asemana.publ.cv/spip.php?article93309&ak=1.

50. Olwyn M. Blouet, *The Contemporary Caribbean: History, Life and Culture since 1945* (London: Reaktion, 2007), 33.

51. Laurent Dubois, *Avengers of the New World: The Story of the Haitian Revolution* (Cambridge, MA: Harvard University Press, 2005).

52. Lumumba Hamilcar Shabaka, "Transformation of 'Old' Slavery into Atlantic Slavery: Cape Verde Islands, c. 1500–1879" (PhD Thesis, East Lansing, Michigan, Michigan State University, 2013); Carreira, *Cabo Verde*.

53. Espen Ronneberg, "Small Islands and the Big Issue: Climate Change and the Role of the Alliance of Small Island States," in *The Oxford Handbook of International Climate Change Law*, ed. Kevin R. Gray, Richard Tarasofsky, and Cinnamon P. Carlarne (Oxford: Oxford University Press, 2016), 761–77.

54. Albert Valdman, "Diglossia and Language Conflict in Haiti," *International Journal of the Sociology of Language* 1988, no. 71 (1988): 67–80; Schieffelin and Doucet, "The 'Real' Haitian Creole."

55. Hubert Devonish, *Language and Liberation: Creole Language Politics in the Caribbean* (London: Karia Press, 1986).

56. C. Jourdan, "Pidgins and Creoles: The Blurring of Categories," *Annual Review of Anthropology* 20 (1991): 187–209.

57. Valdman, "Diglossia and Language Conflict in Haiti"; Albert Valdman, "Language Standardization in a Diglossia Situation: Haiti," in *Language Problems of Developing Nations*, ed. Joshua A. Fishman, Charles A. Ferguson and Jyotirindra Das Gupta (New York: John Wiley and Sons, Inc., 1968), 313–26; Schieffelin and Doucet, "The 'Real' Haitian Creole."

58. Pierre Louis Van den Berghe, "European Languages and Black Mandarins," *Transition: A Journal of the Arts, Culture and Society* 7, no. 34 (1968): 19–23.

59. David D. Laitin, *Politics, Language, and Thought: The Somali Experience* (Chicago: University of Chicago Press, 1977).

Chapter 3

The International Politics
of the Portuguese Language

June 10 is Portugal's national day; officially, it is known as the Day of Portugal, Camões, and the Portuguese Communities (*Dia de Portugal, de Camões e das Comunidades Portuguesas*). It is, along with April 25, the day of the fall of the brutal right-wing dictatorship in Portugal in 1974, one of the most respected and celebrated national days in that European country. In 2019, the events started in the Portuguese district of Portalegre for the official celebrations of this national day. They ended in Cabo Verde, with the Portuguese head of state and head of the government present. On the main day of celebrations in Lisbon, the Cabo Verdean president Jorge Carlos Fonseca was present, and a Cabo Verdean military unit participated in the military parade along with its Portuguese congener.[1] That the Portuguese authorities chose Cabo Verde as the other leg for the celebration of the national day was in any way a coincidence. Instead, it was part of a calculated policy developed over many years to strengthen and deepen Portugal's symbolic influence over Cabo Verde. Through iteration and linkage, Portugal has solidified its connection with Cabo Verde, a condition that facilitates the Portuguese language spread policies in the islands.

In this chapter, I argue that domestic sociopolitical dynamics are not enough to explain the comfortable dominant position of the Portuguese language in Cabo Verde. The chapter's main argument is that international politics of language reinforces and underpins the domestic sociolinguistic situation. The asymmetric situation of the languages is justified and legitimized because one of the languages can better realize international communication. The sociolinguistic and political dominance of the Portuguese language in Cabo Verde—as well as in other African countries with Portuguese as the official language—cannot be solely explained as the outcome of elites' selfish interests and the reproduction of the class system internally. International politics of language also accounts for such a situation. International politics, as such, lays the foundations and creates fertile ground for linguistic encroachment. The deployment of language ideologies, resources of various types, ranging from symbolic to material ones, and the formation of multilateral institutions tasked with promoting the Portuguese language underpin and strengthen the legitimacy of the Portuguese language in Cabo Verde and other African countries with Portuguese as the official language.

This chapter argues that Cabo Verde's international relations reinforce and strengthen the Portuguese language's position as a dominant language in the country. International politics of the postcolonial state in Africa is intimately connected with the former colonial power. The weight of colonial dependency has been too much to be demolished in the postcolonial period, despite radical African leaders pointing out the machinations of neocolonialism.[2] Cabo Verde has maintained solid and intimate links with the former colonial power like its African counterparts. The deepening of diplomatic relations with Portugal has become a means through which the Portuguese language could find the necessary foundations for maintaining its linguistic hegemony in Cabo Verde. International politics is also the realm of the language-politics nexus. Discourses and institutions breeding and sustaining specific language ideologies have helped Portuguese linguistic hegemony.

This chapter includes four main sections. In the first section, I provide a theoretical framework that helps understand the connections between international and domestic politics. This chapter is informed by the argument that international politics influence and shape domestic politics and policies, particularly in language policy and planning. Then, in the second section, I discuss the geopolitics of the Portuguese language. Given Portugal's long history of expansion and colonialism, Portuguese has been disseminated to different continents and is now the official language of several countries and used in many regional intergovernmental organizations. I argue in this section that to speak about the global presence of the Portuguese language is to think about a hierarchy of Portuguese-speaking countries, depending on their capacity and willingness to design and implement Portuguese language policy and planning—chiefly status and corpus planning. The last two sections focus on the dynamic processes of constructing Portuguese linguistic hegemony. On the one hand, I center my analysis in analyzing the role of multilateral organizations, the Comunidade dos Países de Língua Portuguesa (Community of Portuguese Language Countries, CPLP) and the Instituto Internacional da Língua Portuguesa (International Institute of the Portuguese Language). On the other hand, I discuss Portugal's bilateral relations, including its language spread policies, as mechanisms that have assisted in maintaining Portuguese linguistic hegemony.

INTERNATIONAL POLITICS AND
DOMESTIC POLITICS

The literature on the relationship between international and domestic politics is vast and evolving.[3] Though it is rather difficult to establish a clear-cut divide between the two realms, scholars have often engaged in an analytical and disciplinary distinction between international and domestic politics. Thus, comparative politics analyzes domestic political institutions and behaviors, while the other subfield, international politics, focuses on how actors pursuing their interests behave on the international stage. Two schools of thought have developed regarding the symbiotic relationship between these two realms of politics. The first, in which Kenneth Waltz's now-classic *Man, the State, and War* is the main example, suggests that political developments on the international scene result from the state's specific characteristics and domestic politics.[4] Waltz called this perspective the "second image." The other school of thought, called "the second image reversed" by Peter Gourevitch, makes the opposite argument: the international state system shapes domestic political structures.[5] Other theories, ranging from the insights of Alexander Gerschenkron, dependency school, and Immanuel Wallerstein, focusing on political economy, make similar arguments that the structure of international political economy shapes and influences domestic political institutions and behaviors.[6]

Following Gourevitch, I argue that there is an intimate relationship between international and domestic politics of language in the sense that the former substantially affects the latter.[7] International politics, comprising a myriad of state and non-state actors, is quintessentially social; interactions among these actors are established and developed using one or more languages in written or oral formats. To properly communicate their interests, resolve, and foment rapport with others, actors on the international scene have traditionally opted for one of the following strategies: rely on their language, use the language of their counterparts, and communicate through a third language. Since the development of the modern state system in the eighteenth century, international communication and diplomacy have been grounded on monolingualism or bilingualism. Latin and later French were the language of international communication until the 1900s when diplomatic bilingualism became a reality (with English). Since the institution of the UN system, multilingualism and the adoption of non-Western European languages (Russian, Mandarin, Arabic) have become defining features of international politics. Brazil was a founding member of the United Nations, and there was a proposal to make it a permanent member of the United Nations Security Council. Portuguese, the country's official and national language, was not considered one of the organization's official languages.[8] The fact that Portugal was not invited to the founding conference of the United Nations in San Francisco in 1945—and would only become a member of the organization in 1955 after an agreement between the two blocs—did not work for the international advancement of the language. Though the number of states with Portuguese as the official language tripled in the mid-1970s, with the independence of the five African states that were part of the Portuguese colonial empire, very little happened in terms of the international status of the Portuguese language.

English is indeed the de facto lingua franca for international diplomacy and communication and, as such, has carved its arena of global politics. This English-based arena is the main layer of international politics, as state and non-state actors increasingly rely on this language to connect and share views. For this reason, English has been classified as a hyper-central language.[9] The other layer, chiefly in regional international politics, relies on second-tier languages such as French, Spanish, and, to a lesser extent, Portuguese, Russian, and Arabic. To counter the global hegemony of the English language, states like Spain, Portugal, Germany, and others now develop and support policies designed to increase the number of speakers and functions of their respective languages.

Scholars have not paid much attention to the interconnectedness between domestic and international language politics. Different subfields center on analyzing the connections between the two realms. As analyzed by Phillipson and many others, studies of linguistic imperialism connect the domestic politics of anglophone states such as the UK and USA with the global expansion of the English language.[10] Studies of language spread policy also connect domestic political structures with international politics insofar as they analyze domestic interests, actors, and processes involved in disseminating a language in other countries. However, comprehensive studies of language and politics are often locked inside a country, with international factors and variables not given the deserved attention.

A myriad of state and non-state actors intervenes in the international politics of language. Yet, the two dominant actors in this field are the states through the pursuit of their foreign policy and intergovernmental organizations explicitly established by the states to promote and diffuse a specific language. Throughout the twentieth century, and particularly in the aftermath of the Cold War, states have also looked at language as a foreign policy tool to expand their influence on the global stage. The theory of soft power, as suggested by Joseph Nye, posited that the power of states derives not only from traditional sources such as economic and military might but also from the attractiveness of culture and values.[11] Consequently, since the late nineteenth century and throughout the twentieth century, many states began to develop institutions tasked with promoting and diffusion the language. Institutions such as the Alliance française (founded 1883), the British Council (1934), and the Goethe-Institut (1951) were pioneers in this arena. More recently, newcomers also entered this international game of language diffusion and promotion: Spain with its Instituto Cervantes (1991), Portugal with Instituto Camões (1992), and the People's Republic of China with Confucius Institute (2004).

Apart from state-managed institutions of language promotion and diffusion, there is a tendency to form and cement linguistic spaces through intergovernmental organizations. Organisation Internationale de La Francophonie, whose origins can be traced back to the Agence de Coopération Culturelle et Technique founded in 1970, is an intergovernmental organization promoting the French language.[12] The Community of Portuguese Language Countries (CPLP), founded in 1996, is relatively straightforward in its statutes, with the third article describing three main objectives of the organization: (a) political and diplomatic concentration among members; (b) cooperation in all policy domains; and (c) promotion and diffusion of the Portuguese language.[13] The short-lived Three Linguistic Spaces, which combined the Organization of Ibero-American States, the Community of Portuguese Language Countries (CPLP), and the International Organisation of La Francophonie, was more of a united front against the perceived global English linguistic imperialism.

Two dominant characteristics can be observed in the contemporary international politics of language. First, there is the global hegemony of English. Second, the global arena is now characterized by the development of international organizations tasked primarily with assisting the promotion and diffusion of specific languages which have created an additional force that supports the predominance of few European languages in many states around the world. These international organizations coupled with states' language spread policies, channel resources, and ideologies that help construct the linguistic hegemony of the language in question.

To speak about linguistic hegemony, one must first understand the concept of hegemony developed by the Italian philosopher Antonio Gramsci, whose ideas radically changed the meaning of the word. With Gramsci, hegemony became a foundational concept to grasp "the formation and organization of consent."[14] In other words, political domination needs not to rely on brute force, which is very expensive and could easily backfire if used constantly. Gramsci argued that social domination passes through the fabrication of consensus in the sense that subaltern groups identify with and possibly defend the elites' values and norms. Against this theoretical backdrop, linguistic hegemony refers to building consensus regarding a language's status, value, and worthiness, even by those who don't or can't use it. The logical conclusion of linguistic hegemony is to place a language as a *primus inter pares* in a given community, consolidating thus its dominant position and status.

Linguistic hegemony is a form of hidden or covert domination in that the subaltern groups rarely can uncover the situation they are facing. Therefore, a given language is presented as a tool that could generate individual and collective success and advancement. For instance, the idea that people should learn English around the globe is constructed in terms of functional development (English as a tool) and not as "a world order."[15] Other scholars have extended the meaning of linguistic hegemony. For instance, to scholars like Wiley, linguistic hegemony produces self-victimization in that failure is connected with the supposed failings of one's language. In Cabo Verde, Ondina Ferreira, who held government positions in the 1990s (including being minister of education and culture), is perhaps one of the most vocal advocates of this category of Portuguese hegemony. In many of her writings and publications, Ferreira argues that social and academic failure has an identifiable culprit: the Cabo Verdean language. Students' constant use of the mother tongue leads to interference in their acquisition of the Portuguese language and, consequently, hurts their academic and professional future.[16]

THE GEOPOLITICS OF THE PORTUGUESE LANGUAGE

Since the 1400s, the Portuguese language has expanded beyond its original environment, the western corner of the Iberian Peninsula. Portuguese maritime expansion and colonialism facilitated the dissemination of the language to different parts of the world, from Africa to South America and Asia-Pacific. The five-hundred-year expansion of Portuguese occurred not only in geographic dimensions but also in linguistic terms, as the language has historically been the lexifier of many creoles and pidgins in the Atlantic and Asia.[17]

The understanding of the international politics of the Portuguese language entails, first, grasping the sociolinguistic profile of this language. To this end, this section discusses the geopolitics of the Portuguese language. The Portuguese language is the third-largest European language in terms of the number of its speakers (as L1, second, or foreign language), with over 200 million speakers spread across 4 different continents (Africa, South America, Asia, and Europe). The idiom is the official language in eight sovereign states (Brazil, Portugal, Angola, Cabo Verde, Guinea-Bissau, Mozambique, São Tomé and Príncipe, and East Timor) and a sub-national political entity (Macao, where it shares the status of co-official language along with Mandarin). In 2013, by decree of its President Teodoro Obiang, Equatorial Guinea adopted Portuguese as one of its three official languages (along with Spanish and French).

To ease the understanding of the geopolitics of the Portuguese language, I develop a four-concentric language model informed by the insights of Braj Kachru. Kachru proposes a three-concentric circle model to understand better the global diffusion of English—or, as he calls it, *world Englishes*.[18] The inner circle comprises countries like the United Kingdom, the United States, and other countries where English is the first language. The outer circle refers to the former British colonies where English is the second language. Finally, there is the expanding circle, characterized by states where several citizens are now using the language as a foreign language.

The model I propose has four-concentric circles for the Portuguese language (see figure 3.1). Portugal and Brazil make up the inner circle. Portuguese is the first language in these countries, so social and political life happens almost exclusively in that language. Other languages present in these communities are relegated to ethnolinguistic enclaves and, as such, are unlikely to be used in the main domains of social and political life. At the same time, these two states represent the two normative centers of the Portuguese language since Brazil and Portugal are the recognized norm-setters of the Portuguese language.[19] These two states have created and supported language institutions tasked with not only setting but also policing the norms of the language. The Academia das Ciências de Lisboa (Lisbon Academy of Sciences) and Academia Brasileira de Letras (Brazilian Academy of Letters) control the European and Brazilian norms of the Portuguese language. Since the early 1900s, agreements referring to the norms of the language are first discussed between these two bodies.

Moreover, these two countries represent states where most residents have Portuguese as their mother tongue. As an emergent economic power with roughly 200 million inhabitants, Brazil possesses the necessary ingredients to be the hegemon within this Portuguese-speaking space. Nonetheless, the Brazilian norm of the Portuguese language is limited to itself, its diaspora communities, and the extensive Portuguese as Second Language programs it sponsors in North America and Europe.[20] On the other hand, despite its demographic disadvantage vis-à-vis Brazil, Portugal exerts considerable influence over Portuguese used in its former colonies. The accepted norm of writing the language in Africa (and in Macao and East Timor) derive from Portugal, making thus this particular normative system geographically dispersed. In other words, eight out of nine states with Portuguese as the official language follow the norms emanating from Lisbon. This situation, however, will probably change in the future, given the Orthographic Agreement of 1990 that sought to shorten the distances between the two norms.

The second circle corresponds to Angola and Mozambique. Together, these two southern African states have over sixty million habitants; however,

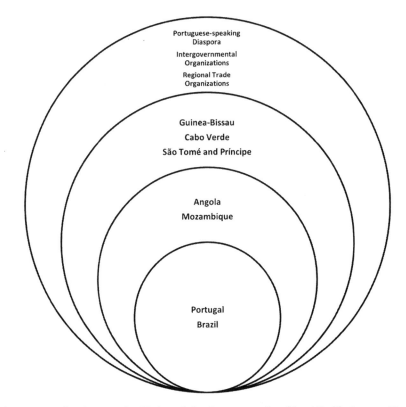

Portuguese-speaking
Diaspora

Intergovernmental
Organizations

Regional Trade
Organizations

Guinea-Bissau

Cabo Verde

São Tomé and Príncipe

Angola

Mozambique

Portugal

Brazil

Figure 3.1   The Concentric Circles of the Portuguese-Speaking World. *Source*: Figure created by author.

the Portuguese speakers in those countries are far below the total population. Moreover, there are two categories of Portuguese speakers in those countries: Portuguese first language and Portuguese second language speakers. The Portuguese first language speakers form what can be called Afro-Lusitanos, in the same way that Ali Mazrui talks about Afro-Saxons.[21] For many years, these two states' political and cultural elite has expressed their intentions to establish their norms of the Portuguese language.[22] However, these two states lack the human, financial, and other resources necessary to fully implement their nativized norm of the Portuguese language. It should also be noted that these two states are the most outspoken critics of the Portuguese Orthographic Agreement, and while they were parties to the agreement, they have not taken concrete measures to implement it.

Cabo Verde, Guinea-Bissau, and São Tomé and Príncipe (as well as East Timor and Macao), the three micro-states in the Portuguese-speaking world, constitute the third circle. Combined, these three states have less than three million inhabitants, of which the great majority use other than Portuguese in their everyday interactions. These states lack the willingness and resources to develop a nativized norm of the Portuguese language. While one or another public intellectual from these states can be heard in their advocacy for a local norm of the Portuguese language, the dominant norm is the one deriving from Lisbon. In other words, there is almost complete adherence to the norms set forth by Portugal. In Cabo Verde and Guinea-Bissau, the share of society that has had Portuguese as its first language is insignificant.

Lastly, there is a relatively thin fourth circle. It corresponds to the different spaces in which the Portuguese language is expanding or seeking to expand. These include countries with a considerable number of Portuguese-speaking immigrants and diasporas, such as France or the United States, and major regional and universal international organizations that have been the target of Portuguese language spread policy. Since the 1990s, it has been a foreign policy of countries like Portugal and Brazil, mainly to assist in the diffusion of Portuguese in regional and universal international organizations. However, the fact that an international organization adopts a language among its repertoire does not mean it will be used for the institution's business. An example is the case of the Economic Community of West African States (ECOWAS), which in the revised agreement of 1993 has added Portuguese as the official language. While this move is quite symbolic, the ECOWAS maintained, as before 1993, a bilingual regional international organization, as English and Portuguese are widely used.[23]

IMPOSING PORTUGUESE LINGUISTIC HEGEMONY: THE MULTILATERAL DIMENSION

To truly understand the encroachment of the Portuguese language as a dominant language in Cabo Verde, one must look beyond the lens of domestic politics. As noted in the first two chapters, domestic politics, in many ways, explain the predominance of the Portuguese language. Yet, I contend that the Portuguese language's international politics substantially affect how it maintains its sociological and political importance in a country where the overwhelming majority either don't speak it or lack comfortable competence. International politics of language contributes to the domestic encroachment of the dominant language for the following reasons. First, through the mechanism of ideological support, various language ideological centers devise, create, reproduce, and disseminate language ideologies that construct and maintain the naturalness of dominance of the language in question and its usefulness in global politics. In the context of the international politics of the Portuguese language, Portugal, and Brazil, and to a lesser extent, the language-promoting organizations, such as the CPLP and IILP, are the language ideological centers. They produce and disseminate ideas on language not only to Portuguese-speaking countries but also to other international audiences, including regional and universal intergovernmental organizations. One of the most potent language ideologies developed within the context of the Portuguese-speaking world is that of *lusofonia*, a topic that will be discussed later in the chapter.

The other mechanism is symbolic support. Political communities need symbols; these are constructed to assist in semiotic abbreviations and miniaturization of the community. Symbols—and language is a great example—are used to be powerful microcosmic representations of the community. A powerful political and language ideology that has taken shape in the past three decades is the notion that the speakers of the Portuguese language constitute a community, leading to celebrations and commemorations in different Portuguese-speaking countries and diasporas. The adoption by UNESCO of World Portuguese language day has become a mnemonic device for this community.

Finally, there is material support. International cooperation and technical assistance have become the vehicle through which countries like Portugal and Brazil weave their language spread policies. Cooperation between Portugal/ Brazil and the African countries with Portuguese as the official language not only has a long history, as will be seen below, but it encompasses all domains of activity, from defense, culture, sports, and so on. Portugal—and, to a lesser extent, Brazil—has been the major exporter of education and artistic materials, cultural products through international radio and television broadcasts, and other elements in which the Portuguese language is embedded.

As a poor, micro-island state, foreign affairs are a crucial dimension of the Cabo Verdean state. Deep linkage with foreign actors, whether states, international intergovernmental organizations, or international nongovernmental organizations, has been cultivated by various Cabo Verdean governments since independence.[24] Foreign policy has been an important tool to procure developmental aid, direct foreign investment, or affirm the micro-state in global politics. In the last fifteen years of the Cold War (1975–1990), characterized by rising tensions between the Soviet Union and the United States, the Cabo Verdean government skillfully maintained a nonalignment position, which made it possible to strengthen cooperation with the communist and western states alike. With the end of the Cold War and the rise of the new world order, the importance of diplomacy was further underscored, with the state becoming more involved in various forums of global politics, from regional intergovernmental organizations such as the ECOWAS to the United Nations.

Deeply entrenched in global politics in the past thirty years, Cabo Verde has thus become unavoidably entangled in international language politics.

The island state has partaken an active role in many language-based international organizations such as La Francophonie, the Latin Union, the Three Linguistic Spaces, and the Commonwealth of Portuguese Speaking Countries (CPLP). These organizations aimed to strengthen Portuguese (as well as French and Spanish) in global politics against what has been described as English linguistic imperialism.[25] Being part of these international organizations means that Cabo Verde has become an ideal target for Portuguese (and French) language spread policies. The country has had access to many programs and projects financed by these organizations, which ultimately have helped to strengthen the position of the Portuguese language in the state and society. Cabo Verde, like most African and Caribbean states, is a target of multilateral and bilateral language spread policy. Portugal, Brazil, and France have developed many actions designed to fortify and consolidate the presence and functions of Portuguese and French, particularly in education and public administration.

The promotion and diffusion of the Portuguese language have two interrelated pathways, multilateral and bilateral. International organizations tasked with defending and disseminating the language regarding the first approach have been created. On the other hand, the bilateral refers to the development of direct language spread policies as part of Portugal and Brazil's foreign policy.

With the end of the Cold War and the subsequent mitigation of the traumas of liberation war and troubled decolonization of the 1960s and 1970s, states with Portuguese as the official language formed multilateral institutions centered on the language. The Community of Portuguese Language Countries (CPLP), founded in 1996, and the International Institute of the Portuguese Language (IILP), established in 2002 as an autonomous body within the CPLP, are the two multilateral organizations grounded on the language. As the name of these organizations undoubtedly indicates, the foundational objective is to promote and advance the use of the Portuguese language not only within its space but also in other areas. To such an end, these institutions have become incubators of language ideologies and font of symbolic, human, and material resources designed to underpin Portuguese language legitimacy in each of these countries and on the international stage. The CPLP and its subsidiary institution, the IILP, have played an important role in strengthening the position of the Portuguese language in Cabo Verde through the dissemination of resources, institutions, and language ideologies, of which the most salient one is that of *lusofonia*.

According to its statutes, the CPLP is a language-promoting intergovernmental organization. The third article of the founding document explicitly states that the organization's objective is to assist in the global promotion of the Portuguese language. To such an end, the CPLP is a language planning institution centering on the two interrelated activities of language corpus planning and status/prestige planning. A political principle guiding the CPLP is that promoting the Portuguese language onto the global stage can be best advanced following corpus planning designed to harmonize the language's different orthographies (Brazilian and European norms). The Orthographic Agreement was initiated in the 1980s and signed in 1990, years before the organization was founded. The agreement is perceived as an essential step in the international promotion of the language. Though there have been complaints that the organization lacks the resources to implement its objectives fully, the CPLP has organized many events and issued many statements and communications to assist in the process of Portuguese language legitimacy.

Unlike many international organizations, the CPLP language policy is monolingualism since Portuguese is the organization's only official and working language. While member states of the organization, chiefly Portugal and Brazil, are vocal proponents of multilingual language policy in other regional and universal intergovernmental organizations to which they belong, there is no discourse to advance any type of such policy within the CPLP. At the same time, other member states do not see any real value in promoting the use of their national languages as part of the activities of the organization, in part because these indigenous languages are confined to the boundaries of these states. The CPLP monolingual language policy advances the hegemonic position of the Portuguese language within its space. Concomitantly, this policy devalues and delegitimizes other languages in the same area.

The Cabo Verdean language is conspicuous within the CPLP space since it can be found among Cabo Verdean diasporic communities in most of the members of the organizations, chiefly Portugal, São Tomé and Príncipe, Guinea-Bissau, and Angola (and to a lesser extent in Mozambique and Brazil). Except for Portuguese, no other language is more visible within this space than the Cabo Verdean language. The success of Cabo Verdean's popular and traditional music within this space adds another dimension to the visibility of the language.[26]

Yet, both the CPLP and the IILP have developed a declaratory language policy regarding other languages found within their spaces. For instance, the project "As Linguas Vivas no Mundo da CPLP" (Living Languages in the CPLP World) centered on languages other than Portuguese was never implemented.[27] The scarce resources at the disposal of these organizations are used essentially to promote Portuguese, while other languages take the back seat. In fact, since the 2010s, the attention and resources of the CPLP have been centered almost exclusively on the international promotion of the Portuguese language. It is against this background that the organization drafted the *Plano de Ação de Brasília para a Promoção, a Difusão e a Projeção da Língua Portuguesa* (Brasilia Action Plan for the Promotion, the Diffusion, and Projection of the Portuguese Language) in 2010, and other plans that were built on this one (Lisboa-PALis 2013, Díli-PADíli 2016, and Praia-PAP 2021).[28] These plans "provide institutional support for the regulation of the form and functions of the language which, in turn, inform the policy on the promotion and dissemination of the Portuguese language, within the scope of the CPLP."[29] Thus, according to the same operation plan, the CPLP language policy and planning stand on four pillars: (a) Promotion and Dissemination of Portuguese Language Teaching; (b) Portuguese, Language of Culture and Creative Economy; (c) Portuguese, Language of Science and Innovation; and (d) Internationalization of the Portuguese Language. By capturing the attention and mobilizing resources of the member states, the current CPLP language policy and planning, resulting from the various action plans as noted above, has two main dimensions: internal, that is, within the CPLP space (a, b, and c) and external, centering on the promotion of the language in the international arena (d), particularly within regional and universal inter-governmental organizations.

The other international organization promoting the Portuguese language is the IILP, headquartered in Cabo Verde. So far, three of seven executive directors were Cabo Verdeans, indicating that the Cabo Verdean sociopolitical elite has been uncompromisingly supportive of this institution.[30] The first article of its bylaws states, "The IILP's fundamental objectives are the promotion, defense, enrichment, and dissemination of the Portuguese Language as a vehicle for culture, education, information, and access to knowledge scientific, technological, and official use in international forums."[31] The keyword here is "vehicle"; the language is presented as an instrument—thus, presumably a neutral, value-free element—whose use can bring positive outcomes to its speakers and nations. The statement, as such, camouflages linguistic hegemony claims by presenting the language simply as a tool. This type of strategy has been identified by scholars studying other languages. For instance, in his study of English linguistic imperialism, Robert Phillipson has persuasively argued that the global dominance of English is presented as a helpful tool and thus "politically and socially neutralized" and never as a "world order."[32] What is hidden is that the international promotion of the Portuguese language benefits Portugal and Brazil far more than the African states with Portuguese as the official language. The deeper the commitment to promoting the language, the more entrenched and naturalized the political order among states where the language is used.

After analyzing the two organizations whose *raison d'être* promotes the Portuguese language, I now focus on an essential ideological dimension of the Portuguese language spread. The most conspicuous language (and social) ideology intimately associated with the CPLP is that of *lusofonia*. The CPLP can be classified as the institutional wing of the ideology of lusofonia, giving it resources and policies. While scholars from various disciplines have addressed the topic, there is no consensual definition or understanding of the term.[33] Lusofonia has become a buzzword in the past three decades among Portuguese-speaking people from different sociological backgrounds. Many political leaders to scholars use the term to signify a pluri-continental and multi-century constructed community whose key determining factors are the common language and the notion of shared history/culture. The term is so pervasive that non-Portuguese-speaking academic communities have adopted it in several parts of the world.

While any proposed definition of the term would not be free from criticism, as it may constitute an "essentially contested term," one can still find some core elements that make up the concept. Lusofonia has been used to refer to different meanings, including linguistic, institutional, geographic, and a "specie of spiritual family."[34] Lusofonia is fundamentally a geopolitical and geolinguistic concept as it fabricates a community whose constitutive members are polities where the Portuguese presence and the adoption of the Portuguese language have been the longest and most pervading. Thus, lusofonia is taken to mean the community of Portuguese speakers, in the same way that Francophonie is the community of French speakers.

Lusofonia entails an imagined community, a geocultural space with fragments from different continents. Many suggest that lusofonia, despite its etymology, is not simply a linguistic community but rather a cultural one. For instance, Armando writes that to speak of lusofonia is to recognize the "existence of a Portuguese-speaking world, which is a world of cultures unified by common traits, despite their great diversity, which linguistic variants reflect and express."[35] Critics note the ideological proximity between lusofonia and lusotropicalism. As noted in chapter 1, lusotropicalism is a social and political ideology developed by the Brazilian sociologist Gilberto Freyre according to which Portuguese colonialism in the tropics, unlike other Europeans, was based on cordiality and miscegenation.[36] Therefore, lusofonia is taken to be the postcolonial resurrection of lusotropicalist ideology.

The ideology of lusofonia fails to mention and describes that the fact the language is used in all different parts of the world is the result of the history of domination, based on symbolic and material violence, through which local languages became victimized by glottophagic language policies advanced and implemented by the colonial state. In other words, Portuguese linguistic hegemony stands on the history of violent imposition. It is well documented that the history of Portuguese colonial language policy was based on violence. Michel Laban's interviews with writers from African countries with Portuguese as the official language are filled with first-person examples of humiliation, bullying, and utter violence applied to them for using local languages.[37] Almost all these writers report being taught during their formative years to despise and reject their native languages, particularly by their teachers. Instead, the discourses of lusofonia, like its colonial counterpart (lusotropicalism), almost always hint at a peaceful acceptance by colonized subjects.

Whether it is understood as a cultural or linguistic community, lusofonia significantly contributes to Portuguese linguistic hegemony within its space. Through its peculiar discourse that emphasizes historical connections (without referring to power asymmetries and colonial violence) and many institutions that accompany it (Lusophone Games, Lusophone University, Lusophone Citizen status, etc.), lusofonia forms a community whose ticket to enter is the acceptance of Portuguese as dominant language within its space. Lusofonia constitutes a substantial international and transnational symbol that shapes and influences the sociopolitical behavior of states, elites, and individuals.

IMPOSING PORTUGUESE LINGUISTIC HEGEMONY: THE BILATERAL DIMENSION

As noted earlier in this book, the modern state developed through a calculated process of language diffusion from political centers to the peripheral areas of the territory under control. France is an illustrative example as the French variety spoken in Paris was disseminated across the territory through carrot and stick policies, chiefly during the French III Republic.[38] Linguistic diffusion from political centers has also seen an international dimension as major states channel different material and symbolic resources to disseminate and maintain their languages in other territories and countries. Scholars of language policy and planning consider this approach as language spread policy. According to Cooper, the language spread policy seek "an increase, over time, in the proportion of a communication network that adopts a given language or language variety for a given communicative function."[39] Language spread policy, therefore, is related to calculated interventions on the language to increase its users and uses as well as changing how the language is perceived by its users, including making it more entrenched in its speakers.[40] Other scholars, who pursue a more critical approach, maintain that language spread policy is related to dominance, power, prestige, and power issues.[41]

Since the end of the Cold War, Portugal and Brazil have developed and implemented language spread policies that were directed at different targets, including the countries in which Portuguese is the official language, the various Portuguese and Brazilian diasporic communities in Europe and Americas, an increasing number of foreigners who are studying Portuguese as a foreign language, and finally, many universal and regional international

organizations. Language spread policy stands on deployment and reinforcement of pro-Portuguese language ideology and the necessary institutions and
resource base, which has ultimately resulted in more profound encroachment
of Portuguese in the countries where it is already being used. The more
entrenched Portuguese linguistic hegemony, the less the chances of ascrib-
ing social value to local languages. In the case of Cabo Verde, Portuguese
linguistic hegemony, which the Portuguese language spread policy has reinforced, has ultimately made efforts to lift the national language a bit difficult.

International cooperation agreements are an important tool of foreign
policy. States use them to enhance their soft power and to advance their
interests. These agreements have been used to strengthen the position of
the colonial language in the postcolonial states, chiefly in the context of the
African continent. These agreements allowed for the crystallization of the
dominant position of the colonial language in the postcolony in two ways:
first, the discussion on these agreements, conducted by the political and
bureaucratic elites from the former metropolitan and African states, was
exclusively in the European language. The outcome is a written document
in one single language. Second, these cooperation agreements assisted in the
dominance of the European language in terms of its content. Cooperation was
to be carried out through the European language. Even the so-called cultural
and scientific cooperation meant, in the last analysis, a tool of the European
language spread policy. The training of African cadres was to be exclusively
in the European language. At the same time, these agreements did not grant
much space for any assistance that could lead to the real development and
modernization of indigenous languages.

Portuguese language spread policy is tied to other foreign policy tools,
mainly official development aid (ODA). Like France, Portugal prioritizes
its ODA to its former colonies, which received 60 percent of all available
funds.[42] For the period 2015–2016, Cabo Verde was the country that received
the largest amount of Portuguese ODA, totaling, on average, 26 million
Euros. Bilateral development aid is linked to the political objectives of maintaining and increasing the influence of Portugal in these states.

It is possible to discern two different moments in the Cabo Verde–Portugal
relationship: (a) 1975–1990 and (b) the 1990s onward. The first moment,
from 1975 to 1990, was marked by relative coldness despite links. As noted
above, political elites in Cabo Verde, though not as radical as their counterparts from Angola or Mozambique, feared neocolonial incursions on the
part of Portugal and, as such, designed policies to maintain relative distance
vis-à-vis Portugal.

The history of Portuguese cooperation with Cabo Verde is quite long and
remotes the period of national independence. On the day of Cabo Verdean
independence (July 5, 1975), Portugal and Cabo Verde signed a Cooperation

and Friendship General Agreement (Acordo Geral de Cooperação e Amizade), where the two parties committed to the principles of cooperation and respect, as laid out in the independence agreement (between the PAIGC and the government of Portugal) of December 19, 1974. The Cooperation and Friendship General Agreement, which had similar versions for the other formerly Portuguese colonies, was in no way similar to the cooperation agreements signed between France and her former colonies in the aftermath of independence. In the case of France, these agreements became a central and important tool through which neocolonial policies could be advanced and implemented. The French cooperation agreements were the cornerstone of what has become *la Françafrique*. Through these agreements, the French could maintain a military presence in Africa and become the "Gendarme of Africa," involved in many military interventions and assistance in the African military coup d'état.[43] In the case of Portugal, national independence resulted from the liberation armed struggle, which in many ways contributed to distrust and distance between the new elites from Africa and Portugal. Moreover, those who acceded power in Cabo Verde (as in other former Portuguese colonies) were, with different intensity and depth, influenced by radical politics: they were pretty aware and often spoke against the specter of neocolonialism.

The Cooperation and Friendship General Agreement was essentially a framework agreement laying the foundations for future sectoral cooperation agreements. Its language was carefully drafted to avoid any misunderstandings of neocolonialism. A guiding principle of the agreement is that both Portugal and Cabo Verde recognized the existence of "special bonds of friendship and solidarity."[44] Since this framework agreement went into force, Portugal and Cabo Verde have signed more than ten separate cooperation agreements, ranging from areas of education and health to that of defense.

On the other hand, Portugal invested far more heavily in its Europe option at the expense of the Atlantic option, which had informed Portuguese policies for over five hundred years—leading to its acceptance into the European Economic Community, now the European Union, in 1986. Moreover, Cold War politics contributed to this relative distance between the two. While it would be reductionist to claim that Cabo Verde belonged to the communist bloc, the country maintained strong links with the Soviet Union and its communist satellites. On the other hand, Portugal was committed to the so-called "free world" under the leadership of the United States. Furthermore, the Cold War proxy wars in Angola and Mozambique, in which the regimes were self-ascribed as Marxists fought Western-supported rebels, put Cabo Verde and Portugal on opposite sides.

From 1975 to 1990, Portugal did not develop an openly stated Portuguese language spread policy in Cabo Verde. Instead, Portuguese language policy directed to Cabo Verde was anchored in other policy sectors, chiefly cultural, scientific, technical assistance, and cooperation. It could be argued that Portuguese policymakers feared that any openly stated Portuguese language spread policy could attract critiques of cultural imperialism and neocolonialism.

The end of the Cold War revamped Portugal's Cabo Verde (and Africa) policy. Having fulfilled its main political objectives since the end of the empire (to become a member of the European bloc), Portugal brought the Atlantic option to the fore by reinvesting ideologically and materially with Cabo Verde. From Cabo Verde's side, considerable sociopolitical changes in the 1990s facilitated further links with Portugal. First, the regime transition from a one-party state to an electoral, multiparty democracy softened political discourses and stances in Cabo Verde. Second, the founding elections of 1991 translated into a humiliating defeat of the radical PAICV and the acceding of power by the "young Turks" organized into a Movement for Democracy (MpD). With the radicals gone, discourses of neocolonialism, cultural imperialism, and other similar tropes lost their appeal and currency. Unlike the Afrophilia stances of the previous regime, the 1990s were characterized by an increased Luso- and Europhilia. The best illustration of this state of affairs was the change in the country's national symbols, chiefly the national flag. In 1992, the new flag, whose colors replicated that of the European Union, replaced the old fag that combined Pan-Africanist colors.

In the 1990s, Portugal entered the club of donor countries, the Development Assistance Committee from OECD, making the country an important actor in the context of the global politics of development.[45] Consequently, the promotion and defense of the Portuguese language became "a priority domain of the Portuguese cooperation policy": cooperation policy became the vehicle for Portuguese spread policy, and Portuguese-speaking countries were the main targets of Portuguese cooperation.[46] Such a policy aligns well with the soft-power orientation of Portuguese foreign policy.[47] To such an objective, in 1992, the Instituto Camões was established with the "fundamental mission and essential vocation to promote, together with other competent State institutions, the Portuguese culture and language in the context of foreign cultural policy."[48]

Since the 1990s, contacts, meetings, and interactions between Portugal and Cabo Verde have significantly increased. Institutions of Portuguese spread policy, such as the Portuguese broadcasting company (RTP-Africa; RDP) and the Portuguese Cultural Center, have solidified their positions in the islands. The deepening of interactions between the two countries led to the development of a new model of diplomatic relations centered on the Cabo Verde–Portugal Summits. The first summit, which took place in 2010, marked the signing of a new cooperation agreement, which replaced the one of 1975 (2022 marked the sixth summit).

Cabo Verde has become an essential target of Portugal's Portuguese language spread policy through iteration and linkage. No other state has far more profound and engaging interactions with Cabo Verde, covering almost all policy dimensions. Iteration, repeated interaction over time, and linkage, connecting and interlocking different policy areas, have created a fertile environment for the diffusion of Portuguese language ideologies and institutions. In fact, given the deepening of the relationship between the two countries, Cabo Verdean's political elites are now suggesting a qualitative change in the interaction with Portugal. In the aftermath of the VI Cabo Verde–Portugal Summit, the Cabo Verdean prime minister Ulisses Correia e Silva suggested that the relationship between the states must advance from that of partnership to an alliance.

Like Portugal, Brazil has also advanced its language spread policy weaved with development aid and assistance. Brazil–Africa relations have historical connections, with millions of enslaved Africans forcefully made to go through the Middle Passage to feed Brazilian plantations and mines from the 1500s to the late 1800s. Yet, diplomatic and political links with Africa were something Brazilian political elites did not consider important interests until the 1990s. Despite relative support given to African independence movements in the early 1960s, Brazil's engagement with Africa, mainly the former Portuguese colonies, was, at best lukewarm. In the 1990s and the first decade of the 2000s, under presidents Fernando Henrique Cardoso and Luiz Inácio Lula da Silva, Brazil emphasized South–South cooperation, which translated into a close relationship with Africa.[49]

Cooperation with African states is in all different sectors, including the sector of defense. Unlike Portugal, Brazil does not prioritize the African states with Portuguese as the official language. While Angola (and Mozambique) was included among the top targets of Brazilian Africa policy, small states such as Guinea-Bissau, São Tomé and Príncipe, and Cabo Verde were put on the back burner. The new administrations (Michel and Bolsonaro) repositioned Brazil's focusses away from the South (and Africa) and into areas such as Western Europe, China, and the USA.[50]

Brazilian language spread policy occurs not only through technical assistance; its cultural products, chiefly its famous TV programs, particularly soap operas, have been the key vehicles through which Brazil influences linguistic development in Cabo Verde as in other African states where Portuguese is also used. The influence of Brazilian soap operas in Cabo Verdean society ranges from imports of Brazilian formulaic expressions to adopting toponymies from these soap operas in the country. For instance, "Sucupira," a fictional city from the soap opera *O Bem-Amado*, has been appropriated as the name of the city of Praia's largest market and soccer stadium.

CONCLUSION

This chapter has focused on understanding the extent that international politics of language inform the domestic language-politics nexus. The case of Cabo Verde, where the Portuguese language has maintained a conformable hegemony, cannot be explained simply with resources of domestic political actors' interests and their dynamic interactions. One must also pay attention to the development of international politics, particularly those that connect Cabo Verde and Portugal, if a correct picture of Portuguese linguistic hegemony is to be drawn.

To fully grasp the dynamic international politics of the Portuguese language, I started by discussing the geopolitics of the Portuguese language. Portuguese, I noted, is a super-central and pluricentric language, with Brazil and Portugal being the two recognized normative centers. Though the language is used in different continents and many regional organizations, Portuguese is far from being accepted as a language of international diplomacy. For this reason, Portugal and Brazil have been at the forefront of the idea of diffusing the language and have indeed advanced policies designed to make the language part of the repertoire of major international organizations.

Two main modes of language spread policies have been carried out, multilateral and bilateral.

Since the 1990s, two main Portuguese-promoting and -diffusing international institutions have been established, the CPLP and the IILP. These organizations, founded on the principle of Portuguese monolingualism, assist the hegemonic position of that language within their spheres. Moreover, both the CPLP and IILP have been significant carriers of the ideology of lusofonia, the idea of a Portuguese-based imagined community, which reinforces the dominant position of this language, particularly vis-à-vis local idioms.

The bilateral approach links development policy with language spread policy. Through international cooperation, Portugal has solidified its close relationship with Cabo Verde—and, to a lesser extent, the other African states with Portuguese as the official language. Cooperation with Cabo Verde has been in all policy domains, from education to security matters. The deepening of this partnership has created a fertile ground for disseminating institutions, such as Portuguese Cultural Centers, and ideologies that prop up Portuguese linguistic hegemony.

NOTES

1. "Comemorações Do 10 de Junho Começam No Domingo Em Portalegre e Terminam Em Cabo Verde," *Observador*, June 8, 2019, https://observador.pt/2019

/06/08/comemoracoes-do-10-de-junho-comecam-no-domingo-em-portalegre-e-ter-minam-em-cabo-verde/.

2. Kwame Nkrumah, *Neo-Colonialism: The Last Stage of Imperialism* (London: Panaf, 1970).

3. Bruce Bueno de Mesquita, "Domestic Politics and International Relations," *International Studies Quarterly* 46 (2002): 1–9; Helen V. Milner, *Interests, Institutions, and Information : Domestic Politics and International Relations* (Princeton, NJ: Princeton University Press, 1997), https://www.worldcat.org/title/Interests-institutions-and-information-:-domestic-politics-and-international-relations/oclc/36178502; David Lumsdaine, "The Intertwining of International and Domestic Politics," *Polity* 29, no. 2 (1996): 293–98.

4. Kenneth N. Waltz, *Man, the State, and War: A Theoretical Analysis* (New York: Columbia University Press, 2010).

5. Peter Gourevitch, "The Second Image Reversed: The International Sources of Domestic Politics," *International Organization* 32, no. 4 (1978): 881–912.

6. Alexander Gerschenkron, *Economic Backwardness in Historical Perspective: A Book of Essays* (Cambridge, MA: Belknap Press of Harvard University Press, 1966), https://www.worldcat.org/title/Economic-backwardness-in-historical-perspective-:-a-book-of-essays/oclc/3356244; Theotonio Dos Santos, "The Structure of Dependence," *The American Economic Review* 60 (May 1970): 231–36; Immanuel Maurice Wallerstein, *World-Systems Analysis: An Introduction* (Durham: Duke University Press, 2004), https://www.worldcat.org/title/World-systems-analysis-:-an-introduction/oclc/54454871.

7. Gourevitch, "The Second Image Reversed: The International Sources of Domestic Politics."

8. Eugênio V. Garcia, "De Como o Brasil Quase Se Tornou Membro Permanente Do Conselho de Segurança Da ONU Em 1945," *Revista Brasileira de Politica Internacional* 54, no. 1 (2011): 159–77; Eugenio V. Garcia and Natalia B. R. Coelho, "A Seat at the Top? A Historical Appraisal of Brazil's Case for the UN Security Council," *SAGE Open*, accessed August 25, 2022, https://doi.org/10.1177/2158244018801098.

9. Calvet, Towards.

10. Phillipson, *Linguistic Imperialism.*

11. Joseph S. Nye, "Soft Power: The Evolution of a Concept," *Journal of Political Power* 14 (2021): 196–208; Joseph S. Nye, "Soft Power," *Foreign Policy* 80 (Fall 1990): 153–71.

12. Margaret A. Majumdar, "'Une Francophonie à l'offensive'? Recent Developments in Francophonie," *Modern & Contemporary France* 20 (2012): 1–20.

13. Edalina Rodrigues Sanches, "The Community of Portuguese Language Speaking Countries: The Role of Language in a Globalizing World," *CIDOB*, n.d.

14. Peter Ives, *Language and Hegemony in Gramsci* (London: Pluto Press, 2004), 2.

15. Phillipson, *Linguistic Imperialism*, 287; Terrence G. Wiley, "Language Planning and Policy," in *Sociolinguistics and Language Teaching*, ed. S. L. McKay and N. H. Hornberger (Cambridge: Cambridge University Press, 2000), 113.

16. Ondina Ferreira, "Crioulês—o Novo Veículo de Comunicação Dos Quadros," *Expresso Das Ilhas*, 2006; "Ondina Ferreira Diz Que Língua Portuguesa Tem Sido Votada Ao Desprezo Na Sua Oralidade e No Seu Uso Quotidiano Em Cabo Verde" (Inforpress, May 9, 2019), https://inforpress.cv/ondinaferreira-diz-que-lingua-por-tuguesa-tem-sido-votada-ao-desprezo-na-sua-oralidade-e-no-seu-uso-quotidiano-em-cabo-verde/.

17. Holm, *An Introduction to Pidgins and Creoles.*

18. Braj Kachru, "Standards, Codification and Sociolinguistic Realism: English Language in the Outer Circle," in *English in the World: Teaching and Learning the Language AndLliteratures*, ed. R. Quirk and H. Widowson (Cambridge: Cambridge University Press, 1985), 11–36.

19. Alan N. Baxter, "Portuguese as a Pluricentric Language," in *Pluricentric Languages: Differing Norms in Different Nations*, ed. Michael Clyne (Berlin: Mouton de Gruyter, 1992), 11–44.

20. Alan Silvio Ribeiro Carneiro, "O Programa Leitorado Do Governo Brasileiro: Ideologias Linguísticas e Práticas de Ensino Em Um Contexto Situado," *Línguas e Instrumentos Línguísticos* 43 (June 2019): 259–89, https://doi.org/10.20396/lil.v0i43.8658373.

21. Ali A. Mazrui, "The Afro-Saxons," *Society* 12, no. 2 (February 1975): 14–21.

22. Gregório Domingos Firmino, "Ascensão de Uma Norma Endógena Do Português Em Moçambique: Desafios e Perspectivas," *Gragoatá* 26, no. 54 (2021): 163–92, https://doi.org/10.22409/gragoata.v26i54.46324.

23. Zuzana Murdoch, Magali Gravier, and Stefan Gänzle, "International Public Administration on the Tip of the Tongue: Language as a Feature of Representative Bureaucracy in the Economic Community of West African States," *International Review of Administrative Sciences* (2021): 1–19, https://doi.org/10.1177/0020852320986230.

24. José Pina Delgado, Odair Barros Varela, and Suzano Costa, eds., *As Relações Externas de Cabo Verde: (Re)Leituras Contemporâneas* (Praia: Edições ISCJS, 2014); Craig N. Murphy, "Cape Verde," in *The Political Economy of Foreign Policy in ECOWAS*, ed. Timothy M. Shaw and Julius Emeka Okolo (London: St Martin Press, 1994), 17–31.

25. Phillipson, *Linguistic Imperialism*; Claudia Piétri, "Les Trois Espaces Linguistiques: Quel Parcours et Quelles Synergies Développer?," *Hermès* n° 75, no. 2 (2016): 147–53, https://doi.org/10.3917/herm.075.0147; Louis-Jean Calvet, "Géopolitique Des Langues Romanes," *Hermès, La Revue* 75, no. 2 (2016): 25–33.

26. Fernando Arenas, *Lusophone Africa: Beyond Independence* (Minneapolis: University of Minnesota Press, 2011).

27. Gilvan Müller de Oliveira, "O Instituto Internacional Da Língua Portuguesa e a Gestão Multilateral Da Língua Portuguesa No Âmbito Da CPLP," *Revista Internacional de Lingüística Iberoamericana* 13 (2015): 19–34.

28. CPLP, "Plano Operacional Para a Promoção e Difusão Da Língua Portuguesa (2021–2026)," 2021, https://www.cplp.org/Files/Filer/1_CPLP/Lingua/Livro-Plano-Operacional-Lingua-Portuguesa-vfinal.pdf; Oliveira, "O Instituto Internacional Da

Língua Portuguesa e a Gestão Multilateral Da Língua Portuguesa No Âmbito Da CPLP."

29. CPLP, "Plano Operacional Para a Promoção e Difusão Da Língua Portuguesa (2021–2026)," 3.

30. Oliveira, "O Instituto Internacional Da Língua Portuguesa e a Gestão Multilateral Da Língua Portuguesa No Âmbito Da CPLP."

31. CPLP, "ESTATUTOS Do IILP," accessed August 31, 2022, https://www.cplp.org/Admin/Public/DWSDownload.aspx?File=%2FFiles%2FFiler%2Fcplp%2FCMNE%2FX_CMNE%2FESTATUTOS_do_IILP.pdf.

32. Phillipson, *Linguistic Imperialism*, 287; Debra Suarez, "The Paradox of Linguistic Hegemony and the Maintenance of Spanish as a Heritage Language in the United States," *Journal of Multilingual and Multicultural Development* 23, no. 6 (December 2002): 514.

33. Moisés de Lemos Martins, "A Lusofonia Como Promessa e o Seu Equivoco Lusocentrico," in *Comunicação e Lusofonia. Para Uma Abordagem Crítica Da Cultura e Dos Media*, ed. Moisés de Lemos Martins, Helena Sousa, and Rosa Cabecinhas (Porto: Campo das Letras, 2006), 79–90; António Bondoso, *Lusofonia e CPLP: desafios na globalização: "ângulos e vértices" ou "defeitos & virtudes" de um processo intemporal* (Moimenta da Beira: Edições Esgotadas, 2013); Carlos Alberto Faraco, "A Lusofonia: Impasses e Perspectivas," *Sociolinguistic Studies* 5, no. 3 (October 21, 2012): 399–421, https://doi.org/10.1558/sols.v5i3.399; Moisés de Lemos Martins, Helena Sousa, and Rosa Cabecinhas, eds., *Comunicação e Lusofonia: Para uma Abordagem Crítica da Cultura e dos Media*, 2a edição (Ribeirão: Húmus, 2018); José Filipe Pinto, *Estratégias da ou para a Lusofonia?: o futuro da língua portuguesa* (Lisboa: Prefácio, 2009).

34. Yves Leonard, "As Ligações a África e Ao Brasil," in *História Da Expansão Portuguesa*, ed. Francisco Bethencourt and Kirty Chaudhiri, vol. V (Lisbon: Círculo de Leitores, 1998), 438.

35. M. L. de Carvalho Armando cited in Faraco, "A Lusofonia," 410.

36. Claudia Castelo, *"O modo portugues de estar no mundo": o luso-tropicalismo e a ideologia colonial portuguesa (1933–1961)* (Porto: Edicoes Afrontamento, 2011); Armelle Enders, "Le Lusotropicalisme, Théorie d'exportation: Gilberto Freyre En Son Pays," *Lusotopie* (1997): 201–10.

37. Michel Laban, *Angola: encontro com escritores* (Porto: Fundação Eng. António de Almeida, 1991); Michel Laban, *Cabo Verde: encontro com escritores* (Porto: Fundação Eng. António de Almeida, 1992); Michel Laban, *Moçambique: encontro com escritores* (Porto: Fundação Eng. António de Almeida, 1998).

38. Weber, *Peasants into Frenchmen*.

39. Robert L. Cooper, *Language Spread: Studies in Diffusion and Social Change* (Bloomington, IN; Washington, DC: Indiana University Press; Center for Applied Linguistics, 1982), 6.

40. Ulrich Ammon, "Language-Spread Policy," *Language Problems and Language Planning* 21, no. 1 (1997): 51; Ofelia García, "Language Spread and Its Study in the 21st Century," in *Oxford Handbook of Applied Linguistics*, ed. Robert Kaplan (Oxford: Oxford University Press, 2011), 401.

41. García, "Language Spread and Its Study in the 21st Century," 399.

42. I. P. Camões, "Estatísticas Da Ajuda Pública Ao Desenvolvimento (APD)," accessed August 1, 2022, https://www.instituto-camoes.pt/activity/o-que-fazemos/cooperacao/atuacao/reportamos/reportamos-2.

43. Victor-Manuel Vallin, "France as the Gendarme of Africa, 1960–2014," *Political Science Quarterly* 130, no. 1 (March 2015): 79–101, https://doi.org/10.1002/polq.12289; Alain Rouvez, Michael Coco, and Jean-Paul Paddack, *Disconsolate Empires: French, British, and Belgian Military Involvement in Post-Colonial Sub-Saharan Africa* (Lanham, MD: University Press of America, 1994), http://bvbr.bib-bvb.de:8991/F?func=service&doc_library=BVB01&local_base=BVB01&doc_number=006628041&line_number=0001&func_code=DB_RECORDS&service_type=MEDIA.

44. I. P. Camões, "Acordo Cultural Entre Portugal e Cabo Verde – Acordo Geral de Cooperação e Amizade of January 27, 1976," https://www.instituto-camoes.pt/component/content/article?id=14690:acordo-cabo-verde, n.d.

45. Clara Carvalho, "Africa and Portugal," in *Africa and the World: Bilateral and Multilateral International Diplomacy*, ed. Dawn Nagar and Charles Mutasa (London: Palgrave Macmillan, 2018), 151.

46. *Cooperação portuguesa: uma leitura dos últimos quinze anos de cooperação para o desenvolvimento, 1996–2010* (Lisboa: IPAD, 2011), 25.

47. Carvalho, "Africa and Portugal," 151.

48. *Cooperação portuguesa*, 33.

49. Adriana Erthal Abdenur, "Brazil-Africa Relations: From Boom to Bust?," in *Africa and the World: Bilateral and Multilateral International Diplomacy*, ed. Dawn Nagar and Charles Mutasa (London: Palgrave Macmillan, 2018), 190.

50. Abdenur, 191.

Chapter 4

Diaspora and the Language and Politics Nexus

In 2016, Sport Lisboa e Benfica won the Portuguese National Soccer League. Among its players were Renato Sanches and Nelson Semedo, born in Portugal to Cabo Verdean parents. After the game, players were joking and celebrating the championship in the bathhouse while reporters from various news outlets were conducting interviews and recording the moment. At one point, Renato Sanches took the microphone from one of the reporters and started interviewing his teammates. When he approached Nelson Semedo, the two engaged in code-switching. The medium of communication switched from Portuguese to the Cabo Verdean language.[1] The short video clip became viral among Cabo Verdeans at home and in the diaspora, driven by the spectacle of two prominent soccer players from a major European team using the Cabo Verdean language while being transmitted live on Portuguese television. This video illustrates how the Cabo Verdean diaspora maintains close and intimate relationships with their mother tongue. The use of the Cabo Verdean language among diasporized Cabo Verdeans is not only a tool of horizontal communication but also a powerful and shining identity marker.

This story is an example of diaspora-led linguistic resistance and empowerment. While independence in Cabo Verde did not translate into any concrete language policy to boost and empower the mother tongue, the Cabo Verdean diaspora in the United States followed a completely different path, aggregating their human and material resources toward recognition of the language. For the first time in history, the Cabo Verdean language entered the realm of formality—though not in its land. The group behind the empowerment of the Cabo Verdean language had to fight all the traditional linguistic stereotypes and prejudices. In many ways, it was an uphill battle to advocate for such a change in the status of the language, both within and without the Cabo Verdean community.

Language is one of the vehicles through which the homeland and its diaspora seek to develop symbiotic relationships. Given that Cabo Verdean diasporic sites are of different shapes and sizes, the influence on homeland political development and policymaking is not even. Resourceful diasporas, measured in terms of the symbolic and/or economic capital at their disposal, are the ones who are most likely to intervene in the homeland's political domains actively. In this chapter, I critically discuss the role of diaspora within the language-politics nexus. Given its economic and social weight, the Cabo Verdean diaspora exercises influence in different aspects of social life in the homeland. Though democratization in the 1990s has given voting rights to the diaspora, homeland political elites have used the dominant language (Portuguese) as a powerful weapon to manage diasporic political participation. Nonetheless, the diaspora uses its economic weight to sway Cabo Verdean society. In this regard, I argue that the diaspora engages in sociolinguistic remittances to reshape the language and, ipso facto, to demonstrate their social power.

Apart from this introduction, this chapter has three main sections. In the first section, I discuss the literature on diaspora as the starting point for understanding the political and linguistic interactions between the Cabo Verdean homeland and its diaspora. I argue that the Cabo Verdean state-diaspora interactions can be better understood using the opposition and transnational models.[2] The second section discusses the political history of the Cabo Verdean diaspora, which is extensive in historical and geographical terms. In the third section, I focus on the role of the diaspora in the context of the Cabo Verdean language-politics nexus. I contend that there are two main categories of diaspora: the resourceful and the resourceless. The first group exercises far more sway in Cabo Verdean society. The influence of diaspora in the language-politics nexus can be noticed in language use and how they influence hostland and homeland language policy and planning. I also maintain that the diaspora has been a powerful resisting force against the linguistic dominance of the Portuguese language in Cabo Verde. Finally, I restate the key points discussed throughout the chapter.

THE POLITICS OF DIASPORA

Studies of diaspora and diaspora politics abound.[3] According to its etymology (from Greek, *speiro* to sow, and *dia* over), diaspora signifies the dispersion of a human group to different parts of the world. The term entered the English language in 1694 and referred to the experience of dispersion among the Jews. After that, the concept began to be applied to other communities dispersed beyond their homelands. The concept of diaspora rests on three main pillars: identity, organization, and contacts.[4] Identity refers to the social processes of maintaining and developing a unique collective identity among "diasporized people." Organization in the sense that the diasporic community establishes its internal organization distinct from both the homeland and the hostland. Finally, Gabriel Sheffer believes that contacts with the homeland, real or symbolic, are at the core of defining the concept. Contra Sheffer, other scholars argue that the concept should be used only for cases involving expulsion or involuntary exile.[5] Despite being scattered in different parts of the world, the diasporized group has maintained a sense of collective, imagined identity.[6]

Some diaspora studies have helped clarify the concept and provide useful taxonomies.[7] Other scholars have paid attention to how diaspora communities seek to influence political development in their homeland and hostland.[8] Still, others have documented how diasporas have formed a formidable auxiliary of homeland economic development.[9] Despite the robustness and dimension of the literature, the literature is silent when it comes to understanding the role of the diaspora in homeland politics of language. Nonetheless, some studies examine the influence of the diaspora on new linguistic developments in the homeland.[10] Against the silence in the literature, this chapter critically analyzes how the diaspora navigates the homeland language-politics nexus.

Given the dissimilarities of diasporic communities, scholars have advanced different typologies to capture the phenomenon. Focusing on the criterion of age, Sheffer distinguishes three categories of diaspora communities: (a) historical (or classical) from the ancient world (as in the cases of Jewish, Greek, Chinese, and Armenian); modern (or recent), since the seventeenth century (black, African American, Italian, Polish, and Irish Diaspora); and (c) incipient, "diasporas in the making, groups of migrants who are in the initial stages of forming organized diasporas."[11] Another typology distinguishes between labor diasporas (e.g., Indians), imperial diasporas (e.g., British), trade diasporas (e.g., Chinese, Lebanese), and cultural diasporas in the Caribbean case.[12]

To grasp how the diaspora intervenes in politics at home and abroad, it is important to briefly discuss the different modalities of relationships between the state and its diaspora. Michel Laguerre discusses five main types of state–diaspora political relations. In the first model—the reincorporation model—policies are enacted in the sending state to facilitate the return and socioeconomic (and even political) reincorporation of its diaspora in the homeland. In the ethnic model, the diaspora reinforces their material and symbolic links with the homeland to strengthen their political position in the hostland. With the economic model, the sending state advances policies toward its diaspora to tap its financial resources, mainly through remittances and other financial transfers. The fourth model is political opposition when the sending state distrusts its diaspora, who are perceived as political troublemakers. Finally, there is the transnational model, which "implies the blurring of the boundaries between state and diaspora, the expansion of the nation, its transformation into a transnation, and the social normalization of border-crossing practices."[13]

Diasporas are now taken seriously as political actors. Governments in both hostland and homeland often use them to shape and influence the policies of the other. The concept of "ethnic lobby" has been used in the literature to discuss the influence of ethnic minorities in shaping and influencing the hostland foreign policy regarding the homeland.[14] Globalization and the dissemination of liberal democracy worldwide have contributed to the added political power of the diaspora. Since the 1990s, several states have amended their constitutions and electoral codes to grant voting rights to citizens living abroad.[15] Other states, such as Portugal, France, and Cabo Verde, have established extraterritorial constituencies through which diasporic communities could elect representatives to the national parliament.[16]

In contemporary African and Caribbean states, the dominant political discourse emphasizes and develops the idea of a *transnation*. States with significant diaspora populations see these communities as an integral part of the nation, however fragmented and extra-territorialized. For this reason, these states now nurture solid and intimate relationships with their citizens living abroad, perceived as untapped resources. Through official and nonofficial discourses and policies, the diaspora is an integral part of the nation. In the case of Haiti, for instance, the diaspora was, until the 1990s, discursively constructed as the "tenth department." Nowadays, Haitian political discourses equate its diaspora as the eleventh department, following a new administrative department (that of Nippes) in the country.

Similarly, it is common in Senegal to identify the Senegalese diaspora as the country's "fifteenth region" since there are fourteen different administrative regions in the country. The case of Nigeria is another illustrative example, as the diaspora is often imagined as the thirty-seventh Nigerian state. In the case under study, Cabo Verde, the dominant narrative considers its diaspora as the eleventh island of the archipelago. These narratives on the diaspora are deployed to assist in developing and maintaining a transnational "imagined community," a condition that would allow close contact between the homeland state and its diaspora for financial and other resources. The diaspora has now been accepted as a source of financing for development that can compete with other primary sources such as the World Bank and the donor states.

The relationship between the Cabo Verdean state and its diaspora spread across the world can be explained as a combination of three main models: ethnic, economic, and transnational.[17] The Cabo Verdean state, its agents, and the political elite, in general, have adopted a discourse that emphasizes the socioeconomic and political significance of the diaspora communities. The diaspora has been accepted as the country's eleventh island to indicate the symbiotic link between the homeland and the various Cabo Verdean communities abroad. Official documents, such as the *Programa do Governo*, highlight the concept of the global nation.[18]

Despite the grand discourses that seek to construct diasporas as monolithic sociological entities, the dispersion of the nation into different countries results in diverse immigrant and diasporic communities, chiefly in terms of the resources at their disposal. The dispersion of the nation to different countries and regions does not happen uniformly or with the same intensity. Some states are more attractive than others—for several reasons, including the socioeconomic opportunities the hostland offers. In this situation, diasporic sites are unequal; instead, a hierarchy among these diasporic sites can be observed.

Diasporic sites are not the same, and they can be distinguished in terms of demographic size, resources they possess, and material links they develop with the homeland. There are different types of resources available to some diasporic sites: financial resources (measured in terms of remittances), relative position in hostland politics (ethnic politics and participation of the community in hostland local and central politics), symbolic resources (how the homeland imagines the diaspora), intellectual resources (professionals of thought), and contacts with homeland (trips, for vacation or business, to the homeland). Thus, it is possible to categorize diasporic communities into two main groups, *resourceful* and *resourceless diasporas*. The first group includes communities that possess significant material and symbolic resources vis-à-vis the homeland. Senegalese communities in the United States or France have far more symbolic and material resources than Senegalese immigrants in Brazil.

Equally, the Indian diaspora in North America enjoys far more resources than its counterpart in East Africa. Cabo Verdean communities in the United States, Portugal, and the Netherlands are resourceful, while their counterparts in Guinea-Bissau, São Tomé and Príncipe, and Angola are resourceless. Resourceful diasporas are the segments of diasporized citizens in specific countries that enjoy a high quality of life and high levels of financial and symbolic capital. Resourceful diasporas are more likely to be engaged by the homeland's state, which seeks to extract resources and can exercise some influence in politics and policymaking.

A BRIEF HISTORY OF THE CABO VERDEAN DIASPORA

The history of modern Cabo Verdean mass migration dates back to the nineteenth century. The colonial state's incompetence and unwillingness to develop policies to mitigate the consequences of cyclical drought had traditionally resulted in the death of thousands across the islands and, consequently, pushed several thousand to move abroad to survive. By the second half of the nineteenth century, colonial authorities began instrumentalizing droughts to find a labor force for the cocoa plantations in São Tomé and Príncipe. This process continued until the last decade of colonial status.[19] The then-colony of São Tomé and Príncipe was not the only destination for Cabo Verdean migration. By the third quarter of the nineteenth century, New England in the United States had become another place that attracted migrants from the islands.[20] By the twentieth century, other countries were added to the list of destinations for Cabo Verdean immigration: Guinea-Bissau, Angola, Senegal (Africa), Brazil, and Argentina (South America)—to name the most significant destination sites. The history of modern Cabo Verde mass immigration, a social phenomenon that developed in the late nineteenth century and the first half of the twentieth century, has constructed what can be called the "Cabo Verdean Atlantic."

There is a long history of Cabo Verdeans leaving home and settling abroad. In a way, Cabo Verdeans have carved out their own Cabo Verdean Atlantic within the Atlantic world, as the nation has its fragments across the region. The political-economic significance of Cabo Verdean communities abroad is widely accepted, and mainstream political discourse often includes expressions such as the "eleventh island" or the notion of a "global nation."

A significant sociolinguistic consequence of Cabo Verdean mass migration is the diffusion of the Cabo Verdean language. In the second half of the nineteenth century, the modern immigration of Cabo Verdeans led to the diffusion of the language to different spaces within and outside the Portuguese colonial empire. Places like Brazil and Argentina in South America; the United States in North America; Portugal, France, Italy, and the Netherlands in Western Europe; and Senegal, Guinea-Bissau, Angola, and São Tomé and Príncipe are now well-known Cabo Verdean diasporic sites. The connections of these diasporic communities with the homeland have made Cabo Verde a transnational archipelago with a worldly language.

One should note that the transnational spread of the Cabo Verdean language did not occur only through mass migration. This process is the most important mechanism through which the language is spread. Cultural diffusion, particularly Cabo Verdean music, has been a significant vehicle through which the language is disseminated to various parts of the world, chiefly in the context of African countries with Portuguese as the official language.[21]

The historical dispersion of Cabo Verdeans in the Atlantic space has transformed a national language into a transnational language; the Cabo Verdean language has become a language used in a myriad of communication between individuals and groups in different countries. Nicolas Quint argues that the Cabo Verdean can be classified as a "symbol of globalization" because of its history as the language that originated from cultural contacts between Europeans and Africans and the dispersion of its speakers to three continents in the contemporary world.[22] He then concludes that Cabo Verdean constitutes a worldly language (*língua mundial*). Crossing the insights of Quint with those of Conrad Brann, I suggest that Cabo Verdean forms an example of a transnational language or a diasporalect.[23] *Diasporalect* languages have gone through a process of dispersion not because of actions of the home state but rather because of their speakers' activities. As such, it is the spread of a language from its historical habitat to various points of the world.

Yet, it should be stressed that the dissemination of the Cabo Verdean language did not occur in every location with the same intensity, and different countries of reception of Cabo Verdean immigration have developed different relationships with the Cabo Verdean language. It is possible to discern two main groups of the Cabo Verdean diaspora. On the one hand, there is the *visible/audible diaspora*, that is, diasporic sites where the Cabo Verdean language has reached relative visibility and audibility in the context of the hostland social and political affairs. The language has been accepted as the educational medium and is used for state–society communications (at least in some significant issues, such as elections, disease prevention, and the like). Additionally, relatively rich diasporic media (radio and television) use the language, and inside the ethnic enclave, the language has become increasingly visible in the linguistic landscape. The visible/audible diaspora includes countries like Portugal, the United States, Angola, Guinea-Bissau, and Senegal. Not Incidentally, the visible diasporic sites are also the spaces with the greatest number of Cabo Verdean immigrants or people of Cabo Verdean descent. On the other hand, invisible/inaudible diasporic sites are where the Cabo Verdean language is minimally present in public, as in the cases of Argentina, Brazil, Italy, and the Netherlands.

The hierarchy of diasporic sites means that the homeland's reception of social remittances from these different sites is unequal and dissimilar. The acceptance of new ideas, beliefs, and values brought through diasporic connections is intimately linked to the perception that the local population develops vis-à-vis the receiving state. The perception created toward different diasporic sites is directly connected with the acceptance of ideas, behaviors, and beliefs emanating from these spaces. In the homeland subconsciousness, diasporic sites are ranked in terms of collective success, fortune, and glory. Some are classified as examples of success, while other sites are classified as the opposite. In the case of Cabo Verdean immigration, the United States and São Tomé and Príncipe represent the two antipodes, with the former accepted as the pathway to success and upward social mobility.

On the other hand, São Tomé and Príncipe is the place that has worsened the social lives of the migrants. These images are reinforced in popular culture. Baltazar Lopes da Silva's *Chiquinho*, Cabo Verde's first novel published by a native writer, recounts the idea of achievement and triumph that the United States represents.[24]

A visible trait of the African and Caribbean postcolonial state is that a European language, Portuguese, English, or French, is the dominant official language. The state, high politics, and other formal arenas of sociopolitical life (schooling, media, administration of justice, and the like) operate almost exclusively in the dominant language, even though only a tiny percentage of the population has a comfortable competence in that language. In the next chapter, I argue that the postcolonial state's overreliance on the European language inherited from colonialism results from a political strategy devised by the elites to keep the state illegible. The phenomenon of state illegibility corresponds to the fact that most people cannot grasp the procedures, operations, and processes of power since these are carried out through a medium they don't fully master. In the case of Cabo Verde, the fact that the state relies extensively on Portuguese has translated into citizens' unwillingness and inability to hold it accountable.

The local elite's strategy of making the state illegible does not end with the country's territorial borders. Instead, state illegibility has also been used as a strategy toward the diasporized citizens. By maintaining the state unreadable to the diasporans, the state elite not only manages to circumvent political accountability but also can assist them in rent-seeking.[25] The elites position themselves as the mediators between the diaspora and the homeland state and use such a position to extract resources from Cabo Verdeans residing abroad. For instance, it is not uncommon for immigrants to complain about fees and other charges at the customs department. Those who migrate tend to be sections of the population with less formal education and, as such, without proper competence in the dominant language. Given that information from and about the state and its operations are kept almost exclusively in the dominant, official language, a considerable percentage of diaspora citizens find themselves unable to navigate the state's domains. Forms, reports, reviews, laws, regulations, and other forms of political and legal output from the state are exclusively in the dominant language.

THE HOMELAND DIMENSION

Scholars have shown that diasporic communities can significantly impact the homeland's political development. Political activities that seek to influence and shape political developments in the homeland can be carried out either from abroad or inside the motherland with the political incorporation of returnees. Democratic development has been linked with the activities of diasporic activists. Similarly, the transference of ideas from diasporic communities to their respective homelands has found a way to become institutionalized in governmental policy. D. Kapur's study on Indian economic policy shows the noticeable influence of ideas brought into the country by diasporic citizens. Migrants can also impact homeland politics through their influence on cultural orientations and social norms.[26] In this section, I critically discuss two main modes of Cabo Verdean diaspora engagement with the homeland regarding the language-politics nexus: their intervention in the language ideological debate and their sociolinguistic remittances.

A dimension of diaspora intervention in the homeland language-politics nexus relates to the intimate connections between language and identity. Contemporary diasporas reconstruct many objective markers to claim cultural and social uniqueness and autonomy. This sociopolitical strategy is more profound in the context of global cities, places that attract groups from all parts of the world. Claims of ethnic uniqueness, as such, are directed not only vis-à-vis mainstream society but also toward other diasporic communities. The mother tongue thus becomes an important tool that facilitates claims of ethnic authenticity and uniqueness. The defense and promotion of the mother tongue are ultimately perceived as a means of ethnic survival.

Diaspora actors participate in the homeland language ideological debates. Since its independence, Cabo Verde has seen different waves of language ideological debate, as analyzed in chapter 2. As noted earlier, language ideological debate constitutes a confrontation of language ideologies that occur in specific times and places.[27] Though abroad, diaspora actors are not passive transnational bystanders to homeland politics. While afar, diaspora actors engage in many political activities, some of which are intense, with the ultimate objective of informing, altering, and influencing homeland political development and policies. Diaspora actors engage in different dimensions of national debates, ranging from the type of political regime to particular policy areas, such as the language question. As a sensitive political and identity topic, diaspora actors participate, with different degrees of success, in the national debate on the roles and functions of the national language.

The engagement of diasporas vis-à-vis their homeland also occurs in other dimensions. The connection that diasporas develop with their homeland can be real or symbolic. Diasporic citizens typically accumulate different capitals, which are then transferred to the homeland, of which remittances are best known and studied. Remittances refer to the transfer of money and goods by immigrants working abroad to relatives, neighbors, or friends in their homeland. Economists and other social scientists debate whether these private financial transfers are used chiefly for consumption or economic development activities. Remittances are an indelible proof of engagement and connection of the diasporas to their homeland.

Notwithstanding the economicist bias of scholars of diaspora and immigration, engagements and connections with the homeland go beyond the above-discussed traditional remittances. Scholars have advanced a new concept of social remittance to focus on the non-material transferences from the diaspora/immigrant communities to their homelands. Social remittances constitute a "migration-driven form of cultural diffusion," including the transference of ideas, behaviors, identities, and social capital from the receiving to the sending state.[28] Diasporic citizens' direct contacts with their family, friends, and neighbors constitute the main pathway through which social remittances are channeled.

Financial remittances, or private income transfers, play an important role in the island's political economy. In relative terms, personal financial remittances sent to Cabo Verde have declined since the early 1980s. In 1980, remittances accounted for 28 percent of the country's GDP; in 2019, the number was about 12 percent. In absolute terms, the total amount of financial transfers made by Cabo Verdean living abroad to their relatives and friends at home has steadily risen since the mid-1980s. In 1980, remittances totaled a little over forty million US dollars. In 2019, that number increased almost sixfold to nearly 236 million US dollars. The numbers indicate that Cabo Verde is an example of a remittance-dependent economy.

The influence of the diaspora in Cabo Verde goes beyond the financial and economic aspects. The diaspora intensely engages in social remittances, significantly shaping the country's sociopolitical fabric. As early as 1915, Eugénio Tavares, one of the most revered public intellectuals in the history of the islands, emphasized the role of social remittances in the political development of Cabo Verde. In his "A Emigração para a América," Tavares talks about how Cabo Verdean immigration to the United States did not constitute simply a "journey of labor" but also a "physical and *psychic* training."[29] Through their uncompromising engagement, the diaspora has played crucial roles in Cabo Verdean political history, including anticolonial mobilization, the fight for national independence, and democratization in the 1990s. Ideas from hostland societies were packaged and sent to the homeland and helped reshape conversations while simultaneously serving as pressures on the political system.

Sociolinguistic remittances are a subset of social remittances as they constitute the transfer of ideas, values, and beliefs regarding language. Sociolinguistic remittances operate in different dimensions, for they can be about the transference of linguistic elements of the mainstream language from the hostland, or they can include sending new ideas and perceptions about the homeland language to the homeland itself. Ultimately, sociolinguistic remittances have the language of the homeland as its primary target, seeking to alter its structure and the people's perception. Sociolinguistic remittances, therefore, happen in three primary modalities: (a) linguistic knowledge, (b) language-use experience (bilingual education), and (c) language-use transferences.

Over the past four decades, Portugal and the United States have become a veritable reservoir of Cabo Verdean language scholars and intellectuals who research and publish about the corpus of the language and topics that have dismantled century-old myths regarding the mother tongue. Later in this chapter, I will discuss the role of language scholars and intellectuals. For now, it is important to mention that these researchers and intellectuals have maintained close relationships with the homeland and use these connections as the bridge through which linguistic knowledge is transferred to their peers and other interested parties in the islands. Language laws in Cabo Verde often pinpoint the role of these individuals and, as such, indicate the extent that their ideas might have informed or influenced language policy and planning in Cabo Verde. The Decree-Law number 8/2009 of March 16 explicitly mentions the name of the Cabo Verdean poet who resides in Lisbon, José Luis Tavares, who has done translations into Cabo Verdean of "great classics of the Portuguese literature."

Another dimension of sociolinguistic remittances refers to the transference of applied linguistics or language-use experience in bilingual education. Cabo Verdean bilingual education is far more developed and entrenched in the United States (Massachusetts) than in the homeland. In fact, discussions on the elaboration of Cabo Verdean bilingual education in Cabo Verde often take the US experience as a guide.[30] Narratives about the experience of using the Cabo Verdean language in bilingual education transferred directly through personal contacts or participation in conferences, language commissions, study groups, and so forth have been incorporated into legal norms emanating from the Cabo Verdean government. Moreover, the first bilingual education experience attempted in Cabo Verde in the early 2010s was elaborated on and coordinated by a Cabo Verdean-Portuguese teacher and researcher from Portugal, who had extensive contact with those involved in similar programs in Massachusetts.

Finally, there is the last dimension of sociolinguistic remittances, which refers to how diasporic citizens influence the mother tongue by introducing linguistic elements from their hostland dominant languages. Andrea Lobo has carefully analyzed the phenomenon of exchanges and borrowings of language expressions between emigrants and locals.[31] Cabo Verdean these days includes many expressions, words, and phrases deriving from English, Italian, and French, brought in by diasporized citizens in their contacts with their relatives or while visiting the islands on vacation. The influence of foreign expressions in everyday language is more substantial in the islands of Brava and Fogo, where the historical diasporic community in the United States has exerted much influence. In everyday Creole from Brava and Fogo, for instance, it is not uncommon to hear words like "zip" (from *zipper*), "droma" (from the *drum*), "troba" (from *trouble*).

THE HOSTLAND DIMENSION

Scholars have shown that immigrants frequently have trouble maintaining their first language. It has been argued that the immigrants' language is replaced after two or three generations, a consequence of adopting the mainstream societal language. Policies designed and implemented by the state, chiefly bilingual language education, can either mitigate or retard such a process. Helder de Schutter has argued that there is a direct correlation between people's self-respect and dignity and how the state actors perceive their language. Any official status, whether formal or informal, granted to their language is taken by its speakers as a status bestowed upon them. Bilingual education is one of the channels through which the state confers special recognition of the immigrants' language. The state considers and admits the worthiness of their language to fulfill one of the most significant functions of modernity—schooling. The dignity of the immigrants' language can also be uplifted through its use in political communication.

The dispersion of Cabo Verdeans across the Atlantic has led to the internationalization of their language, which can now be heard in the streets of Dakar (Senegal), Lisbon (Portugal), Paris (France), and Boston (USA). However, one should note that linguistic activism has been far more entrenched and more profound in some Cabo Verdean diasporic sites. Thus, Cabo Verdeans in the United States and Portugal have been far more open and engaged in promoting their language in different arenas of social life, from literature to formal education.

Linguistic activism is "a genuine case of language planning."[32] In analytical terms, two main modes of linguistic activism can be discerned, one centering on corpus planning and the other on status planning. An example of the first mode of linguistic activism centering on the linguistic corpus is the campaign by feminists in the 1970s that eventually led to the reform of the English language that represented a more balanced representation of men and women.[33] Expressions, phrases, and words that indicated a gender bias (e.g., police*man*) were deleted, and new gender-neutral ones were introduced (police *officer*).

The other mode of linguistic activism seeks to center its action on reformatting the functions of a given language. This type of linguistic activism is formed to reject the historical language ideologies that reject using a particular language in specific domains or for certain functions. Consequently, linguistic activists develop counter-ideologies to emphasize the sustainability of a language to fulfill functions that were hitherto negated to it.

There is a long history of linguistic activism grounded on status and corpus planning among the Cabo Verdean diaspora, particularly in the United States and Portugal. Many factors explain why Cabo Verdean linguistic activism tends to be more intense in those two diasporic sites. First, there is demographic weight. The United States and Portugal represent the two largest Cabo Verdean communities. In the context of Portugal and Massachusetts (USA), Cabo Verdeans represent one of the most significant ethnic minorities. Cabo Verdeans are the second-largest immigrant community in Portugal.

Thousands of Cabo Verdeans hold Portuguese citizenship. As in the case of Portugal, it is difficult to come up with the correct number of Cabo Verdeans in Massachusetts. As a historical community in New England, thousands have been born in the United States and/or hold US citizenship. In fact, if citizens of Cabo Verdean descent are included, the number is way above 100,000. In Boston, the Cabo Verdean language is the third most spoken language in its public schools—after Spanish and English.

A second factor that explains the intensity of Cabo Verdean language activism in Portugal and the United States is the high concentration of language intellectuals and scholars. In these two diasporic sites, many Cabo Verdean public intellectuals write on/in the Cabo Verdean language. In Portugal, writers such as José Luis Tavares and José Luis Hopffer Almada have been quite prolific in using the Cabo Verdean language in poetry. Diasporic language scholars are an integral part of a larger epistemological community on Creole languages in general, and through these connections, experiences from other Creole islands are shared and compared. Through formal and informal meetings with other Creole language scholars, Cabo Verdean scholars have played the role of mediators between cutting-edge research as carried out by scholars around the globe (chiefly from/on the Caribbean cases) with the work done by Cabo Verde-based researchers. A practical approach to this mediating role is through research co-authorship, in which diaspora-based scholars partnering with those in Cabo Verde.[34]

I present two examples to illustrate the case of language scholars and their role in promoting the language in the United States. Professors Donaldo Macedo and Marlyse Baptista are perhaps the best-known Cabo Verdean language scholars. Macedo was the first Cabo Verdean to write a doctoral dissertation on the Cabo Verdean language and has published widely on the Cabo Verdean language and bilingual education.[35] Baptista has also written extensively on the Cabo Verdean language and has maintained a close relationship with Cabo Verde-based scholars.[36] Through their scholarship, both Macedo and Baptista have helped to empower the language by deconstructing many of the myths that were traditionally attached to the language. Moreover, these scholars have also shaped Cabo Verdean language-in-education policy through consulting work and involvement with the Cabo Verdean community in New England.

Apart from these language scholars, one should also mention an army of educators who have contributed significantly to the advancement of the Cabo Verdean language in bilingual education. As will be shown later, the role of Cabo Verdean educators in paving the way for Cabo Verdean bilingual education cannot be underrated. The fight to recognize the Cabo Verdean language in the United States started primarily in bilingual education. The contribution of this group is not only in language use in education but also through their reflections and studies on bilingual education. I will discuss this point later in this chapter when I examine the history of Cabo Verdean bilingual education.

Cabo Verdean linguistic activism is also part of grassroots and community politics, with Cabo Verdean community-based organizations placing themselves on the political battlefront to defend the community's interests. Cabo Verdeans in the United States understand that realizing the community's interests passes through grassroots mobilization and organization. As such, like other ethnic and immigrant communities, Cabo Verdeans are forming community-based organizations and networks to enhance and increase their social visibility. Numbers, whether in demographic or financial terms, are the main foundations of the modern political system. Community organization is one of the main pathways to construct those numbers. These Cabo Verdean community-based organizations have worked tirelessly in advancing Cabo Verdean interests, including, as it can be assumed, promoting the Cabo Verdean language. Many services these organizations provide are in the Cabo Verdean language. These groups have increasingly relied on the written Cabo Verdean to disseminate essential information from the local, state, and federal governments. Moreover, these community-based organizations have also developed language spread policies by promoting classes on the Cabo Verdean language directed to second-generation Cabo Verdeans and non-Cabo Verdeans.

A significant consequence of the decades of promoting and empowering the Cabo Verdean language has been increased linguistic self-esteem. The advent of social media deepened the use of the Cabo Verdean language as a medium of communication by these community organizations. Scholars have noted that social media offer new opportunities to minority languages.[37] Given their status as representatives of the community, these organizations play an important role when it comes to language planning. Their decision to relay information in the mother tongue permits the non-English-speaking Cabo Verdeans to capture the message in the shortest possible time, thus reducing or eliminating transaction and translation costs. At the same time, that decision can transform people's perception vis-à-vis their language.

Finally, it is important to discuss the role of local government—at the state and city levels—in advancing the Cabo Verdean language. Following decades of its promotion and empowerment, the Cabo Verdean language is now a language that is widely used in different formal domains, from bilingual education to information from the public authorities. Local governments (chiefly in the city of Boston) have used the Cabo Verdean language to pass the information on elections, public health, and other socially relevant domains. The experience of Boston and Massachusetts, in general, has spread to the state of Rhode Island, where local governments have begun to use the Cabo Verdean language to transfer critical information to the community. The COVID-19 pandemic has given new impetus to the Cabo Verdean language, as public health information on how to deal with the latest virus and ways to minimize its spread were also put in the Cabo Verdean language. For instance, the Massachusetts Department of Public Health has translated critical information about COVID-19 into the Cabo Verdean language (see figure 4.1).[38]

Given the rise of multilingualism in American society, which has informed and influenced language policy and planning at the state and local levels, one

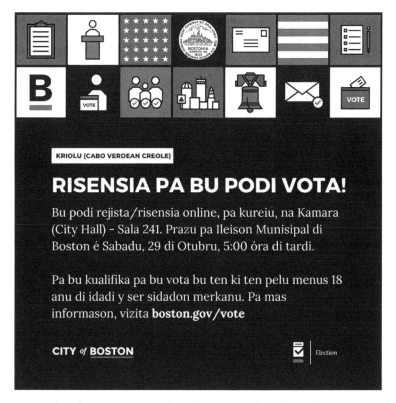

Figure 4.1   City of Boston, Voter Registration Message in Cabo Verdean. *Source*: Photo taken by author.

should also discuss how minority languages have made significant inroads in electoral politics. American electoral politics, chiefly at the state and local levels, is no longer a reserved realm of English. It has become multilingual or, at least, bilingual, with Spanish used widely by candidates across the country. This new linguistic situation in electoral politics has trickled down from the federal to the local levels. At the local level, electoral politics in many parts of the country have become genuinely multilingual, with many different languages being used by candidates to communicate their policy proposals with other language communities that make up the polity (figure 4.1).

The inclusion of the Cabo Verdean language emphasizes symbolic representation insofar as it can produce radical changes in how the general public—and the Cabo Verdean community—perceive the group in the context of Boston local politics. Very few non-European social groupings can claim a multigenerational history in the city of Boston (or in southern New England, more broadly). As noted earlier, Cabo Verdeans in the region—and in Boston, more particularly—date back to the late nineteenth century.

The 2010s were indeed the decade of Cabo Verdean-American political awakening. Though Cabo Verdean-Americans have always had some degree of active political participation in their local and state politics, there was a qualitative and quantitative increase of Cabo Verdeans in the political arena in that decade. Until the 2010s, Cabo Verdean ethnic politics were mainly directed toward community organizing, grassroots politics, and forming coalitions with dominant political agents. Many Cabo Verdean grassroots and community organizations were founded decades before. They were veritable schools of political leadership, allowing ambitious individuals to rehearse leadership skills while making a name for themselves.

In the past decade or so, many young Cabo Verdeans have entered the field of local politics, running for office, as city councilor or even mayor, in different cities such as Boston, Brockton, and New Bedford (Massachusetts), and Pawtucket, Central Falls, and East Providence (Rhode Island). Many new generations of political actors born in the islands have approached the language question from a different perspective from the past. To these young political actors, the Cabo Verdean language is far from a problem, as it was often conceived in the past. Instead, they approach the language as a powerful asset that can assist in their plan to win elections. The Cabo Verdean language thus has become an electoral language, used widely in different forms of political advertisements, websites, and door-to-door electioneering. Take, for instance, the case of John Barros, who ran for mayor of Boston in the 2021 elections. His electoral campaign website, now taken down, was multilingual, with information in all of the major languages spoken in the city, including the Cabo Verdean language. Other Cabo Verdean-American candidates, such as Evandro Carvalho, who ran for city councilor in 2021, have distributed multilingual literature, where the Cabo Verdean translation was also included.

When they use the Cabo Verdean language, these political actors often prefer to have their message transcribed according to the rules defined by the Cabo Verdean Alphabet. In so doing, their actions assist in promoting and, perhaps more importantly, legitimizing the writing system. One should ask why these political actors use the Cabo Verdean language. Three possible explanations can be advanced. First, there is the identity dimension. The use of the Cabo Verdean language constitutes a means through which to indicate their social identity. Language, after all, is one of the most objective identity markers. It can be argued that the demonstration of Cabo Verdean identity constitutes a strategy to attract ethnic voters and to have the political actor as the agent of descriptive representation of the community.

Second, the Cabo Verdean language is a tool for political mobilization. It is known that many Cabo Verdeans in the United States hold US citizenship and, as such, are entitled to participate in electoral politics. Many of these Cabo Verdeans, chiefly the elderly, have a rudimentary or no understanding of English. Using their mother tongue allows for faster transmission of the electoral message and could inspire this particular electorate to partake in the electoral game.

Finally, there is the pedagogical dimension to using the Cabo Verdean language in the electoral political game. It is well documented that naturalized Americans are less likely to register to vote than their native counterparts.[39] Candidates understand that the Cabo Verdean electorate traditionally does not engage much in electoral politics. The transmission of political information in a language that the electorate is more comfortable using constitutes part of a political pedagogy: to train the voters in the complex web of local politics.

A word must be said regarding the rather complex relationship between the Cabo Verdean and English languages. In the context of the Cabo Verdean community in the United States, Cabo Verdean *Kriolu*, a minority language, poses no threat to English—unlike the case of Spanish, which many see as a potential menace to English.[40] An understanding of how the Cabo Verdean language interacts with English in the context of New England, where the presence of Cabo Verdeans and their language is historical, warrants a discussion of a linguistic hierarchy model of the region. New England has historically attracted immigrants from all over the world, first from Europe and, since the second half of the twentieth century, from South and Central America, Asia, and Africa. The region is fundamentally multilingual, characterized by various language communities of different sizes and historical presence.

The linguistic hierarchy model is constructed in terms of the size of the language community, the sociopolitical status of the language, the economic value of the language, and linguistic activism on the part of their speakers. As such, it is possible to construct a four-strata model of linguistic hierarchy in the city of Boston (figure 4.2). On top of the pyramid is English, the language of political and economic power and prestige. While Massachusetts does not have any legal or constitutional provision about the official language, English is the language of power, officialdom, and mainstream economic interactions. Spanish is right below English, with its speakers increasing significantly in the past few decades. The political significance of Spanish is such that it has become common to find official communications in that language.

One finds many language communities in the third tier of the pyramid of languages, ranging from Mandarin, Haitian Creole, Vietnamese, and Cabo Verdean Creole. These languages are somehow—if not informally—recognized by the city as locally significant communities, including in the public schools' bilingual education. Therefore, city and state officials sometimes rely on these languages to transmit important communications and instructions, mainly information about public health or elections. Finally, at the bottom tier, other minority languages are yet to be recognized and utilized as a medium of communication by the city or in bilingual education. Examples of language communities at the bottom of the pyramid include new Yoruba and Bengali.

Having discussed the politics of linguistic empowerment of the language, I now elaborate on the development of Cabo Verdean bilingual education in the United States (Massachusetts) and Portugal, the two countries with vast experience in Cabo Verdean bilingual education. The demographic weight of the community, along with pressures and lobbying by community-based organizations, networks, and individuals, explains the change in the language-in-education policy in those two diasporic sites to include Cabo Verdean as a medium of education. The experience of bilingual education in Massachusetts is far more entrenched and profound, with origins dating to

Figure 4.2 The Hierarchy of Languages in the City of Boston. *Source*: Figure created by author.

1975, as noted at the beginning of the chapter. In the case of Portugal, Cabo Verdean bilingual education was a recent phenomenon tried in the second half of the 2000s. In what follows, I provide a sketch of the Cabo Verdean language bilingual education development in those two territories.

Cabo Verdean bilingual education in Massachusetts traces back to 1975 when the state legislature classified Cabo Verdean as a "living foreign language." The classification made the language a medium that could be included in bilingual education, as mandated in the 1971 Transitional Bilingual Education Act. The educators and community activists who spearheaded the process were influenced by the politics of the civil rights movement and its quest for ethnic origins and ethnic revival.[41] Despite the status planning, the Cabo Verdean language was not readily accepted in bilingual education, including among its speakers.[42] Nonetheless, community persistence made Cabo Verdean bilingual education a reality in many Massachusetts school districts, particularly in Scituate, Brockton, New Bedford, and Boston.

By the late 1980s and early 1990s, Cabo Verdean bilingual education had already consolidated across southeast Massachusetts. To assist in the formulation of materials and other curriculum resources, a group of language scholars and educators founded the Capeverdean Creole Institute (CCI) in 1996 in the city of Boston. The CCI, a nonprofit organization, was the first-ever Cabo Verdean language promoting organization. Its primary objectives entailed language activism not only in the United States but also in the motherland. Thus, it proposed to provide "active support for the recognition of Capeverdean Creole as an official language in the Republic of Cape Verde, the implementation of a standardized orthography (ALUPEC), and curriculum development in Capeverdean bilingual programs in the US and abroad."[43]

However, in the same period, bilingual education was targeted across the United States, with the rise of English-only movements and high-profile individuals such as Ron Unz. He provided material and symbolic resources to shatter bilingual education programs in California, Arizona, and Massachusetts. Following the steps of California and Arizona, where voters passed anti-bilingual education initiatives, in Massachusetts, voters also approved the 2002 "Question 2" that drastically reconfigured the program in the state.

A decade and a half later, it became clear that non-English speakers face an achievement gap.[44] Consequently, a new law, the LOOK Act, was passed by the state legislature in 2017, which provided more resources for bilingual education in the state. The new law has led the Cabo Verdean community in Boston to reorganize to better advocate for Cabo Verdean bilingual education. In this context, a think tank was founded by language scholars and educators, the Cabo Verdean Center for Applied Research. The organization has worked closely with the Boston Public Schools in developing Cabo Verdean bilingual education materials.

The experience of bilingual education in Portugal is more recent. Like other European states, Portugal had maintained a monolingual language policy in education for centuries. Thus, in Portugal, Portuguese has historically been the sole medium through which learning could happen in the context of public schools. However, in 2007, for the first time in its history, Portuguese public schools embarked on a bilingual experience informed by the experiences of other countries.[45] The bilingual project, *Turma Bilingue* (Bilingual Classroom, 2007–2013), was developed and coordinated by scholars affiliated with the ILTEC (Instituto de Linguística Teórica e Computacional— Institute of Theoretical and Computational Linguistics), a research unity from the University of Coimbra. The project's main objective was literacy through immersive Portuguese bilingualism and an hour/day of Cabo Verdean. In the 1990s, two Cabo Verdean bilingual projects were developed for preschool children.[46]

This experience was based on the Cabo Verdean language, given the demographic weight of the Cabo Verdean student population within the public school system.[47] Additionally, the choice to use the Cabo Verdean in this pilot experience had to do with the fact that it is a Portuguese-based Creole and linguistically related to the dominant language in Portugal. Cabo Verdean bilingual education was legitimized on the grounds of assisting in maintaining the vitality of the dominant language.[48]

Unlike the case of Cabo Verdean bilingual education in Massachusetts, there was relatively little input and pressure from the community. The experimental policy was top-down, involving researchers and the Portuguese Ministry of Education, with the Gulbenkian Foundation funding the project. Nonetheless, the Cabo Verdean language bilingual project in Portugal proved that the language could be used effectively in children's education.[49] Moreover, the project contributed to augmenting linguistic self-esteem among its speakers. Furthermore, the experience led Ana Josefa Cardoso, a teacher-scholar of Cabo Verdean origin who was directly involved in the project in Portugal, to persuade the Cabo Verdean Ministry of Education to develop a pilot bilingual education in Cabo Verde.[50]

The experiences of bilingual education in the United States and Portugal have helped to reshape the general perception of the Cabo Verdean language, not only among those in the diaspora but also in Cabo Verde. In the case of the United States, thousands of Cabo Verdean students have passed through bilingual education, many of whom are professionally accomplished. This situation has helped to disprove further the notion that learning through Cabo Verdean is a dead end. Furthermore, as was shown above, the development of Cabo Verdean bilingual education has also assisted in the entry of the language into other domains, particularly local government communications, and electoral politics. Finally, the experiences of bilingual education have been used to pressure the homeland government into adopting a similar system for its children—a process that occurred from 2013 to 2016.

CONCLUSION

This chapter has analyzed the role of the Cabo Verdean diaspora in the context of the language-politics nexus. Their actions have helped mitigate the consequences of economic downturns and other crises, such as drought. However, the Cabo Verdean diaspora is far from a monolithic sociological entity. The material and financial engagement levels with Cabo Verde are directly related to the resources available to the specific diasporic community. For this reason, I distinguish between resourceful and resourceless diaspora. I argue that the former are the ones who have exerted far more significant influence on the political economy of the islands.

My analysis of the actions of diasporic actors in the context of the language-politics nexus follows two dimensions. In the first dimension, I discuss how diaspora citizens have influenced language politics in Cabo Verde. In this aspect, I center my investigation on understanding sociolinguistic remittances, the transference of linguistic materials and ideologies to the homeland. In so doing, diaspora communities are reconstructing themselves as soldiers who work tirelessly to promote and defend the mother tongue. As the illegibility of the state is also directed against diasporic communities, their reliance on the Cabo Verdean language constitutes a strategy of resistance. In other words, the fact that the state in Cabo Verde is unreadable to most of them, who may not have the linguistic competence to navigate in the dominant language (Portuguese), the emphasis on the mother tongue is a technique to overcome such hindrance.

Diaspora engagement in the Cabo Verdean language-politics nexus also includes a hostland dimension. I argue that two diasporic sites will be highlighted in this case: Portugal and Massachusetts in the United States. Historically, these two diasporic sites have contributed a significant number of linguistic activists and scholars who have assisted in the public promotion of the language in these sites. One of the domains through which the Cabo Verdean language has been promoted is bilingual education, a process whose origins are traced back to 1975. I argue in the chapter that the success of Cabo Verdean bilingual education has allowed the diffusion of the language into other domains of public life, including public health and electoral information from the local and state governments.

NOTES

1. Do You... Papia Kriolu ?, "RENATO SANCHES Ku NELSON SEMEDO TA DA KEL KRIOLU de CABO VERDE," May 15, 2016, https://fb.watch/f2DTjVK49n/.

2. Michel S. Laguerre, *Diaspora, Politics, and Globalization* (New York: Palgrave Macmillan, 2006), 43–53.

3. Gabriel Sheffer, *Modern Diasporas in International Politics* (London: Croom Helm, 1986); Gabriel Sheffer, *Diaspora Politics: At Home Abroad* (New York: Cambridge University Press, 2010); Lisa Anteby-Yemini and William Berthomière, "Diaspora: A Look Back on a Concept," *Bulletin Du Centre de Recherche Français à Jérusalem* 16 (2005): 262–70; Laguerre, *Diaspora, Politics, and Globalization*; Ronald Lee Cohen, *Global Diasporas: An Introduction* (Seattle, WA: University of Washington Press, 1997); Michel S. Laguerre, *Parliament and Diaspora in Europe* (New York: Palgrave Macmillan, 2015).

4. Anteby-Yemini and Berthomière, "Diaspora."

5. Sheffer, *Modern Diasporas in International Politics.*

6. Anderson, *Imagined Communities*; Abel Djassi Amado, "Whose Independence? Cabo Verdean-Americans and the Politics of National Independence Of Cabo Verde (1972–1976)," *Journal of Cape Verdean Studies* 5, no. 1 (2020): 36–53.

7. Sheffer, *Diaspora Politics*; Anteby-Yemini and Berthomière, "Diaspora"; Cohen, *Global Diasporas.*

8. Laguerre, *Diaspora, Politics, and Globalization*; Charles King and Neil Melvin, "Diaspora Politics: Ethnic Linkages, Foreign Policy, and Security in Eurasia," *International Security* 243 (1999): 108–38.

9. João Resende-Santos, "Cape Verde and Its Diaspora: Economic Transnationalism and Homeland Development," *Journal of Cape Verdean Studies* 2, no. 1 (2015): 69–107.

10. Andréa de Souza Lobo, "Bambinos and Kassu Bodi: Comments on Linguistic Appropriations in Cape Verde Islands," in *Creolization and Pidginization in Contexts of Postcolonial Diversity: Language, Culture, Identity*, ed. Jacqueline Knörr and Wilson Trajano Filho (Boston: Brill, 2018), 272–87; Bernard Spolsky, *The Languages of Diaspora and Return* (Boston: Brill, 2016).

11. Sheffer, *Diaspora Politics*, 75.

12. Cohen, *Global Diasporas.*

13. Laguerre, *Diaspora, Politics, and Globalization*, 40–54.

14. David M. Paul and Rachel Anderson Paul, *Ethnic Lobbies and US Foreign Policy* (Boulder: Lynne Rienner Publishers, 2009).

15. Andrew Ellis et al., *Voting from Abroad: The International IDEA Handbook* (Stockholm: International Institute for Democracy and Electoral Assistance: Instituto Federal Electoral, 2007); Laguerre, *Parliament and Diaspora in Europe.*

16. Ellis et al., *Voting from Abroad.*

17. Laguerre, *Diaspora, Politics, and Globalization.*

18. Governo de Cabo Verde, "Programa Do Governo. IX Legislatura" (Governo de Cabo Verde, 2016).

19. António Carreira, *The People of the Cape Verde Islands: Exploitation and Emigration* (London; Hamden, CT: C. Hurst; Archon Books, 1983); Batalha and Carling, *Transnational Archipelago*; Jørgen Carling and Lisa Åkesson, "Mobility at the Heart of a Nation: Patterns and Meanings of Cape Verdean Migration," *International Migration* 47, no. 1 (2009): 123–55.

20. Deirdre Meintel, "Cape Verdean Transnationalism, Old and New," *Anthropologica* 44, no. 1 (2002): 25; Raymond A. Almeida, *Cape Verdeans in America: Our Story* (Boston, MA: The American Committee for Cape Verde, 1978).

21. Arenas, *Lusophone Africa: Beyond Independence*.

22. Quint, "O Cabo-Verdiano: Uma Língua Mundial."

23. Brann, "The National Language Question"; Quint, "O Cabo-Verdiano: Uma Língua Mundial."

24. Baltasar Lopes da Silva, *Chiquinho: Romance* (Lisboa: Livros Cotovia, Lda, 2008).

25. Robert D. Tollison, "Rent Seeking," in *He Encyclopedia of Public Choice*, ed. C. K. Rowley and F. Schneider (Boston: Springer, 2004), https://doi.org/10.1007/978-0-306-47828-4_179.

26. Devesh Kapur, "Ideas and Economic Reforms in India: The Role of International Migration and the Indian Diaspora," *India Review* 3, no. 4 (2004): 364–84.

27. Blommaert, *Language Ideological Debates*.

28. Peggy Levitt, "Social Remittances: Migration Driven, Local-Level Forms of Cultural Diffusion," *The International Migration Review: IMR* 32, no. 4 (1998): 926; Peggy Levitt and Deepak Lamba-Nieves, "Social Remittances Revisited," *Journal of Ethnic and Migration Studies* 37, no. 1 (2011): 1–22.

29. *Eugénio Tavares: pelos jornais ...*, 2a Edição, Coleção Os clássicos (Praia, Cabo Verde: Biblioteca Nacional de Cabo Verde, 2017).

30. Jose Hopffer Almada, "O Bilinguismo Oficial Caboverdiano – Bilinguismo, Diglossia e Problemáticas Relativas Às Políticas de (Co)Oficialização Da Língua Caboverdiana," *Santiago Magazine*, March 27, 2019, https://santiagomagazine.cv/cultura/o-bilinguismo-oficial-caboverdiano-bilinguismo-diglossia-e-problematicas-relativas-as-politicas-de-cooficializacao-da-lingua-caboverdiana.

31. Lobo, "Bambinos and Kassu Bodi: Comments on Linguistic Appropriations in Cape Verde Islands."

32. Anne Pauwels, "Linguistic Sexism and Feminist Linguistic Activism," in *The Handbook of Language and Gender*, ed. Janet Holmes and Miriam Meyerhoff (Malden, MA: Blackwell Pub., 2003), 552.

33. Christine Mallinson, "Language and Its Everyday Revolutionary Potential: Feminist Linguistic Activism in the U.S.," in *The Oxford Handbook of U.S. Women's Social Movement Activism*, ed. Holly J. McCammon, Jo Reger, Rachel L. Einwohner, and Verta Taylor (Oxford: Oxford University Press, 2017), 419–39; Pauwels, "Linguistic Sexism and Feminist Linguistic Activism," 554.

34. Marlyse Baptista et al., "Language Contact in Cape Verdean Creole: A Study of Bidirectional Influences in Two Contact Settings," in *Oxford Handbook of Language Contact*, ed. Anthony Grant (Oxford: Oxford University Press, 2019), 713–40; Marlyse Baptista, Inês Brito, and Saídu Bangura, "Cape Verdean Creole in

Education: A Linguistic and Human Right," in *Creoles and Education*, ed. Bettina Migge, Isabelle Léglise, and Angela Bartens (Amsterdam/Philadelphia: John Benjamins, 2010), 273–96.

35. Macedo, "A Linguistic Approach to the Capeverdean Language"; Donaldo P. Macedo, "Cape Verdean Language Project: Final Report" (Washington, DC: Department of Education, 1985).

36. Marlyse Baptista, *The Syntax of Cape Verdean Creole: The Sotavento Varieties*, Linguistik Aktuell (Amsterdam: John Benjamins Pub., 2002).

37. Elin Haf Gruffydd Jones and Enrique Uribe-Jongbloed, eds., *Social Media and Minority Languages: Convergence and the Creative Industries*, Multilingual Matters (Series) (Bristol: Multilingual Matters, 2013); Daniel Cunliffe, "Minority Languages and Social Media," in *The Palgrave Handbook of Minority Languages and Communities*, ed. Gabrielle Hogan-Brun and Bernadette O'Rourke (London: Palgrave Macmillian, 2019), 451–80.

38. Mass.Gov, "Informason Sobri COVID-19 (COVID-19 Information in Cape Verdean Creole)," accessed August 16, 2022, https://www.mass.gov/info-details/informason-sobri-covid-19-covid-19-information-in-cape-verdean-creole.

39. Louis DeSipio, "Making Citizens or Good Citizens? Naturalization As a Predictor of Organizational and Electoral Behavior among Latino Immigrants," *Hispanic Journal of Behavioral Sciences* 18, no. 2 (1996): 194–213.

40. Jack Citrin et al., "Testing Huntington: Is Hispanic Immigration a Threat to American Identity?," *Perspectives on Politics* 5, no. 1 (2007): 31–48; Samuel P. Huntington, *Who Are We?: The Challenges to America's National Identity*, First Simon & Schuster (New York: Simon & Schuster, 2005).

41. Marilyn Halter, "Cape Verdeans in the U.S.," in *Transnational Archipelago: Perspectives on Cape Verdean Migration and Diaspora*, ed. Luís Batalha and Jørgen Carling (Amsterdam: Amsterdam University Press, 2008), 35–46; Amado, "Whose Independence? Cabo Verdean-Americans and the Politics of National Independence of Cabo Verde (1972–1976)."

42. Donaldo Macedo, "A Língua Caboverdiana Na Educação Bilingue," in *Issues in Portuguese Bilingual Education*, ed. Donaldo Macedo (Cambridge, MA: National Assessment and Dissemination Center for Bilingual/Bicultural Education, 1980), 183–200.

43. Capeverdean Creole Institute, "CAPEVERDEAN CREOLE INSTITUTE," *Capeverdean Creole Institute* (blog), accessed July 5, 2022, http://www.capeverdeancreoleinstitute.org/.

44. Miren Uriarte et al., "English Learners in Boston Public Schools: Enrollment, Engagement and Academic Outcomes of Native Speakers of Cape Verdean Creole, Chinese Dialects, Haitian Creole, Spanish, and Vietnamese," Gastón Institute Publications. 130. (Gastón Institute. UMass Boston, 2009), https://scholarworks.umb.edu/gaston_pubs/130.

45. Dulce Pereira, "Aprender a Ser Bilingue," in *Múltiplos Olhares Sobre o Bilinguismo: Transversalidades II*, ed. Cristina Flores (Húmus: Universidade do Minho, 2011), 20; Ana Josefa Cardoso, "Falar Cabo-Verdiano e Português: A Educação

Bilingue Em Cabo Verde e Na Diáspora," *Iberografias: Revista de Estudos Ibericos* 15 (2019): 41–52.

46. Ana Josefa Cardoso, "As Interferências Linguísticas Do Caboverdiano No Processo de Aprendizagem Do Português" (Masters Thesis, Lisbon: Universidade Aberta, 2005), 56.

47. Pereira, "Aprender a Ser Bilingue," 20.

48. Pereira, 21.

49. Cardoso, "Falar Cabo-Verdiano e Português," 47.

50. IILP, "Por Uma Educação Bilíngue Competente," February 27, 2017, https://iilp.wordpress.com/2017/02/27/por-uma-educacao-bilingue-competente/; Cardoso, "Falar Cabo-Verdiano e Português," 47–48.

Chapter 5

The Illegible State in Cabo Verde

António Domingo Gomes Fernandes, known by his nickname "Totinho," is a famed sax player from Cabo Verde. For many years, he was a member of the famous local band, "Os Tubarões," and accompanied Cesária Evora, the world-renowned singer from Cabo Verde, on her tours around the globe. After a January 8, 2016 car accident, Totinho was taken to court, where the legal proceeding was in Portuguese, the state's official language. During his trial, the state district attorney demanded that Totinho speaks Portuguese and even prohibited the Cabo Verdean language from being used.[1] Like its African counterparts, the Cabo Verdean state, as noted above, uses a European language inherited from colonialism to conduct its business, including the administration of justice. Totinho later accused the legal system of partiality by noting that he was ordered to speak Portuguese, which he didn't fully master.

Situations like this happen constantly, and those with more significant influence and power in society instrumentalize the dominant language to further entrench their high status and privilege. Despite the constitutional precepts against language-based discrimination, the rights of citizens are often trampled because the state uses a language that most don't understand or employ.[2] The state-society linguistic divide serves the interests of the elites and, in many ways, facilitates and advances the processes of domination over the great masses. The case of Totinho illustrates how the inability to comprehend the state because of linguistic differences could cause irreparable damage to citizens' rights and privileges.

In this chapter, I advance the concept of the *illegible state* as an essential heuristic device to understand state-society relations in postcolonial Cabo Verde, a concept that can be applied to most cases in Africa and the Caribbean. Simply put, the idea of an illegible state refers to the fact that the postcolonial state, the epicenter of political power, is a black box to most of the population. I argue that language policy—a combination of language ideology, practices, and planning—is one of the main reasons for state illegibility.[3] The state in Cabo Verde is "unreadable" to most citizens since it relies extensively on Portuguese, a language that most either don't know or aren't comfortable using. The phenomenon of state illegibility is further deepened by the role played by the media, an important actor in constructing Portuguese linguistic hegemony. Furthermore, the chapter also discusses two main political consequences of state illegibility: disengagement and decreasing surveillatory power over the state.

ON THE CONCEPT OF THE ILLEGIBLE STATE

The state has long been a central subject of study in comparative politics, particularly in the first half of the twentieth century. However, in the 1950s and 1960s, with the so-called "behavioralist revolution," dominant approaches in the field of political science rejected the idea of the state as a significant variable; it was only in the 1980s that the field began to pay close attention to the state.[4] Notwithstanding this fact, the centrality of the state in political analysis has been deeper in African political studies. In fact, the state in Africa has been through so many analytical representations and characterizations, a situation that has no comparison in other areas of study. The African state has been defined as "warlord," "rhizome," "criminal," "rapacious," "vampire," and "neopatrimonial," to cite a few examples.[5] As an external imposition resulting from colonialism, the African state has been said to be neither "African" nor "state."[6] These studies nonetheless point out the centrality of the state in African politics; any serious study of politics in an African country, as such, must include a clear understanding of the processes of power within the state. Yet, despite all this attention given to the state, few political scientists have analyzed and examined the role of language and language policy in state formation and reproduction. The few exceptions include works from Ali Mazrui, David Laitin, and Victor Webb.[7] The topic has attracted more attention from sociolinguistics, who have extensively commented on the region's links between politics and language.[8] An extensive and in-depth analysis of the postcolonial state in Africa must focus on the critical examination of language policy. The state and its elites use language policy as a tool for self-construction and reproduction while instrumentalizing it in societal domination. Language, more than a simple instrument of communication, is a medium through which asymmetric social relations are constructed and consolidated.

Understanding the concept of the *illegible state* entails unpacking its two constitutive terms: the state and illegibility. First, it is important to discuss the idea of the *state*. The concept of the state is not equivalent to that of government. While the "government" and the "state" are used interchangeably in popular and media discourse, the two are different sociopolitical entities.[9] Institutionally, functionally, and in terms of personnel, the two are quite distinct: the government is just one portion of the state institutions, perhaps the most important. In most of the world, the expression "government" is typically reserved for the central executive authority of a sovereign political entity. As a collective body, the government in places like Cabo Verde includes the prime minister, the head of government, and many ministers, vice-ministers, and secretaries of state. The government, as such, sits at the top of the state's bureaucracy, with powers to supervise, superintend, manage, and control a complex network of other bureaucratic entities, many of which are independent. The government is but the executive and the key administrator of the state. The other institutions that make up the state include the different autonomous public organizations and enterprises, the judicial and legislative branches, and the head of the state.

Comparative political studies on the state have been informed by the insights of Max Weber, according to whom the "state is a human community that (successfully) claims the monopoly of the legitimate use of physical force within a given territory."[10] This Weberian conceptual operationalization served as the guide for further understanding the contemporary state. Alfred Stepan notes that the state "is the continuous administrative, legal, bureaucratic and coercive systems that attempt not only to structure relationships between civil society and public authority in a polity but also to structure many crucial relationships within civil society as well."[11] The state is the supreme locus of power in society and, ipso facto, with normative and often empirical domination over its respective community.

The illegible state constitutes an "unreadable" state to many of its citizens. This concept is essential for analyzing contemporary political development in Cabo Verde, Africa, and the Caribbean since it can serve as an important analytical tool for understanding state–society relations. The illegible state is a state that demands citizens' huge investments, intellectual or otherwise, in their process of deciphering it. The illegibility of the state derives from a culture of secrecy and lack of transparency among its elite, the type of political regime, and language policy. The postcolonial state's insistence on using only or relying extensively on the dominant language for its communication and record-keeping has resulted in the political exclusion of a significant segment of the population who can't grasp information deriving from public authorities. The illegibility of the state, as such, is constructed through the official language policy, which, explicitly or implicitly, mandates that the language inherited from colonialism be the sole medium through which the procedures, operations, and processes of the state can be conducted. In Africa—as in the Caribbean—the state relies almost exclusively on English, French, or Portuguese. As the postcolonial state in Africa and the Caribbean is a Europhonic and Eurographic construction, it is an entity that is legally and constitutionally defined by a language inherited from colonialism.

The concept of the illegible state borrows heavily from the insights of James C. Scott, who has extensively discussed and analyzed political legibility. For Scott, political legibility refers to the "state's attempt to make society legible, to arrange the population in ways that simplified the classic state functions of taxation, conscription, and prevention of rebellion."[12] In other words, the state maintains its preponderance over society through resource extraction and demands for political acquiescence. Interested in state–society relations from a historical point of view, Scott analyzes ways and strategies created by the state to control, manage, and direct its society. The ultimate political goal of the state and its elite is to facilitate the state's penetration into its community for the extraction and mobilization of human and material resources. This process ultimately results in the state taming society to conform to its interests.

Making society legible thus accelerates the rule of the state. The state is the Trojan horse deployed in its society with discourses, practices, and policies. Scott's point of departure is the following: the premodern state lived with an unordered society, or what he prefers to call "social hieroglyph" to hint at the enigmatic characteristics of the society—from the perspective of the state elite. The key distinguishing feature between the premodern and modern states is that the latter are engaged in ordering, classifying, cataloging, and controlling the population and its territory. Therefore, "legibility [becomes] a central problem in [modern] statecraft."[13] Through its activities and actions, the state becomes more knowledgeable of its society; the knowledge of the social supports power.

Turning Scott's theory upside down, I focus on the state itself and examine how it has been made illegible to most citizens. When the lines of communication between the state and society are clear of interference, the former is legible to the latter. A language widely used by its population constitutes a fundamental mechanism for making the state open and transparent to the public. When the state uses a language that is the population's mother tongue, citizens are more likely to understand and supervise the procedures, operations, and processes of power. In other words, when the state speaks the mother tongue, citizens can amplify their political knowledge. Inversely, the constant and permanent use of a language that most people either don't grasp or have a limited understanding can hinder and mitigate their political knowledge. While the state puts out information about itself, the message may not be readily absorbed since it is packaged in a medium that the majority don't understand. When there is a difference between the language of the state (*politolect*) and that of citizens (*demolect*), the lines of communication between the state and society are affected.[14] When the politolect coincides with—or is minimally distant from—demolect, information put out by the state is more likely to be grasped by the general population. Consequently, these citizens can significantly and qualitatively increase their overall political knowledge.

In a liberal democratic order, information about the state's procedures, operations, and processes are readily available—online or through a visit to a library. The modern state is based on the notion that it must publicize how it operates—a situation amplified by modern technology and social media and the rise of what many call e-government.[15] The problem, as such, is not the scarcity of information but rather how data is packaged. The illegible state is hidden in plain sight. While there have been some incursions of an indigenous mother tongue in some domains of the postcolonial state, there are two things to note: first, these incursions occur almost exclusively in the oral domains; second, the written domain has been maintained as a reserved domain for French, English, and Portuguese. In simple terms, the state is illegible when its operations, procedures, and processes, while publicized and made available in the oral and written domains, cannot be understood or used by the overwhelming majority of the population. State illegibility is a byproduct of language policy: fluency in the dominant language constitutes a necessary condition for an enlightened understanding of the state and its actions, much less to participate in them. When it is not the population's mother tongue, the state's continuous use of and reliance on the dominant language makes it a black box. The state is linguistically shielded, and only those who have mastered the dominant language can circumvent the shield.

The phenomenon of state illegibility is directly related to the postcolonial state language policy. Through institutions, regulations, and practices, the postcolonial state dictates the linguistic medium through which it operates. Across the African continent, with few exceptions, there is an uninterrupted continuity in language policy from the colonial to the postcolonial state. One should note that independence in sub-Saharan Africa brought the processes of Africanization and indigenization across many policy areas; little by little, with a degree of success, the postcolonial state in Africa sought a rupture with the previous colonial state by Africanizing itself. Such a phenomenon is evident in terms of the personnel of the state bureaucracy. However, in terms of language policy, the postcolonial state has been rather conservative, maintaining, often without much changes, the colonial state's linguistic regulations and practices.

That the state uses a language that citizens don't use for everyday social interactions is an indication of and a pathway for its illegibility. However, the state's reliance on a given language alien to most citizens provokes a cultural short circuit. State illegibility also leads to cultural differences between state elites and society, derived from the fact that the former relies on a language distinct from what the latter typically uses. The continuous reliance on a language inherited from colonialism has made the postcolonial state culturally alien to its society; the problem of state illegibility is also cultural. In other words, the constant reliance on the dominant language shapes the state elites' views and behaviors in multiple ways.

Scholars have noted a direct and interconnected link between language and culture. Philosophers and scholars of language have argued that the language we speak directly influences how our worldview is formed. In such a view, language is not a neutral instrument of communication; language shapes and even limits how we see the world and, as such, can directly impact our learning and cognitive processes. As formulated by Robert Miller, "each language was said to contain a peculiar Weltanschauung, which causes *its speakers to 'see' the world in a way different from the speakers of other languages.*"[16] In a similar vein, Franz Fanon also writes that "To speak means to be in a position to use a certain syntax, to grasp the morphology of this or that language, but it means above all to assume a culture, to support the weight of a civilization."[17] Therefore, the use of a language formats how one sees the world. The illegibility of the state, thus, is not simply a linguistic issue. The use of a language that is not the nation's language constitutes a powerful hindrance to grasping and participating in the operations of the state. Further, by relying extensively on a language that is not the language of the community, the state becomes culturally distinct. The dominant language, inherited from colonialism, is not simply an instrument of communication; it is, at the same time, a tool for reproducing the postcolonial as an alien entity vis-à-vis the local community.

The phenomenon of state illegibility in postcolonial Africa is reinforced by two sociopolitical phenomena, namely, the official-language privilege and institutional linguicism. Official-language privilege refers to the accruing of benefits and privileges from the public authorities (and society at large) simply from being a fluent speaker of the state's official language. In the postcolonial African state, having the language of the former colonial power as the official means of conducting state business constitutes the medium through which privileges can be made effective and experienced by the few. The official-language privilege may be reflected either in the quickness of the response following an inquiry and/or in access to material and non-material benefits that nonofficial language speakers may find difficult to access. This concept is valid as it helps to understand state–citizen relationships. The greater one's command of the official language, the more privilege one extracts from the state, namely accessing information and/or assuming a higher social status. To master or to be fluent in the official language is to enjoy significant social capital or "property."[18]

State illegibility is legitimized by the ideology of state monolingualism, the idea that the modern state must rely on a single language in order to be an effective apparatus of authoritative control, decision-making, and management. As an invention of European political history, the modern state was developed on the notion of linguistic oneness—the language of the state must be dispersed throughout the territory, and all citizens must use it.[19] This single language, historically derived from the dialect spoken by powerholders and the elites, is then imposed across the nation.

The second mechanism that reinforces the illegibility of the state is institutional linguicism. Linguicism refers to "ideologies and structures which are used to legitimate, effectuate, and reproduce unequal division of power and resources (both material and non-material) between groups defined on the basis of language."[20] Linguicism is a language-based ideology and practice of social domination. It is, as such, correlated to other systems, ideologies, and practices of social domination, such as racism, classism, sexism, and ageism, in which oppression is based on race, social class, gender, and age, respectively. This ideology forms the basis for classifying and hierarchizing individuals and social groups based on their language. The language that one speaks is the marker of one's social position. Like any other political system of classification and hierarchization, there is a construction of an ideal speaker who becomes a standard measure. Access to resources, material or otherwise, depends on one's position relative to this ideal speaker—the further linguistically one is from the ideal speaker, the more exclusion one is likely to experience.

The development of institutional linguicism centers on the state's role as the critical agent in developing and nurturing ideologies, practices, and institutions that create asymmetric and hierarchical relationships among languages found in the polity. Given that the state controls immensurable resources, financial and otherwise, its actions and omissions often translate into supporting one language at the expense of others. Take, for instance, the case of language in education policy. When the state designates a language as the medium through which schooling in public schools is conducted, plenty of public resources, ranging from symbolic to financial ones, are thus channeled toward that specific language. The ultimate consequence of this situation is the construction or maintenance of asymmetry among the languages found in the community.

Institutional linguicism derives from colonial linguicist language policy, a topic analyzed in chapter 1. The modern colonial state, developed in the late nineteenth century, designed the linguistic arena of the colony through the construction of two publics, each of which was reserved for specific languages. Several scholars and thinkers on the colonial state have noted its bidimensional characteristics: for Fanon, it was about Manicheanism; Peter Ekeh talks about "two publics"; and Mahmood Mamdani discusses what he terms the "bifurcated" state.[21] The formal public—that of the state—became the reserved arena for the European language, in which indigenous languages were relegated to the private, communitarian, and rural arenas.

Institutional linguicism occurs at the state level, where its policies and actions produce a classification of citizens. In other words, the state effectively creates social hierarchy and access to itself through its action and policies, particularly its official language policy. A linguicist language policy can be considered a diglossic language policy writ large. Such a language policy reinforces the diglossic situation that characterizes society. The dominant language, employed by the public authorities for its primary functions, becomes the key and often the only medium for formal, official sociopolitical, and economic life. It becomes the "language of high politics" insofar as the elite and the ruling classes' major political battles are conducted in the dominant language. In state institutions, such as the bureaucracy, the parliament, the judiciary, and so on, official business is conducted through the dominant language. In the African context, these are Portuguese, English, or French. It is the language that the state considers the medium for most, if not all, of its critical political transactions—through various legislative, rule-making, norming, and judicial review processes. High politics, therefore, is not in the vernacular. In postcolonial Africa, the vernacular is rarely the language of high politics.

To better understand the concept of the illegible state, it is imperative to comprehend the communicative interactions between the state and society. Traditionally, information about the state processes, procedures, and operations is made available by the state itself or through mass media. State–society communication can be either direct or indirect. The state makes itself known to the public through various channels, including its official gazettes, websites, bulletins, posters, billboards, reports, and so forth. Additionally, information from the state is direct whenever there is a direct encounter with a street-level bureaucrat, such as between a police officer and a citizen. Alternatively, the state indirectly transfers information about itself, often through the media.

In many African postcolonial states, direct oral communication between the state and citizens often occurs in low language. State agents such as police officers, public administration clerks providing detailed information and/or services to the population, and many other low-ranking state officials perform their duties in the mother tongue. These low-ranking state officials often do not have a fluent command of the high language—thus, their subaltern position within the state hierarchy. Direct communication between the state elite and the ordinary citizen is scarce, except for election campaigns or visits to the community by the elected state elite. Public hearings can be conceived as a mechanism that would increase or facilitate the communicative encounter between the high-echelon state official and the ordinary citizen. Nowadays, different states, from states with a long history of democratic experiences to one-party states, such as China, are creating and developing mechanisms of public hearings to support citizens' participation.[22]

Information and commentary on the political processes and power architecture are often channeled into the dominant language. Language ideologies and practices distinguish between languages of modernity and tradition, and they influence the choice of the medium to diffuse the performance of power. The language of modernity is accepted as the *medium* to transmit political modernity. According to the mainstream ideology in many postcolonial states, other languages lack the necessary components or status to perform such tasks of modernity.

To properly understand how linguistic exclusion becomes political, I develop a model linking the monoglossic citizen to the state (figure 5.1). Often the information is made available in the state's channels (e.g., the public speech of a state leader, the state's official newspaper, or, more recently, the government's websites, among other channels). Alternatively, the information coming from the state may be disseminated through the mass media.

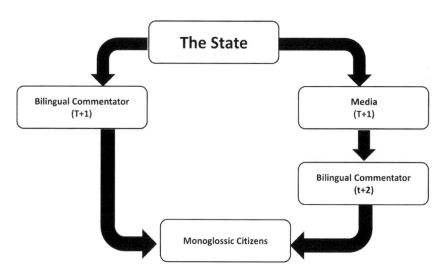

Figure 5.1 The Flow of Information and Control between the State and Citizens. *Source:* Figure created by author.

The media would fill in the vacuum of incomprehension by facilitating the interpretation of the processes of power. In modern democracies, the mass media are crucial devices that simplify already-complex political processes.[23] By following diglossic language ideologies and practices, the media contribute to the further illegibility of the state. The model represents the flow of information between the state and citizens. The model does not apply to situations in which the citizen, who is proficient in the high language, can access the information by going directly to the state without any linguistic intermediary.

For nonofficial language speakers to grasp the meaning and content of information about political processes, they must have access to those proficient in the high language. The flow is as follows: information about the political processes of the state is acquired by a commentator/translator—a citizen proficient in the two languages, that is, the low and the high languages, and has personal relations with the monoglossic citizen. This commentator cum translator, in turn, passes the information to the monoglossic citizen. The direct linkage between an average citizen and an informed and genuinely bilingual citizen who can explain the processes of government and politics can be through family relations or some nongovernmental organizations. More often than not, the monoglossic citizens lack access to bilingual citizens. The latter use different social spaces vis-à-vis the former—thus, the direct contact is relatively minimal. This situation is worse in rural areas—or the peripheral regions of urban Africa. Ordinary rural folks rarely engage with bilingual citizens, the linguistic brokers. The likelihood of engaging in politics increases with more knowledge about political processes and operations. In other words, a citizen with a high degree of political knowledge is more likely to participate actively in community affairs. Possessing high levels of political knowledge translates into lower costs of participation.

THE ILLEGIBLE STATE IN CABO VERDE

The state is concealed from many Cabo Verdean citizens because it is illegible. The linguistic gap between the state and society makes it challenging for citizens to properly supervise the state, its institutions, and its personnel. The state has developed a linguistic shell that a sizeable proportion of its citizens find challenging to penetrate. The use of the Portuguese language provokes a political short circuit between the state and a significant percentage of the population, whereby the power of control of the latter over the former is significantly reduced. Comprehending the state and its operations is a grueling task for many. Yet, gathering information about the state is a sine qua non for the citizens' proper supervision and democratic control.

As noted earlier, a sizeable portion of the Cabo Verdean citizens lacks mastery of the Portuguese language. In general terms, nonelite does not possess complete linguistic competence in Portuguese. The increasingly complex and abstract processes of politics that characterize the contemporary state take place almost exclusively in Portuguese. This situation may hinder ordinary citizens' ability to act politically to exercise democratic control over their representatives and political leaders.

To put it differently, the linguistic difference between the ordinary citizen and the state leads to the waning of *surveillatory* political participation. The concept refers to citizens' full engagement in making the state agents accountable for their actions (or lack thereof). The state is defined as a political entity grounded in the Portuguese language. In other words, the predominance of the Portuguese language is double: first, it is the medium through which the state defines, classifies, and orders itself via the constitution and ordinary legislation. Second, an explicit official language policy guarantees the predominance of the Portuguese language. As noted in chapter 2, the official language policy was amended with the 1999 revision of the constitution. What was a de facto linguistic predominance has become a de jure linguistic predominance. As discussed earlier, the country's constitution enshrines the Portuguese linguistic hegemony.

The state agents, particularly those placed in the higher echelons of the public administration bureaucracy, use primarily Portuguese in their official capacity. The higher a state agent is on the administrative ladder, the more linguistic distance they have vis-à-vis the ordinary citizen. For instance, in the courts, the working language is Portuguese, even when the defendant does not speak the language (in which case, they must count on the translation or explanations from their attorney).[24] During field research in Cabo Verde, I often asked my informants about their linguistic interaction with the state's offices. During one of the focus group interviews, a male high-school graduate in his early twenties told me: "There are state agencies in which if you didn't speak Portuguese, you would not go further. I have been through so many constraints for not knowing to speak Portuguese correctly."[25] Institutions such as the Ministry of Foreign Relations, which does not interact with ordinary citizens, communicate with the public in Portuguese. Yet, people respond in their native language even when Portuguese is used. A young female informant told me that in the state offices where Portuguese is the primary language, many citizens conducting business with the state would retort in the Cabo Verdean language. She said: "Creole has a lot of [social] weight. It isn't easy to go to the [public] administration [offices] and speak Portuguese. We often respond [in] Creole even when they communicate with us in Portuguese."[26]

State agents also use the Cabo Verdean language. Many state agencies that interact daily with citizens use the Cabo Verdean language in their oral and direct communication with the public. As part of my research, I visited some of the state's agencies to observe the sociolinguistic behavior of citizens and state employees. One of the state offices I often visited during my research stay in Cabo Verde was the Conservatory of the Records in the neighborhood of Txada Santu Antoni in the city of Praia. Direct communication between citizens and the clerk was exclusively in the native language.

Bilingual citizens possess a social advantage. Fluency in the high language is in itself a form of symbolic capital. To be proficient in Portuguese is to be fully equipped with *linguistic capital*: high social value and distinction deriving from being proficient or a native speaker of a dominant and prestigious language.[27] Ultimately, a fluent Portuguese speaker enjoys preferential treatment from the state agent. Cabo Verdeans view language and speech styles as markers of social identity and status markers. Being fluent in the language is an asset that translates into tangible advantages. Speaking the dominant language often means a drastic improvement in the services provided by the state. Linguistic differences incur different levels of access to the state. A female informant in her mid-twenties who works for the community radio station in her neighborhood of Pónta d'Agu recounted an experience she had at the Conservatory of the Records in the neighborhood of Txada Santu Antoni:

> Like everybody else, I was waiting for my number to be called to be attended to by the clerk. Then, a gentleman came in and went straight to the clerk. He began to speak in Portuguese, and things changed automatically. The clerk became friendlier. About ten minutes later, he took the paperwork he came in for and left—while we were all waiting for our turn.[28]

Similar situations like the one described above are typical. It was no surprise for me to learn that my informants had experienced such discrimination either directly or had heard of it. Being a native of the islands, I recall how speaking Portuguese in public was an asset that opened doors and made services faster. Consequently, there is a general perception that the state categorizes and establishes a hierarchy among its citizens based on their competence in the dominant language. It leads to a common understanding that some citizens are effectively more equal than others.

Accessing information about and from the state is also problematic. Monolingual citizens are doubly disadvantaged. On the one hand, they cannot access the information about the state directly since they lack the proper skills to grasp the data, which are locked in a language different from what they use for everyday social life. On the other hand, as a speaker of the subordinate language, the language of low prestige, ordinary citizens often find themselves with a limited capacity to extract information from/about the state—and/or from its agents. Using one language or the other results in either political inclusion or exclusion. A young man told me that:

I believe [communication] in the Cabo Verdean language is far better [. . .] some of my colleagues may understand it better in the Cabo Verdean language than in Portuguese. [Moreover] there are many words in Portuguese that many people often don't understand what is discussed.[29]

Another young male with a high-school diploma searching for a job went further:

In the Cabo Verdean language, people better understand [. . . and] interpret the sentences [uttered] better. The Portuguese language has many words that one has a hard time understanding. So, when you are around a politician [who speaks Portuguese], you are pointlessly clapping your hands as you may not know what you are supporting.[30]

A third informant, a young woman in her early twenties, commented: "I believe that both Portuguese and the Cabo Verdean languages should be made the official language [of the country]. Sometimes, many people face embarrassment in many state offices as they can't speak Portuguese."[31]

In Cabo Verde's case—and the model can be applied to other former Portuguese colonies in Africa—this social mechanism of domination corresponds to what I call "Lusophone privilege." To be a fluent and proficient speaker of the Portuguese language is powerful symbolic capital that can easily be translated into other forms of capital, chiefly economic. Lusophone privilege manifests in different domains of society. It manifests with the agent uttering, with the audience learning that the former is a fluent Portuguese speaker.

Many of my informants have told me that using different languages in public administration means preferential treatment. Some of them have even recounted their own experiences regarding this. An anecdotal experience is worth sharing here:

My friend [a proficient bi-lingual] asked me to go with him for some errands, including various stops at different state offices for documents he needed to take to the port authorities to get some of the stuff imported from Portugal. My friend spoke the Cabo Verdean language with the clerks in the first few offices we visited. While he obtained the necessary paperwork, they gave him a hard time. He then decided to speak Portuguese in the other offices and Port Authority. Not only did it become relatively easier for him to get what he was looking for, but the office manager came from the inside to talk to him to ensure everything was fine.[32]

Citizens generally understand the state to be a linguistic construct. The state is the realm where one language (Portuguese in Cabo Verde) assumes the predominant role and is used for its functions. Though my informants note the disadvantages that monolingual citizens endure, they note that the top state agents *must* be fluent in the official language, the language of wider communication that permits the linkage between the country and the international community. Many see the state as the device to muster material and moral support from abroad. The process of seeking foreign aid implies that the state agents be proficient in an international language. A young man in his twenties, with a high-school diploma and looking for a job, told me that one of the roles of the president of the republic is to engage with foreign governments to procure developmental aid. In his own words: "The president of the republic is a person who travels abroad searching for aid, doing this and that. They should not be in that position if they speak only [Cabo Verdean] Creole. A person that speaks only Creole should not exercise such a post."[33]

Along the same lines, another young man who had not concluded high-school education considered that:

> a president of the republic, a prime minister, or a minister who speaks only Cabo Verdean Creole is not good since there are times when it is good to talk in Creole, but there are also times when one needs the Portuguese language more than Creole [. . .] But to speak just Creole, even for us who are not the president of the republic, sometimes when we go someplace, we feel frustrated, let alone a president. A president who is not able to speak Portuguese is too bad.[34]

Still, another informant said, "A president of the republic who speaks only in Creole can't be possible. It is not good. [It is] too negative. Too negative as many presidents come to Cabo Verde [for state visits]."[35]

These quotes show how ordinary citizens think about and understand the state. To these citizens, the state and its key personnel should (or perhaps must) use the language with more prestige and power. These quotes also make clear the pervasiveness of high language ideology. There is a notion that the state needs Portuguese for international communication, a role that the native language cannot fulfill. Against this backdrop, the elites have positioned themselves as the *interlocuteur valable* to the global world.[36] Information and resources coming from abroad pass through the gatekeepers. Their social value is increased by controlling access to foreign news and resources.

THE MEDIA, AUXILIARY OF THE ILLEGIBLE STATE

The main point of this section is that the media furthers the illegibility of the state by reporting almost exclusively in Portuguese, a language that most people can't grasp or understand. The media, as such, becomes an instrument of the society's elite, designed to construct further the invisible wall that keeps the majority of the people outside the realms of public debate. The media in Cabo Verde can be classified as local when an outlet is owned by and serves national citizens and foreign when programming has almost nothing to do with the country's social reality. Globalization has had a tremendous impact on the Cabo Verdean mediascape. While the global media are very influential and important, they are accessible only to a minority of citizens: those with linguistic or economic capital.

The media constitute another critical vehicle through which communication between the state and citizens can be carried out. While available, online media do not get as much audience, given the high internet costs in Cabo Verde. Print media circulation is relatively small, limited to thousands per week (consumed by the *culturati* and highly educated class). The media that have more impact are television and radio broadcasters. Most radio stations are locally based, limited to an island or a group of islands. The National Radio of Cabo Verde (RNCV), the state-owned national radio station, is the exception, as it has nationwide coverage. As for the television broadcasters, only the national television (TCV) station has nationwide coverage.

Through media, citizens encounter the Portuguese language daily. Different "Portugueses" are available to the Cabo Verdean audience since Portuguese is a *pluricentric* language, given that it has two main and recognizable standard versions, both in spoken and written forms: the European and American (Brazil).[37] Cabo Verdeans encounter Brazilian Portuguese mainly through entertainment programming such as Brazilian soap operas, which are popular with the audience. The "erudite" Portuguese and the Standard European Portuguese (the norm from Portugal) are used mainly by the local cultural and political elite for their oral and written communication needs. The employment of uncommon and unfamiliar words marks distinction and social prestige. The local elite's use of "erudite" Portuguese accomplishes many political and social objectives. It also constitutes a technique for manipulating social perception. Using "difficult language" is perceived at face value as a marker for other socially rewarded qualities such as intelligence and technical competence.

Television is far more attractive than traditional media, such as print or radio, because of its bi-dimensionality (voice and image). Entertainment programs constitute most of what is broadcast on national television in Cabo Verde. Most of the programs presented on the national television broadcast, be they national or foreign, are about musical or other noninformative shows. Discussions of domestic socioeconomic and political affairs are confined to two types of television shows: first, the news, particularly the 8:00 p.m. news, presents the most important political developments of the day or week. The prime-time news report takes about fifty minutes. Current political issues do not go through careful or in-depth analysis. The second type of program is those in which informed commentators are invited to discuss some critical issues of the week (e.g., "A Grande Entrevista" [The Great Interview] or

"Conversa em Dia" [Updating Talk]). These two types of programs are almost exclusively presented in the Portuguese language.

The informed commentator interviews are almost exclusively in Portuguese. Almost always, the invited commentators are members of the leading strata of the society (i.e., members of the local cultural and political elite). The use of the Portuguese language in these TV programs legitimizes the commentator as an authority on the subject under discussion. Second, it allows the individual to demonstrate their capacity to manipulate the Portuguese language. Linguistic exhibitionism leads to using esoteric Portuguese: uncommon lexicography, unusual grammatical and sentence constructions, and so forth. Esoteric language is a marker of expertise. Its use creates an environment conducive to monolingual citizens' political passivity. When these informative programs are on, monoglossic citizens have few incentives to follow them. Little can be retained by those citizens who don't have a complete mastery of the Portuguese language. Unless someone proficient in Portuguese can translate or provide the gist of what is being discussed, the monoglossic citizens find themselves in a difficult situation. The information is not presented in a form that allows them to grasp the contents to form an opinion about the subject matter. Instead, a "veil of ignorance" is imposed upon monoglossic citizens. Thus, linguistic exclusion becomes political exclusion insofar as not being proficient in the high language hinders access to vital information and/or political processes. In other words, linguistic choices in the media impact citizens' enlightened understanding—another pillar of modern democracy, the source for proper and active civic and political engagement.

THE ILLEGIBILITY OF THE STATE AND DIMINISHED SURVEILLATORY POWER

In Cabo Verde, the state and its agents use mainly Portuguese, chiefly when communicating through writing. The state uses the dominant language as the language of expertise, characterized by specific jargon and structures that are understandable only by those familiar with that language. The mother tongue speaker's encounter with the state is superficial. This superficial communication often happens when citizens deal with street-level bureaucrats or seek to acquire a service or a good provided by the state (e.g., a copy of the certificate of live birth in the Conservatory of the Records).[38] Understanding the operations, processes, and procedures of power entail going to the core of state actions and omissions. Citizens' control over and supervision of the state implies understanding the institutional and legal architecture underpinning the state apparatus. To question and inquire about the actions carried out (or failed to be carried out) by state officials, one must know the institutional limits the state imposes upon itself.

In the previous sections, I argued that the state is a linguistic black box. It is illegible in that ordinary citizens, who lack linguistic competence in the Portuguese language, find it extremely difficult, if not utterly impossible, to decipher, decode, and interpret the procedures, processes, and operations of power conducted mainly through Portuguese. In this section, I contend that this results in diminished surveillatory power for these citizens. My argument builds on the insights of many political scientists, such as Robert Dahl, who argue that a precondition for active citizenship is an enlightened understanding of politics.[39] Along the same lines, David Laitin notes that speaking the language of the state is a "critical condition enabling the citizen to participate in the political arena of the state."[40] This argument is supported by Will Kymlicka, who argues that "democratic politics is politics in the vernacular," a crucial medium that mitigates anxieties and other psychological costs of participation.[41] The linguistic approximation between the state and citizens foments and fosters political engagement. On the contrary, the linguistic distance between the state and society tends to lead citizens to disengage from the state.

Yet, the state in Cabo Verde over-relies on Portuguese, a situation that has led to political exclusion and disengagement. In other words, to many citizens in Cabo Verde, Portuguese constitutes an "instrument of deprivation."[42] The state-controlled portion of public space has been a domain of the Portuguese language for many decades—despite recent inroads by the Cabo Verdean language. Non-Portuguese language speakers cannot navigate that portion of public space, given that available materials are in a language in which they lack competence. In this aspect, it can be argued that the constant use of Portuguese as the state's medium of communication deprives many citizens of their right to information and negatively impacts the principle of political equality before the law. The comprehension of the Portuguese language is hindered not only by the "difficult words" that my informants mention in their interviews. Sentence and grammatical constructions may also hinder understanding a message passed through Portuguese by those who are not fully trained in that language.

State illegibility increases the likelihood of societal disengagement. By disengagement, political scientists mean an increasing political gap between the state and society. Disengagement from the state occurs at different levels and aspects of social life. It affects the political economy as "economic activities turn to outlets less easily regulated by the state."[43] Additionally, "cynicism, satire, ridicule of both the state and the difficulties of everyday life, and a whole array of popular art forms that develop around them provide an important psychological outlet for the population."[44] In its most profound form, societal disengagement leads to parallel structures that compete with the state.[45] Disengagement constitutes a mode of state–society interaction in which the latter distrusts and moves away from the former. Through disengagement, ordinary citizens prefer to maintain distance from the state in material and symbolic terms. Therefore, disengagement is not distinct from "exit." As analyzed by Albert O. Hirschman, society responds with either voice or exit when they perceive that their interaction with the state is far from bringing them material, symbolic, or other benefits.[46] Exit constitutes a strategy of removing from the interaction, whether behavioral or symbolic.

Despite the relative success of the liberal democratic order in Cabo Verde in the past three decades, the inability of society to properly read the state and, ipso facto, exert surveillatory power over it has resulted in continuous disengagement. While language policy and practice are not the only reason for such a situation, the state's extensive reliance on a language most people don't grasp has contributed to this condition. Two proxies can be brought to demonstrate the continuous societal disengagement in Cabo Verde: political trust and contact with state officials.

The inability to "read" the state has translated into a growing gap between the state and society. The state is culturally strange to the citizens; thus, it may not correctly represent the interests and will of the general population. The political radiography of the country can be reconstructed after a careful reading of the Afrobarometer survey conducted in Cabo Verde in 2019.[47] An overwhelming percentage of respondents believe the National Assembly "never" or "only sometimes" listens to citizens. Three out of four are either "not at all satisfied" or "not satisfied" with how democracy functions in the islands. Contacts with state officials, mainly those elected into office, are almost nonexistent. Eighty-five percent of the population has never contacted local government officers. The percentage is slightly higher for a member of parliament (88 percent). Trust in key political officers is also concerning, as 59 percent and 60 percent of the population have shown little to no trust in the government (prime minister) and the National Assembly.

In the last analysis, the illegibility of the state constitutes a threat to the quality of democracy. The fact that the state relies on a language that most citizens either don't know or lack the necessary competence in results in the crystallization of language-based inequalities. This condition hinders political participation and democracy. Democratic legitimacy has been eroding, so electoral apathy has become a norm.

CONCLUSION

In Cabo Verde, there is a clear distinction regarding the roles and functions of the languages used by the community and the state. As produced during colonial times and reproduced by the postcolonial elite, the predominant language ideology and practice maintains that the citizens' mother tongue is the language of tradition—in opposition to the Europhone language, which is the language of modernity. It is the medium through which tradition finds its way into the present. The language of tradition continues to thrive because of popular cultural manifestations. However, such a language has profound limitations. It simply cannot perform tasks of modernity. That is reserved for the Portuguese language. Such a language position reproduces the exclusion of Cabo Verdean citizens, who don't actively participate in the country's political processes as they do not possess the necessary linguistic tools to understand and comprehend those processes.

Such linguicist language policy and planning have made the state unreadable to most citizens. The high language can only be learned in formal schooling. In Africa, the state is the primary provider of formal schooling. Unfortunately, the political and economic crises of the 1980s and 1990s, coupled with the impositions of international financial institutions such as the World Bank and the International Monetary Fund, have significantly reduced the state's capacity to provide this type of public good to the citizens. Few people have access to education, the medium through which mastery of the high language could be attained. Therefore, the linguistic divide between the exoglossic (foreign language) state and the vernacular society widens.

A large number of citizens cannot effectively communicate nor comprehend messages transmitted in the high language, the language of the state. This situation hinders the process of surveillatory participation. Information about the processes, procedures, and operations of power does not trickle down to the monoglossic citizens; information is constructed, reproduced, and transmitted through the medium of the dominant language. This situation seriously impacts ordinary citizens' enlightened understanding of politics and its actors. In other words, the inability to properly read the state often translates to the inability to effectively track and supervise the actions carried out on their behalf by the state and its agents.

There is a political incentive for the elite to keep the state illegible. The circle of those who can hold the elite accountable for their actions (or omissions) is kept to a minimal and   usually from people the same social stratum. Moreover, political benefits and economic and material rewards can be extracted from the illegibility of the state. The elites can position themselves as the intermediaries or brokers between the local population and the international system. Such "elite closure," as noted by Carol Myers-Scotton, manages and limits political (and thus economic) participation by nonelites.[48]

NOTES

1. Onda Kriolu, "Conjunto 'Os Tubarões' Recorri a Empréstimo Bancário Pa Salva Totinho Di Bai Cadeia," *Facebook Post*, January 16, 2016, https://www .facebook.com/onda.kriolu/photos/conjunto-os-tubar%C3%B5es-recorri-a-empr%C3 %A9stimo-banc%C3%A1rio-pa-salva-totinho-di-bai-cadei/1147313268614046/.

2. Onda Kriolu.

3. Shohamy, *Language Policy*.

4. Evans, Rueschemeyer, and Skocpol, *Bringing the State Back In*; Robert A. Dahl, "The Behavioral Approach in Political Science: Epitaph for a Monument to a Successful Protest," *The American Political Science Review* 55, no. 4 (1961): 763–72.

5. Michael Bratton and N. Van de Walle, "Neopatrimonial Regimes and Political Transitions in Africa," *World Politics (Print)* (1994): 453–89; Gareth Austin, "National Poverty and the 'Vampire State' in Ghana: A Review Article," *Journal of International Development: Policy, Economics and International Relations* (1996); Kenneth Kalu, "State-Society Relations, Institutional Transformation and Economic Development in Sub-Saharan Africa," *DPR Development Policy Review* 35 (2017): O234–45; Jean-François Bayart, *The State in Africa: The Politics of the Belly* (Cambridge: Polity, 2017); Jean-François Bayart, Stephen Ellis, and Béatrice Hibou, *The Criminalization of the State in Africa* (Oxford: James Currey, 2001).

6. Pierre Englebert, "The Contemporary African State: Neither African nor State," *Third World Quarterly* 18, no. 4 (1997): 767–75.

7. Laitin, *Language Repertoires and State Construction in Africa*; Laitin, *Politics, Language, and Thought*; Victor N. Webb, *Language in South Africa: The Role of Language in National Transformation, Reconstruction and Development* (Amsterdam: Benjamins, 2002); Ali Al'Amin Mazrui, *The Political Sociology of the English Language: An African Perspective* (The Hague: Mouton, 1975); Mazrui and Mazrui, *The Power of Babel*.

8. Ayo Bamgbose, *Language and Exclusion: The Consequences of Language Policies in Africa* (Munster; London; Piscataway, NJ: Lit Verlag; Global; Distributed in North America by Transaction Publishers, 2000); Alamin M. Mazrui, *English in Africa: After the Cold War* (Clevedon, England; Toronto: Multilingual Matters, 2004); Kamwangamalu, *Language Policy and Economics*; Paulin G. Djité, *The Sociolinguistics of Development in Africa* (Clevedon: Multilingual Matters, 2008).

9. Evans, Rueschemeyer, and Skocpol, *Bringing the State Back In*; Max Weber, Hans-Heinrich Gerth, and Charles Wright Mills, *From Max Weber: Essays in Sociology* (New York: Oxford University Press, 1972); Alfred C. Stepan, *The State and Society: Peru in Comparative Perspective* (Princeton: Princeton University Press, 2015).

10. Weber, Gerth, and Mills, *From Max Weber*.

11. Stepan, *The State and Society*.

12. James C. Scott, *Seeing like a State: How Certain Schemes to Improve the Human Condition Have Failed* (New Haven: Yale University Press, 2020).

13. Scott, 2.

14. Brann, "The National Language Question."

15. Gregory G. Curtain, Michael H. Sommer, and Veronika Vis-Sommer, *The World of E-Government* (New York, NY: Haworth Press, 2004).

16. Robert L. Miller, *The Linguistic Relativity Principles and Humboldtian Ethnolinguistics: A Historical and Appraisal* (The Hague: Mouton, 1968), 10.

17. Fanon, *Black Skin, White Masks*, 8.

18. Bourdieu, *Language and Symbolic Power*; Cheryl I. Harris, "Whiteness as Property," *Harvard Law Review* 106, no. 8 (1993): 1707–91.

19. Weber, *Peasants into Frenchmen*.

20. Skutnabb-Kangas, "Multilingualism and the Education of Minority Children," 13.

21. Frantz Fanon, *The Wretched of the Earth* (New York: Grove Press, 2021); Peter P. Ekeh, "Colonialism and the Two Publics in Africa: A Theoretical Statement," *Comparative Studies in Society and History* 17, no. 1 (1975): 91–112; Mahmood Mamdani, *Citizen and Subject: Contemporary Africa and the Legacy of Late Colonialism* (Princeton: University Press, 2003).

22. R. Kemp, "Planning, Public Hearings, and the Politics of Discourse," in *Critical Theory and Public Life*, ed. John Forester (Cambridge, MA: MIT Press, 1985), 177–201.

23. James Curran, *Media and Democracy, Communication and Society* (Oxford: Routledge, 2011), http://www.dawsonera.com/depp/reader/protected/external/AbstractView/S9780203406878.

24. Márcia Rego, *The Dialogic Nation of Cape Verde: Slavery, Language, and Ideology* (Lanham, MD: Lexington Books, 2015), http://site.ebrary.com/id/11047976.

25. Abel Djassi Amado, Focus Group Interview, Neighborhood of Brazil (Praia, Cabo Verde), August 11, 2011.

26. Abel Djassi Amado, Focus Group Interview, Neighborhood of Ponta d'Agu (Praia, Cabo Verde), August 13, 2011.

27. Bourdieu, *Language and Symbolic Power*.

28. Abel Djassi Amado, Focus Group Interview, Neighborhood of Achada Santo António, Artica (Praia, Cabo Verde), August 12, 2011.

29. Amado, Focus Group Interview, Neighborhood of Ponta d'Agu (Praia, Cabo Verde).

30. Amado, Focus Group Interview, Neighborhood of Ponta d'Agu (Praia, Cabo Verde).

31. Amado, Focus Group Interview, Neighborhood of Ponta d'Agu (Praia, Cabo Verde).

32. Abel Djassi Amado, Focus Group Interview, Neighborhood of Txada Riba, August 7, 2011.

33. Amado, Focus Group Interview, Neighborhood of Brazil (Praia, Cabo Verde).

34. Amado, Focus Group Interview, Neighborhood of Brazil (Praia, Cabo Verde).

35. Amado, Focus Group Interview, Neighborhood of Brazil (Praia, Cabo Verde).

36. Jose Carlos Gomes dos Anjos, *Intelectuais, Literatura e Poder em Cabo Verde: Lutas de Definiçao da Identidade Nacional* (Porto Alegre: UFRGS Editora, 2006).

37. Michael G. Clyne, *Pluricentric Languages: Differing Norms in Different Nations* (Berlin: Mouton de Gruyter, 1992); Baxter, "Portuguese as a Pluricentric Language."

38. Peter L. Hupe, Michael Hill, and Aurélien Buffat, eds., *Understanding Street-Level Bureaucracy* (Bristol, UK: Policy Press, 2015), http://site.ebrary.com/id/11084104.

39. Robert A. Dahl, *On Democracy* (New Haven: Yale University Press, 2020).

40. Laitin, *Politics, Language, and Thought*, 3.

41. Will Kymlicka, *Politics in the Vernacular: Nationalism, Multiculturalism and Citizenship* (Oxford: Oxford University Press, 2000), 214.

42. Weinstein, *The Civic Tongue*.

43. Victor Azarya, "Reordering State-Society Relations: Incorporation and Disengagement," in *The Precarious Balance: State and Society in Africa*, ed. Donald Rothchild and Naomi Chazan (New York: Routledge, 1988), 7.

44. Azarya, 7–8.

45. M. A. Animashaun, "State Failure, Crisis of Governance and Disengagement from the State in Africa," *Africa Development* 34, nos. 3–4 (2009): 47–63.

46. Hirschman, *Exit, Voice, and Loyalty*.

47. Afrobarometer, "Cabo Verde Round 8 Resumo Dos Resultados, 2019," 2021, https://www.afrobarometer.org/publication/cabo-verde-round-8-resumo-dos-resultados/.

48. Myers-Scotton, "Elite Closure."

Chapter 6

Language Policy and Political Participation

In 1986, while visiting the islands of Cabo Verde as part of the Brazilian presidential delegation, the writer Jorge Amado noted that "life in Cabo Verde happens in [Cabo Verdean] Creole."[1] In everyday social relations, the common man and woman engage each other almost exclusively through the vernacular. The Cabo Verdean language, despite its regional and class variations, is the language of affection, friendship, and family relations. In general, local intellectuals and culturati have adopted a positive posture vis-à-vis the national language, concurring that the vernacular is the "soul of the people" in that it is the most visible trace of Cabo Verdean identity.[2] Yet, as noted in previous chapters, diglossia, the social and political predominance of one language over the other, has the norm.

This chapter explores how diglossic language policy leads to the political passiveness and submissiveness of a significant portion of the citizenry, namely those possessing little or no knowledge of the dominant language. The division of the political field into different linguistic fields, that of the dominant language at the state level and that of the vernaculars at the grassroots level, impacts people's participation in the political dialogue and debate—beyond electoral participation. In chapter 5, I argued that the language of the state excludes its non-speakers from engaging in political discussions about policymaking or changes to existing policies.

The diglossic situation mitigates political participation on the part of monoglossic citizens, individuals who are not proficient in or have only a rudimentary understanding of the dominant language. In the case of Cabo Verde, the lack of competence in the dominant language, Portuguese, is politically and psychologically consequential. It leads to political apathy through two fundamental mechanisms that I call the *politics of ridicule* and the *politics of inaudibility*, which will be discussed below (figure 6.1).

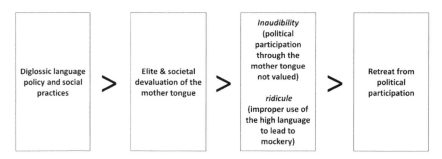

Figure 6.1   Pathway to Retreat from Initiatory Participation. *Source*: Figure created by author.

Full-fledged democracy is realized when citizens have few or no structural barriers to active participation in the political decision-making process.[3] Lack of language fluency is one of the fundamental limitations to the average citizen's full engagement in formal politics. Whenever the language of politics is distant from the language that the citizen uses more recurrently, they are more likely to be cast out of the political equation (see figure 6.1).

In this chapter, I examine the language-politics nexus with a clear focus on society. Unlike chapter 5, which centered on analyzing the state, I provide an understanding of how language policy, practices, and ideology impact ordinary citizens' political participation in the following pages. To that end, I first describe what I call the politics of ridicule in Cabo Verde, the whole business of mockery based on the improper use of the Portuguese language. Then, I look at the issue of inaudibility. This situation is related to the monoglossic citizens' voices being muted since they do not speak the *right* language. One's engagement in the debate at the societal level is the consequence of the language one speaks. In the third part of this chapter, I touch upon the extent to which the politics of ridicule and inaudibility encourages people to retreat from active engagement in the political business of the community. In conclusion, I highlight all the significant points of the chapter.

THE POLITICS OF RIDICULE

Without citizens' political participation, the democratic experience cannot be realized. In their 1995 study, Sidney Verba and colleagues start their book by noting, "Citizen participation is at the heart of democracy. Indeed, democracy is unthinkable without the ability of citizens to participate freely in the government process."[4] Political participation has been understood by political scientists as collective action that seeks to influence the government's composition or policies emanating from it.[5] Political participation ranges from canvassing for and supporting a candidate to voting and less conventional modes of action such as protests and riots. This chapter focuses on the involvement in political debates, chiefly about national issues. I argue that language policy, which includes language practices, is one of the most potent hindrances to citizens' full participation in the national conversation. Full political participation, particularly in effectively partaking in the public debate about a politically relevant issue, is not without a cost. The cost can be exacted in material or psychological terms. That is to say, the cost can be in terms of a supposed loss of free time—which could have been devoted to other activities, including productive activities that bring in material advantages or leisure. To participate in the political life of the community implies, as such, a cost of opportunity.

The socioeconomic status model informs the model I propose to understand the extent to which postcolonial language policy constitutes a powerful hindrance to effective formal participation in political affairs. According to this theory, a great predictor of an individual's political participation level is the resources they possess, such as time, money, and civic skills.[6] Like Pierre Bourdieu, I suggest that being fluent in the dominant language is a capital or a resource: those who have it the most are most likely to be "invited" to participate in politics.[7] However, the use of the mother tongue, mainly as a tool to populate the community's political language, is a form of political participation insofar as it constitutes a medium through which the powers that be are linguistically resisted. In other words, using the Cabo Verdean language is—as it was in the past—a form of political resistance.[8]

In this section, I start by discussing a few illustrative examples of the politics of ridicule. A video posted on YouTube titled "Falando Português ou Brutuguês?" (Speaking Portuguese or Brutuguese?) went viral in 2012 among Cabo Verdeans.[9] The video, which has over 95,000 views and more than 80 comments, is about a fisherman being interviewed about marine turtles. As the interview is being conducted in Portuguese, the fisherman attempts to respond in the same language. Lacking knowledge and training in Portuguese, the interviewee failed to respect basic grammatical rules, such as the rule of agreement. The video provides various examples of syntactic, lexical, and phonological errors.

The video's title is very suggestive of the dominance of a particular language ideology, revealing attitudes and beliefs regarding the use or function of a language. Accordingly, not following the rules of standard Portuguese is to be a subhuman. After all, as discussed in previous chapters, Portuguese has been historically classified as the language of modernity and civilization. Not following the rules of agreement and other grammatical rules is to assume a monster-like figure. According to the video title, engaging in ungrammatical Portuguese is engaging in a language appropriate to a monster, a *Brutuguês* (a portmanteau between "bruto," *brute*, and "Português," Portuguese). The persistence of colonial ideology is evident in the title of the video. As noted by one of its most critical students, Franz Fanon, Colonialism was essentially Manichean. The dichotomy between savage and civilized is implied in the title (the Portuguese word for savage is "bruto"): savagery, the condition of being *un*civilized, means the distorted use of the civilized language.[10] According to one commentator, the video was an example of a language "killer." For another commentator, just one word was necessary to classify the situation: "Pretoguês" (*blackguese*)—clearly, a play on words, whereby "*por*tuguês" becomes *preto*guês (preto means black in Portuguese), a link with the expression "língua dos pretos" (the language of the blacks), deriving from old colonial language ideology.

Another video that has gone viral recently is an interview on the national television station. A municipal officer from the local government of Santa Catharina, Santiago Island, was questioned about the condition of stray dogs that were found to roam around the city freely.[11] While explaining the policy to the reporter, who interviewed in Portuguese, the official made a simple and noticeable mistake: he kept referring to "cãos" as the plural form for cão (dog) when the correct form is *cães*. While the plural form in the Portuguese language is often formed by adding an "s" at the end of the noun, there are some exceptions, as in the case of "cão."

Deviation from the standard Portuguese leads to mockery. This situation is mainly observable in domains like school. Among the youth, it is common to find examples of friends and/or classmates who are mocked for language errors while speaking Portuguese in the classroom. While conducting a focus group interview in the neighborhood of Brazil, one of the informants told me about an interesting case. He said that one day, while in a class, a school official came to his classroom while the teacher was lecturing. This official did knock on the door, but the teacher did not hear him. Another student, trying to get the teacher's attention, said someone was knocking on the door. However, the problem is how he said it. He used a Creole language word—"konku" is a Creole word for "knocking on the door."[12] My informant further noted that his fellow student is often derided for this language error.

Similarly, another informant, who had recently graduated from high school, told me that he and many of his classmates would shy away from responding to questions asked by teachers in the classroom. He noted that:

> When the teacher asks a question and asks for a volunteer to respond, most of us sit quietly and do not venture to respond. Often it is not because we don't know the answer. It is because we fear that our classmates will make fun of us if we make a mistake [in the Portuguese language] as we attempt to respond to the question.[13]

Another informant described the above situation from a different neighborhood (Ponta d'Agu). My informant, a twenty-two-year-old with some college education, recounted that sometimes students know the answer to the question posed by the teacher but have difficulty putting the answer in standard Portuguese. She stated that often the answer is "under the tongue," and once the teacher permits her to respond in Cabo Verdean Creole, the student often gets to the point.[14]

What happens in the classroom is just a microcosmic representation of society. There is a general condemnation of deviation from standard Portuguese. This condemnation is mainly carried by some sectors of the political and cultural elite who often claim that the Cabo Verdean language is being contaminated in form and content. For instance, Ondina Ferreira, a former minister of culture and overt lusophile, talks about the development of a new form of talking that she coins as "creoulese" (or "crioulês" in original, a portmanteau of "Crioulo" and "Português").[15]

The above examples illustrate the culture of ridicule, the popular predisposition to focus on the form and not the content of the message, with the intent to mock and deride the speaker. The content of the message is put aside—regardless of its importance, relevance, and significance. The focus is on linguistic mistakes. As part of this culture of ridicule, the video goes viral. The Internet, which has made possible the construction of online social communities and the rise of online commentators, has significantly fueled the phenomenon of ridiculing people for language mistakes.

As the dominant language enjoys social value, individuals are socially evaluated based on their competence in that language. In most postcolonial states, proficiency in the dominant language is acquired through formal education. It is also through schooling that one develops technical competence. Linguistic proficiency and technical competence thus overlap. Competence in the dominant language is the yardstick for measuring general (technical) competence. Individuals' social respectability and prestige are often linked to their capacity to be at ease when speaking the dominant language. As it is more complicated to judge the technical competence of an individual, their comfort with the dominant language is used as the gauge for their overall competence.

Non-speakers of the dominant language are negatively judged regarding their linguistic competence. The politics of ridicule have become quite common: failure to follow the basic rules of grammar or the orthography of the dominant language is an invitation to public ridicule. Ridicule is a mechanism and strategy to minimize the political role of the individual or their ideas by focusing not on the message's content but its form (e.g., grammatical red herrings). Modern information technologies worsen matters by permitting instantaneous, anonymous, and globally reachable ridiculing comments.

Consequently, it is not uncommon for monoglossic citizens to shy away from participating in public debate when it is carried out in Portuguese, lest they be ridiculed for common linguistic mistakes.

Modern societies have developed complex languages, that is, languages that can be used in different and diverse domains, with a developed and rich lexicon and a multitude of rules regulating syntax, phonology, and semantics. While there is a vibrant subfield of language error analysis, scholars have yet to analyze the political implications of language errors.[16] In postcolonial Africa, the language of education, government, and the formal public sphere is often the language of the former colonizer. As mentioned earlier, only those who go through extensive and widespread formal education acquire the necessary competence to use the language without language errors. Cabo Verde is no exception, as Portuguese is the language of the state and instruction. Acquiring this language occurs almost always through formal education, as it is the medium of schooling. The Portuguese language is used in Cabo Verde as if it were not a foreign language—a state of affairs that has led, as some scholars have noted, to disastrous consequences for learners. Germano Almeida, a renowned Cabo Verdean writer, argues that Portuguese in Cabo Verde should be taught in the same manner as any other foreign language.[17] This idea seems to be gaining traction, as the government has changed the Portuguese language-in-education policy, in which it will be taught as a foreign language.[18]

Making language errors in public often results in ridicule. Those who commit language errors become the center of attention. The error (or errors) becomes the focus of all comments, while the content of the message often receives little attention. Public ridicule based on language errors is proportional to the depth of those errors: the more they deviate from the standard norms, the more jokes and anecdotes are derived from the experience. This language error-based culture of ridicule is exceptionally prevalent in the realms of primary and secondary education. Not infrequently, primary and secondary school students are the target of ridicule by their peers because of speech errors while addressing or responding to a question posed by the teacher. This situation creates a withdrawal from active class participation, lest those speech errors are translated into a public joke. From personal experiences in Cabo Verde and information gathered during several focus interviews, I know many cases in which individuals are jokingly nicknamed for their mistakes (speech errors).[19]

The politics of ridicule are mainly focused on the improper use of the Portuguese language. Not following the rules of the grammar, or pronouncing words with an accent that is perceived to be distant from standard continental Portuguese, invites mockery, scorn, and ridicule. Often the process of ridicule can include nicknaming, as noted above. It is common for individuals who have made highly noticeable public mistakes in the Portuguese language to be nicknamed after the error made.

The issue with the politics of ridicule is that the message is never made the focus of an individual's conversation. Instead, attention is focused on the form and the general mistakes, often at the expense of the message, even when this is socially significant. Mimicking the mistakes becomes the topic of conversation among close friends or family members. Whenever the conversation is about the incident, the message is put aside—the focus becomes the individual and their attempt to speak Portuguese.

Because the politics of ridicule may lead to the decline of individual self-esteem and self-confidence, people who are not proficient in the Portuguese language may think twice before engaging in public debate when the medium of the debate is a language they poorly master. Consequently, it is very likely that to these citizens, politics happen in the realm of silence and head-nodding. Members of the Cabo Verdean society understand that mockery is a primary cultural trait and that the community is often looking for an individual to be the butt of its jokes, scorn, and ridicule. Whenever a case of improper language use occurs, it instantly becomes a social joke shared by almost all members of society. Contemporary popular music is a powerful vehicle for transmitting these social jokes about language use. Examples abound of musical hits which are about these social jokes. What was presented above is in no way peculiar to Cabo Verde. For instance, a study conducted in Mozambique notes that when noneducated people attempt to speak Portuguese, they often fall victim to mockery on the part of the state agents.[20]

THE POLITICS OF INAUDIBILITY

The mechanism of inaudibility is the other psychological constraint to public political participation on the part of Cabo Verdean monolingual citizens. By the concept of inaudibility, I mean the extent to which the voice of an individual engaged in public discourse is not considered by others. "Being heard" means more than the ears capturing the sounds uttered by the speaker—or the eyes reading the words written by the writer. Instead, it is a perception that others take what one says and writes seriously. The mainstream language ideology, which sustains the notion that the high language is the language of science, modernity, and logic, influences how the general audience accepts or rejects a serious message by a given speaker. Monolingual citizens' inaudibility is also stressed by their lack of access to the media, which historically has been biased toward high-language speakers. The mechanism of inaudibility often affects the perception of whether one is taken seriously or not, leading to partial or total withdrawal from the public sphere.

The democratization of the 1990s and 2000s did not result in the opening of the political arena, and politics is still tightly controlled by the elite. The fall of the one-party state meant the opening of high politics, with the sections of the social elite previously barred from competing for power now vying for state control.[21] For the most part, the masses are still blocked from active political participation—other than voting. This is particularly visible in areas of policymaking and implementation. The discourse of professionalism, meritocracy, and development transforms the majority into a "silent majority," the passive reactors to the actions taken at the higher levels of state politics.

Contemporary electoral democracy restricts the people's choice of who gets to rule over them. Consequently, the number of actual, direct actors in high politics is kept at a minimum. The exclusion of the masses from this domain supposedly makes politics a faster decision-making process. The logic is as follows: the more actors involved in the process, the more arduous and troublesome the process of gathering support for a given policy line. Consensus building can be easier and faster if only a few people are involved in the discourse.

Being socialized in a society with two or more languages, one internalizes from an early age that one language is more equal than others. Without being told explicitly, a person quickly discerns that the languages are used in different domains. The people, in general, have a clear idea about the linguistic divide that exists in the country. As one of my interviewees stated:

> There are places where the Cabo Verdean language can be spoken, where only the Portuguese language can be spoken, and where both can be spoken. The mother tongue is that language [in which] we feel more at ease expressing [ourselves]. It is the language we are fluent in, and often it influences the spaces where only the Portuguese language is to be spoken, for instance, in school. Sometimes when one talks, a word in the Cabo Verdean language comes out with force. Thus, Creole has too much weight in our speech pattern (*linguagem*). And it has too much interference even in the places that are to speak only the Portuguese language.[22]

As Cabo Verdean is the language from the cradle to the grave, the language of everyday use, one must be fluent in Portuguese to avoid mixing the two codes. It is relatively easier to combine the two codes for two main reasons: first, the Cabo Verdean language is a Portuguese-based Creole. This means that the bulk of the lexicon derives, in one way or another, from Portuguese. Even today, this latter language is the supplier of lexicon to the former. As such, there is always a temptation to mix the two languages. Second, the two languages have a long history of sharing the same social space—though in two different domains. Young citizens from the city's peripheral areas where I conducted most of my interviews showed rudimentary knowledge of Portuguese. While most of them have attended high school, they know they are not fluent in Portuguese. Increasingly though, people understand that the Cabo Verdean language is the language of social and political relations. Another youth told me about the social weight that the Cabo Verdean language has in society.

> Creole has weight. It is rare for one to go to public administration and speak Portuguese. And even if we are talked to in Portuguese, we often respond in Creole (. . .). Some MPs (*deputadus*) use the Cabo Verdean language to be adequately understood. In the classroom, sometimes we may know something, but we cannot explain it in Portuguese. We find ourselves saying to the teacher, "I know about the topic, but it is 'under the tongue' (*baxu lingua*)." It is not that it is "under the tongue"; it is about explaining it [in Portuguese]. Sometimes a down-to-earth teacher may allow us to describe the topic in the Cabo Verdean language, and a good explanation follows. If you say it in Portuguese, it comes out totally different. Rarely what comes out as spoken word is what you think.[23]

Language is, *par excellence*, a site of domination; communication often reflects power relations. Power relations are embedded in linguistic interchanges. It is through the use of language that the relations of power are made effective and efficient. Through different linguistic strategies and manipulations, the power of one social group over the others is constructed and reconstructed. The power relation, thus, derives from the internalization of the linguistic hierarchy accepted as given in society.

In the communicative encounter between the state representative and the people, the former has two alternatives: (a) either using the language or a variety of language that is closer to the vernacular and, ipso facto, avoiding any static in the message to be passed to the audience; or (b) using the dominant language/variation to play up their supposed academic and social superiority. Sometimes the use of the vernacular is a calculated strategy. Pierre Bourdieu talks about the *strategy of condescension* to demonstrate the instrumentalization of the vernacular in a diglossic community by political leaders.[24] The strategy of condescension refers to a political actor from a higher socioeconomic and political class (in one word, the elite) taking up a language, speech, or style linked with the lower socioeconomic classes. The strategy implies that the elite can temporarily accept and use a style or variation that is not part of their typical linguistic repertoire. Ultimately, such a strategy is designed to conquer "the hearts and minds" of the lower socioeconomic class. The actor engaging in such a strategy presents himself/herself as "a man/woman of the people." In other words, this strategy can bring political advantage to the elite by temporarily removing the existing inequality and social hierarchy conditions.

The use of Portuguese may well be a tactic of silencing contestation. Regardless of the political regime or historical conditions, the elite seeks to maintain their dominance over the nonelite. The more citizens' contestations the elite can avoid, the more entrenched their dominance. It is precisely at the level of language that the elite seek to maintain supremacy over the masses. Language policy becomes a tool at their disposal to manage how and when the subalterns, or the nonelite, speak. Distance from the centers of power (both social and geographical) is simultaneously a linguistic distance. The peripheral area is the domain where linguistic power can be further exercised. In this regard, one of my interviewees presented her interpretation of the linguistic situation in the peripheries:

> Take, for instance, the case of towns and villages outside the city. People in those areas have less access to radio, newspapers, television, and the like. Little attention is aroused when a politician arrives (or even broadcasts on tv) and begins his "lectures" in Portuguese. For these people, it is just the same old things. However, when a politician starts to speak Creole, attention is aroused among these people. Things communicated in Creole call people's attention.[25]

Language is a powerful tool. It can be used either to open channels of communication and dialogue or to impose a monologue. More often than not, political actors use the dominant language precisely to block any attempts at critical questioning, especially when such questioning is direct and bottom-up. One cannot avoid asking why a bilingual politician would choose to communicate in the dominant language when they know that the message passes faster and better if conveyed through the mother tongue. The use of the dominant language justifies and reproduces the position of the social and political elite. There is a history of the Portuguese language as the dominant language that dates back to the last hundred years of colonial rule, and the use of that language justifies the position of dominance. The dominant language becomes the identifier of social leadership and dominance. Fear of being ridiculed demobilizes many from the political arena. Ridicule is essentially a product of a social situation or relation. It is perceived as any naïve deviation from the norms (i.e., peer-like) of social behavior.

A state official or representative may elect to speak in the dominant language—or a variation closer to the dominant language or dialect. This, in itself, is a political statement. Using a particular variant of Creole corresponds to a specific social discourse. The choice for the mesolect, mixed with a catalog of words traditionally not part of the Cabo Verdean language, indicates that the speaker could be highly educated. The utterer presents him or herself, *via* language, as someone untrained minds need not question. Even when the discourse is started in the vernacular, the official often resorts to upward code-switching (changing from the vernacular to the dominant language) to dodge direct queries. By alternating the linguistic code in certain situations, code-switching can constitute a powerful mechanism for avoiding responding to accountability demands. An interesting example of code-switching, from the lower to the higher language, is given by Donaldo Macedo after an encounter with a high-echelon state official from the Ministry of Education of Cabo Verde. Macedo, a world-renowned scholar and a member of the Cabo Verdean diaspora in the United States, recounted how the meeting's language was the Cabo Verdean language, for most Cabo Verdean immigrants and Cabo Verdean–Americans do not grasp Portuguese. Then, the official switched to the Portuguese language, arguing that, in a type of philosophical debate, he makes much more sense in Portuguese than in Creole, as he was educated in that language. It turns out, as noted by Macedo, that "as soon as he started to speak Portuguese, the dialogue ended."[26]

Like other former Portuguese colonies, Cabo Verde inherited a specific Lusitanian culture, which can be called the culture of "mister doctor" (*senhor doutor* in Portuguese). There is an overuse of the title "doctor" by those who managed to finish college studies. Calling oneself a doctor has increasingly become more of a social title than an academic title. A college graduate is often referred to by the abbreviation of doctor (Dr.), while for a person with an academic doctoral degree (Ph.D.), the title is fully spelled out ("doutor" in Portuguese). However, at the level of oral speech, there is no way of distinguishing between the two. To have a bachelor's degree is to be a doctor—and to require others to call one doctor. Language, that is, the Portuguese language, is the medium that reinforces such a culture. The more erudite, esoteric, and impenetrable the language, the more one boasts one's "doctor-ness." The use of the dominant language in the public sphere is a means to reinforce the social hierarchy, thereby creating relations of power and authority. Put another way, social relations become relations of power insofar as one of the participants uses language to symbolize their higher social, economic, and political standing.

The culture of "mister doctor" overlaps and is reinforced by the language ideology that considers Portuguese the only language capable of transmitting knowledge, science, logic, philosophy, and the like. The result of this ideology is that, due to its inherent limitations, the vernacular cannot, in any way, be used for transmitting complex and abstract messages.

SILENCING AND MANAGING CITIZENS' POLITICAL PARTICIPATION

To use the high language, the Portuguese language, in the case of Cabo Verde, is an invitation to passivity. Although more people are now in contact with Portuguese, it is not their everyday language. Only a tiny minority of the social and political elite are genuinely fluent in Portuguese (see chapter 5). To most people, the language is a foreign language that can only be learned in school, and its command is a sign of upward mobility and education. Interviews with people from different sections of Cabo Verdean society support this view. A young male from one of the peripheral areas of the capital city of Praia tells me that sometimes the political audience's role is nothing more than to clap hands, as the message is often not understood.[27] There is a "disconnect" between the politician and the general population. Even when the former uses the Cabo Verdean language, they frequently mix it with the Portuguese language, making comprehension of the message daunting for a person whose knowledge of Portuguese is rudimentary.

On a different occasion, a female informant elaborated further on this situation. She noted that:

> [There is the] question of peripheral areas [from the countryside, for instance] . . . People from these far regions have limited access to radio, newspapers, television, and the like. [When a] politician arrives, or even [when they are] on television, and they begin reading in Portuguese, with all their posture, it simply does not bring any awakening in these people. For him, it is politics, as usual.[28]

Her focus was obviously on the rural and peripheral areas where access to education is relatively tricky. In these areas, formal education is harder to come by. As a consequence, ordinary citizens from rural areas have trouble understanding statements made in the Portuguese language. This situation is also because their contact with the language is often limited. Modern technologies, such as radio, television, and the internet, are not part of the daily life of a sizeable portion of the rural population (even though the country is tiny).

To most of my informants, using Portuguese in public communication and politics, in general, is somewhat alienating. Using the dominant language keeps some portions of the population out of the circle of understanding. She further elaborated on this, stating:

> People feel more integrated when listening to what is being said in their language. They think that whatever is being discussed is related to them. But when it is in Portuguese, they may feel that the message has nothing to do with them— sometimes, they do not even bother to listen.[29]

Elections may be one of the few times the political and social elite use the vernacular for public communication. Seeking to attract electoral followers and votes implies that the candidate—or the party or the political organization competing in the elections—portrays itself, both in the content and in the form of the message, as closely as possible to the everyday, ordinary citizen.

Increasingly, the language of electioneering is the Cabo Verdean language. Candidates are increasingly relying on the Cabo Verdean language. As will be discussed in chapter 7, the presence of the vernacular is visible from party slogans, billboards, election jingles, and other communicative electoral paraphernalia. Yet, things change during elections. The use of the Portuguese language is associated with technical and scientific thought. On the opposite side, the Cabo Verdean language links the speaker with the simplicity of ideas. A well-educated person can make poetic use of the Portuguese language to the point that a few only understand the message. The vast majority of the population is thus kept out of communication. In this regard, an informant from the peripheral area of the capital city said that

[There is the] question of which *type* of Portuguese to be used—even among journalists who do [sic] the interviews. They use very difficult vocabulary that most people are unfamiliar with or do not know.[30]

The use of the vernacular in public discussion is linked to citizenship and participation. Even though there is a widespread belief that Portuguese is the language of modernity and prestige, it is the use of the Cabo Verdean language that brings people into the debate. It is the language they best understand, for it is their mother tongue and the language of everyday use. Moreover, a public debate in the vernacular allows citizens to participate naturally. The Cabo Verdean language, as the mother tongue, is quite natural, flowing without constraints. In this regard, an informant tells me that "[when it is in Cabo Verdean Creole, a person] feels even a better citizen, [capable of] ask[ing] questions."[31] As different languages are given different statuses and convey different sets of symbols, the choice of language by the person of authority (in this case, the politician) may determine whether hearers withdraw or adopt an integrative attitude.

Postcolonial diglossic language policy is a powerful hindrance to effective political participation by many citizens. As the dominant language is acquired through education, the distinction among the members of the society reflects the individual level of education. A person fluent in the dominant language will likely be part of the elite. Alternatively, the individual who can only communicate in the mother tongue is likely to be cast outside the main circles of economic and social power.

In third-wave electoral democracy in sub-Saharan Africa, language policy has significantly hindered the real and effective political participation of a sizeable portion of the population. With few exceptions, the language of the state is the language of the former colonial power. The Portuguese, French, and English languages, as such, are the official languages and the medium of politically and socially important functions. As the official language is often other than the language of the population, this significantly impacts the people's input in designing and implementing state policies.

Diglossic language policy defines and maintains language hierarchy regarding their functions, roles, and value in a given community.[32] This type of language policy ultimately leads to the formation of two arenas of politics: one in which the official language of the state, the language inherited from colonialism, is dominant—and sometimes is the only one—and the other arena of the low, subordinated languages. To visualize the distinction, one can think of the first arena as the main circles of power (the state institutions). This realm can conveniently be called "high politics"—in the sense that it happens above the people, and the decisions emanating from it supposedly are authoritatively binding.

The arena of "low politics" is at the level of ordinary citizens. In this arena, people share ideas and perceptions about the political situation, organize collective action to defend their community interests, and engage in the local associational life. Politics, as such, takes place in the vernacular.[33] The two-arena politics reinforces the political marginalization of monoglossic citizens. Political marginalization has to do with the "establishment" of structural constraints that "lock" specific segments of the population. The structural conditions may be based on social constructions such as class, gender, race, ethnicity, religion, or language. A person's inability to perform comfortably in the dominant language will likely push them to the margins of politics.

The postcolonial linguistic condition, as described above, negatively impacts monolingual citizens' political participation. The linguistic and structural factors demarcate the domains in which each language can/should be used. Path dependence, individual strategies, and institutional legacies mark off the social and political arenas for the employment of a specific language. For instance, language and education policies determine which languages will be used in the formal school system or the language of the state bureaucracy. It follows that employability or upward mobility within the bureaucratic ranks is proportional to one's proficiency in the official language. The postcolonial state bourgeoisie, often through a calculated strategy but sometimes unconsciously, seeks to perpetuate this linguistic situation, forming itself also what David Laitin calls the "linguistic elite."[34]

BLOCKING INITIATORY POLITICAL PARTICIPATION

As noted above, political participation constitutes all the social activity that ultimately results either in the composition of government—at the local or national levels—or in the outcomes or policies that emanate from the governing bodies. Political participation may be as simple and direct as voting or as complex and indirect as partaking in a mass movement for or against policies or the government. In this section, I argue that what I call initiatory political participation is relatively low in Cabo Verde. By the concept of *initiatory participation*, I mean the ability to engage in public debate about issues, policies, rules, and other governmental output. Despite the legal and political system, which may be constructed to guarantee free and open participation by all, the reality is different. Formal and informal institutions, chiefly language policy, are practical elements that ultimately hinder ordinary citizens' free and direct partaking in the affairs of the polity.

I have noted above that the actual sphere of politics is indeed limited. Elections may be one of the few channels of political participation for the general population. Participation in the general public debate, leading to either the formation of the government or the creation and implementation of public policies, particularly at the national level, involves few people. For one thing, there are infrastructural limits. In Cabo Verde, a deficit of political infrastructures and institutions restricts the free entry of people into the whole process of debating policies and their implementation. Political institutions such as public hearings, initiatives, and referenda that can be effectively used as the channels for active and engaging initiatory participation either are not present or exist only on paper. For instance, the current Cabo Verdean Constitution refers to the institutions such as referenda and citizens' legal initiatives. Yet, over three decades after the constitution was approved, there is still no law regulating these processes—let alone the actual referendum experience in national or local politics. Engaging in the question of the structures is to get into the very complex and somewhat convoluted question of learning what the causes are and their effects.

There are few incentives for the political elite to open another debate channel. That is to say, the sphere of public debate is, at best, frozen—if not shrinking. Ordinary citizens are kept out of the circle. This state of affairs, in one way or another, has something to do with the language question—and the ideologies that underpin it. First, many believe that modern politics is very technical and complex. As such, the whole process of debating and discussing, including their form and content, are to be left in the hands of professionals and technicians. The general public, therefore, is left only the option of choosing which "package," already constructed, should be implemented. The idea is that by choosing one candidate or party, citizens automatically legitimize all of the public policies they implement. Second, the political elite fears the entrance of competing forces from the general society. The opening of the public sphere produces a quantitative change—measured in terms of an increase in the number of participants. Subsequently, this quantitative change may ultimately lead to a qualitative shift in the public sphere and the form, content, and manner in which the debate is carried out.

Logically speaking, the power of persuasion would have to go through a radical transformation with an increased number of participants in the debate. If the debate is limited to the political elite, the participants would probably put less effort into persuading the other participants to follow a particular line of action or thought. Because they are part of the same social group and, as such, share the same cultural subsystem, the communicative process can afford to be somewhat superficial without the need to explain small details, such as body language. Instead, there is an emphasis on *thick description*, that is, cultural understanding that results from sharing the same culture, where the group members are likely to know and understand these unspoken details.[35] To enter into a debate with a member of the lower socioeconomic classes is to open Pandora's box, where everything would probably need to be explained and clarified.

The entry of citizens would alter this state of affairs. Like most African elites, the Cabo Verdean elite finds their legitimacy to rule in terms of their role as intermediaries between the local and the international. The access to linguistic and cultural capital makes them capable of serving as the link between the general mass of citizens and the overall global market and politics.[36] One of the key discourses legitimizing the sole reliance on the Portuguese language as the language of the state and education has to do with the notion that that language may constitute a bridge with the international world and scientific and technological development. I have noted in chapter 2 that even radical anticolonial nationalists, such as Amílcar Cabral, did not see any contradiction in using the Portuguese language in national liberation and postcolonial state building. As the country is heavily dependent on foreign aid and assistance, from the elite perspective, ultimately, the language question boils down to the capacity to link the country with foreign donors. Yet, these outside-in notions of development tend to alienate the local population and disregard all the locally produced knowledge and social experiences as expendable.

It is essential to understand the mental atmosphere in which politics takes place. One needs to learn about the general cultural context of politics, for culture shapes politics and, at the same time, is the arena within which politics is shaped. To investigate this cultural context, I gathered a group of five college-educated individuals (all male). All of them are employed in the mid- to high-echelons of the public bureaucracy, with some of these individuals also teaching in secondary and higher education institutions.[37] My goal was to learn about the characteristics of political leadership at the national level. There was a consensus among the interviewees that political leadership at both national and local levels should be reserved for the well-educated. A forty-three-year-old male participant, a college graduate who teaches history at one of the high schools in the city of Praia, argued that:

Politics is too complicated a business. The modern state is very intricate and complex. Only those with the necessary academic tools should be in state leadership positions—such as ministers and other elected officials in the local and central government. Political leadership is technical leadership.[38]

Behind this notion is the idea that the modern state is highly complex and challenging and that only those with higher education can effectively lead the state. The other side of the coin is that while an uneducated individual may not be fit for public office, they may have the capacity to decide *which* policies are best for the community—but can't come up with these ideas or implement them.

Following the discussion, another participant, also a college graduate, who works in the Ministry of Tourism and Energy, maintained that:

One cannot expect anybody to perform the jobs of a medical doctor or an engineer. These jobs require expertise from years of sitting on the college bench and understanding the theories and approaches. Similarly, one does not expect anybody to be in charge of the Ministry of Economy. One must be an economist to guide the Ministry properly. Without a college education, I am afraid you wouldn't get the necessary tools to serve the government appropriately.[39]

Individuals with little or no formal education also share this notion, particularly elderly citizens who may not have had the opportunity for schooling. In this regard, the sentence uttered by an elderly female citizen during a focus group interview in the neighborhood of Paiol is illustrative. She noted, "I have no schooling [and, thus,] I need only to follow what they say."[40] This attitude is typical among those who lack formal education.

CONCLUSION

The key objective of this chapter has been to note that the diglossic situation that characterizes Cabo Verde fosters a situation of political withdrawal. Those citizens who are not proficient in the dominant language, Portuguese language, have a psychological disincentive to active engagement and citizenship. For one, they cannot make a valuable contribution to the public political debate, which is most often conducted in Portuguese. At the same time, given the language ideology and the long history that considers the mother tongue unsuitable for modern domains and tasks, its speakers are not taken seriously—at least not to the same extent as the dominant language speakers.

I also noted that one of the primary motivations for the self-removal from political participation is what I have defined as politics of ridicule. Those brave enough to speak up are all but forced to attempt to speak in the dominant language if they have any hope of being taken seriously. As they often lack the knowledge and experience of speaking Portuguese, their spoken language is far from the norm of standard Portuguese. As a result, a wave of ridicule, mockery, and jokes soon follows—directed, as we have seen, at the speaker.

Withdrawing from active political participation, that is, to remove oneself from the public political debate, is the consequence of what I call inaudibility: speakers of some language, chiefly those who speak a non-prestigious language, are not taken seriously. Their political complaints, suggestions, and grudges often go unheard—and, as such, left unaddressed. Speakers of the mother tongue in Cabo Verde, particularly those who speak the basilect, the dialect far removed from the Portuguese language, find it difficult to engage in public debate. The (erroneous) idea that their language is not capable of translating complex thoughts is accepted as a given by many. Ultimately, ordinary citizens' initiatory political participation is curtailed.

NOTES

1. Almada, *Bilinguismo ou diglossia?*, 21.

2. Abel Djassi Amado, Andre Corsino Tolentino, Praia (Cabo Verde), August 10, 2011.

3. Barber, *Strong Democracy*; William R. Nylen, *Participatory Democracy versus Elitist Democracy: Lessons from Brazil* (New York: Palgrave Macmillan, 2003), http://site.ebrary.com/id/10135680; Laurence Bherer, Pascale Dufour, and Françoise Montambeault, "The Participatory Democracy Turn: An Introduction," in *The Participatory Democracy Turn*, ed. Laurence Bherer, Pascale Dufour, and Francoise Montambeault (London: Routledge, 2018), 1–6.

4. Sidney Verba, Henry E. Brady, and Kay Lehman Schlozman, *Voice and Equality: Civic Voluntarism in American Politics* (Cambridge, MA: Harvard University Press, 2002), 1; Robert Alan Dahl, *Polyarchy: Participation and Opposition* (New Haven, CT: Yale University Press, 1978); Sidney Verba and Norman H. Nie, *Participation in America: Political Democracy and Social Equality* (Chicago: The University of Chicago Press, 1991); Lester W. Milbrath and Maden Lal Goel, *Political Participation: How and Why Do People Get Involved in Politics?* (Lanham: University Press of America, 1982).

5. Joan M. Nelson and Samuel P. Huntington, *No Easy Choice: Political Participation in Developing Countries* (Cambridge, MA: Harvard University Press, 1976), http://www.degruyter.com/search?f_0=isbnissn&q_0=9780674863842&searchTitles =true.

6. Sidney Verba, Henry E. Brady, and Kay Lehman Schlozman, "Beyond SES: A Resource Model of Political Participation," *American Political Science Review* 89, no. 2 (1995): 271–94.

7. Bourdieu, *Language and Symbolic Power*.

8. Katherine Carter and Judy Aulette, *Cape Verdean Women and Globalization: The Politics of Gender, Culture, and Resistance* (New York, NY: Palgrave Macmillan, 2009).

9. Rui Sanches, "Falando Português Ou Brutuguês?" YouTube. Online Video Clip (a—," Video), *YouTube*, accessed November 21, 2012, http://www.youtube.com /watch?v=YX8bqYplfjM.

10. Bill Ashcroft, Gareth Griffiths, and Helen Tiffin, *Postcolonial Studies: The Key Concepts* (London: Routledge, 2013), 209–10; Fanon, *Black Skin, White Masks*.

11. "Sem Verbas Para Canil, CM de Santa Catarina de Santiago vê Como Única Solução Abater Cães Vadios," *Noticias* (RTC), accessed November 21, 2012, http:// rtc.cv/index.php?paginas=13&id_cod=16281.

12. Amado, Focus Group Interview, Neighborhood of Brazil (Praia, Cabo Verde).

13. Amado, Focus Group Interview, Neighborhood of Brazil (Praia, Cabo Verde).

14. Amado, Focus Group Interview, Neighborhood of Ponta d'Agu (Praia, Cabo Verde).

15. Ferreira, "Crioulês – o Novo Veículo de Comunicação Dos Quadros."

16. Wenfen Yang, "A Tentative Analysis of Errors in Language Learning and Use," *JLTR Journal of Language Teaching and Research* 1, no. 3 (2010): 266–68; Carl James, *Errors in Language Learning and Use* (London: Routledge, 2014).

17. "Língua: Português Deve Ser Ensinado Em Cabo Verde Como Língua Estrangeira, Defende Germano de Almeida," (Portugal), *Expresso*, March 27, 2010, http://expresso.sapo.pt/lingua-portugues-deve-ser-ensinado-em-cabo-verde-como -lingua-estrangeira-defende-germano-de-almeida=f573370.

18. IILP, "CABO VERDE: PORTUGUÊS PASSA A SER ENSINADO COMO LÍNGUA ESTRANGEIRA," *IILP* (blog), December 8, 2016, https://iilp.word-press.com/2016/12/08/cabo-verde-portugues-passa-a-ser-ensinado-como-lingua -estrangeira/.

19. Amado, Focus Group Interview, Neighborhood of Brazil (Praia, Cabo Verde).

20. Judith Marshall, *Literacy, Power and Democracy in Mozambique: The Governance of Learning from Colonization to the Present* (New York: Routledge, 2018), https://search.ebscohost.com/login.aspx?direct=true&scope=site&db=nlebk &db=nlabk&AN=2085052; Christopher Stroud, "Portuguese as Ideology and Politics in Mozambique: Semiotic (Re)Constructions of Post Colony," in *Language Ideological Debates*, ed. J. Blommaaert (Berlin: Mouton de Gruyter, 343AD).

21. Schumpteter and Swedberg, *Capitalism, Socialism and Democracy.*

22. Amado, Focus Group Interview, Neighborhood of Ponta d'Agu (Praia, Cabo Verde).

23. Amado, Focus Group Interview, Neighborhood of Ponta d'Agu (Praia, Cabo Verde).

24. Bourdieu, *Language and Symbolic Power*, 68.

25. Amado, Focus Group Interview, Neighborhood of Ponta d'Agu (Praia, Cabo Verde).

26. "Donaldo Macedo: 'A Nossa Língua é Viável Como Instrumento Pedagogico,'" *A Semana*, December 10, 2005, http://www.asemana.publ.cv/spip.php ?article14036&var_recherche=Procurar&ak=1.

27. Amado, Focus Group Interview, Neighborhood of Brazil (Praia, Cabo Verde).

28. Amado, Focus Group Interview, Neighborhood of Ponta d'Agu (Praia, Cabo Verde).

29. Amado, Focus Group Interview, Neighborhood of Ponta d'Agu (Praia, Cabo Verde).

30. Amado, Focus Group Interview, Neighborhood of Ponta d'Agu (Praia, Cabo Verde).

31. Amado, Focus Group Interview, Neighborhood of Brazil (Praia, Cabo Verde).

32. Ferguson, "Diglossia."

33. Kymlicka, *Politics in the Vernacular: Nationalism, Multiculturalism and Citizenship.*

34. Laitin, *Politics, Language, and Thought,* 10.

35. Clifford Geertz, *The Interpretation of Cultures: Selected Essays* (New York: Basic Books, 1973).

36. Anjos, *Intelectuais, literatura e poder em Cabo Verde*; Jean-François Bayart, "Africa in the World: A History of Extraversion," *African Affairs* 99, no. 395 (2000): 217–67.

37. Amado, Focus Group Interview, Neighborhood of Achada Santo António, Artica (Praia, Cabo Verde).

38. Amado, Focus Group Interview, Neighborhood of Achada Santo António, Artica (Praia, Cabo Verde).

39. Amado, Focus Group Interview, Neighborhood of Achada Santo António, Artica (Praia, Cabo Verde).

40. Abel Djassi Amado, Focus Group Interview, Neighborhood of Paiol (Praia, Cabo Verde), August 15, 2011.

Chapter 7

The Politics of Linguistic Landscape

Plateau, Platô, or "Riba Praia" is the historical part of the city of Praia, built during colonial times and standing on a plateau—thus the name. To this day, Riba Praia is the political and economic center of the city; it is the district that attracts people from around the island. Every morning, its population increases manifold, with people coming to work, running errands, or simply visiting the district. There are three main ramps to get to the district, northern, southwestern, and eastern. As one enters the city from the southwestern ramp, a huge sign "PRAIA," lighted at night, welcomes you. Traditionally, the southern ramp has been used by different sociopolitical actors as an arena to disseminate information and messages to the population of Praia. At the southwestern entry to Plateau, there is now (as of June 2022) an antimalaria mural. Against a white background, the mural consists of three elements: a short message in Cabo Verdean, placed at the top, in the larger blue font; a red prohibition sign, resembling that of road traffic signs, over a mosquito; and finally, there is small white font disseminating a message in Portuguese.

The message in Cabo Verdean reads, "NU KABA KU PALUDISMO NA NOS TERRA," which can be translated as "Let's terminate malaria in our country" (figure 7.1). The Portuguese message reads, "ZERO PALUDISMO COMEÇA COMIGO!" "Zero malaria starts with me!" Though there is no indication of who is behind the mural, it was most likely done by an agency of the state focusing on public health, either the Ministry of Health or the various autonomous public health institutes. The mural is bilingual, and the dominance of Cabo Verdean over Portuguese is indicated by its size, type, and placement. The mural is an example of how public authorities manipulate the public space to communicate with the city and its population. It is part of what sociolinguists call the linguistic landscape, a topic of this chapter.

Figure 7.1 "Nu Kaba ku Paludismo na nos Terra," a Mural in Praia, Cabo Verde. *Source*: Photo taken by author.

The urban space, more than semi-urban and rural areas, has become a sphere that many social actors seek to control and shape through the display of written messages. Though these actors have diverse and often contradictory interests, they share the same instrument: the written language and other semiotic devices. The written word and the semiotic elements that often accompany it have become important sociopolitical tools as they seek to reshape the public space. This chapter approaches the linguistic landscape from the point of view of political linguistics, focusing on and analyzing language in public as an alternative approach to studying power, the quintessential phenomenon that motivates political science.

Language is a powerful instrument through which the control of space can be exercised. A critical examination of the Cabo Verdean linguistic landscape makes it clear that it is an arena of durable yet subtle, including intra-elite and inter-class, sociopolitical conflict. The conflict is manifested in different ways, including the choice of the medium through which a political message is displayed to the public. For instance, what language (Portuguese or Cabo Verdean) should be used in public as the medium through which messages are carried? Moreover, suppose the choice falls on the use of the Cabo Verdean language. In that case, additional issues include the dialect or variety used and the chosen written system. The political consequences of these choices include issues related to national and social identity, diglossia, monolingualism or bilingualism, and marginalization and political exclusion. In this chapter, I focus on the political linguistic landscape, centering my analysis on discourses that are either displayed by political actors such as the state or that have an observable political message.

FROM LINGUISTIC LANDSCAPE TO
POLITICAL LINGUISTIC LANDSCAPE

Scholars have analyzed and examined language and other semiotic units in the public arena for many decades. However, the origin of the concept of linguistic landscape is recent and can be traced back to the late 1990s. Rodrigue Landry and Richard Y. Bourhis coined the term in their 1997 seminal paper, defining it as "public road signs, advertising billboards, street names, place names, commercial shop signs, and public signs on government buildings."[1] The two scholars invited others to pay close attention to how the urban space communicates with its citizens through the written word displayed in public. Since then, studies on the linguistic landscape have flourished and boomed, and countless papers and books have been published on the topic.

Consequently, the definition proposed by these two scholars has been expanded to include an analysis of any establishment that displays language signs on "any piece of the written text within a definable frame."[2] The importance of studying the linguistic landscape of a region or polity derives from the fact that it can assist in understanding how identity is constructed and reproduced.[3] Given the centrality of language in the social construction of identity, examining the linguistic landscape sheds light on how the community presents and communicates with itself.[4] The presence or absence of a language in public not only provides an understanding of the perception of the worthiness of a language within the area but also could index to other issues such as powerlessness, minority status, and exclusion. At the same time, the introduction and use of a minoritized and powerless language in the linguistic landscape forms a strategy of resistance and linguistic empowerment on the part of its speakers.

Studies of the linguistic landscape are interdisciplinary as they combine insights and theories from many fields, such as sociolinguistics, geography, political science, and sociology. Over the past thirty years, the study of the linguistic landscape has abounded with different geographic scopes, ranging from analysis of small areas such as one street or a neighborhood to subnational regions, the whole nation, and a group of countries; scholars have studied the linguistic landscape of different cities from around the globe, including Jerusalem (Palestine/Israel) and Montréal.[5] However, very few studies have focused on African cities. In many ways, this chapter addresses this void in the literature by critically analyzing how Cabo Verdean social actors, pursuing their ideological and other interests, construct and reconstruct the space through the written words and other semiotic devices.

The linguistic landscape is a subset of the semiotic landscape, the display of signs and other artifacts in public that are filled with meanings and, for this reason, communicate with citizens often through their subconsciousness. To study the linguistic landscape of a region is to focus on the following aspects: (a) signage, (b) the language in which they are written, (c) who produced them, and (d) to whom they are directed.[6] The written word displayed in public accomplishes two functions in a bilingual (or multilingual) setting. The first of these functions is the message itself; the content of information passed to the community is codified in a given language. The other function, more subtle and hidden, refers to the choice of language to carry the message, indicating the authors' views regarding the languages spoken in the community. Placing a public message in a given language says a lot about the authors' view on that language and the other languages that were not chosen as the medium to disseminate information—as such, studying the linguistic landscape uncovers the belief systems regarding the worthiness and value of a language. Signs are placed in the public space with clear political significance or function. These signs form implicit (sometimes explicit) statements of power or counterpower; as such, they are, in essence, political instruments. A sign that provides information about something that is not openly political is, however, political insofar as the choice of language reinforces or negates the linguistic status quo—and thus power relations within the community.

A critical analysis of a polity's—or a community's—linguistic landscape is an open window that allows the investigator to capture the reality of asymmetric power relations between languages and their speakers. Jasone Cenoz and Durk Gorter note that "the linguistic landscape reflects the relative power and status of the different languages in a specific sociolinguistic context."[7] A linguistic landscape can, in many ways, be the informal statement of the community's language policy, even when no such policy exists in the realm of formality.

When the signs are placed by the state or its agents, these are called top-down; on the other hand, when private citizens and nongovernmental entities are the social actors behind a sign in public, the situation is that of a bottom-up sign. Whether at the local or the national level, the state is the legitimate authority to place signs (top-down signs) and regulate the proper display of private signs in public (bottom-up signs). The official language used to conduct state business displays the names of places, buildings, streets, and monuments. As stated above, the urban space has become a sphere that many actors seek to control and shape by displaying their written messages. The written word and its semiotic elements are essential sociopolitical tools they employ as they seek to reshape the public space.

As a sociopolitical construct, the linguistic landscape of a region is not a neutral phenomenon. On the contrary, it defines, redefines, and counterdefines power relations. It has been suggested that the linguistic landscape is a site of conflict or an arena of contestation insofar as ideologies are produced and propagated through textual, linguistic, and semiotic artifacts.[8] The linguistic landscape of a region or polity is, by its nature, an arena of disputes. Different sociopolitical actors of the community make calculated uses of the space through written words and signs to mark off their territory, solidify their identity, or even silence other actors' voices. Focusing on the linguistic landscape is to unearth the ongoing and yet implicit disputes. The choice of a language as the medium to disseminate messages, or even a particular manner of writing the message in public, is part of a strategy to enhance a social group's ideological or material interests. Social groups populate the space with their written words to enhance intra-group communication and channel ideas to the community.

It is possible to discern intra- and inter-class linguistic disputes. Regarding the first category, the dispute is often between two different sections of the elite, namely the national elites and regional elites, particularly those of major cities that compete with the capital city. The other dispute over the linguistic landscape is between the elites and the nonelites of the polity. The state's different agencies and institutions, political parties, and urban and semi-urban youth are the main actors constructing a political linguistic landscape. Of all these actors, the state has far more capabilities and resources to define—and redefine—the linguistic landscape of the community. As an apparatus of power and political epicenter of the policy, the state makes itself visible through written words and signs in public. Signs sanctioned by the state tend to be a particular form and often adhere to a particular format, giving the idea of uniformity and centralism. Take, for instance, road and street signs. These are uniformly made and placed in public and respect strict rules regarding the chosen language, font, size, and color.

Political parties are another significant actor in constructing a political linguistic landscape. The intensity through which political parties engage in such a construction is not temporally even; electoral campaign periods are when these actors use their resources to transform the space to appeal to the voters. In the weeks preceding the elections, political parties and their candidates put out different semiotic signs in public as part of their electoral strategy to enhance visibility, recognition, and, as such, success.

THE CABO VERDEAN STATE AND LINGUISTIC POLITICAL LANDSCAPE

This section explores the state as an important and conspicuous actor in constructing a community's linguistic landscape. As an actor that presents itself as the hegemonic power in a society, regulating behavior and setting standards of social action, the state, as the supreme locus of political authority, makes itself present in all domains and aspects of social life.[9] Frequently, the presence of the state is not noticeable; through action, it defines and redefines collective identity, spheres of power, and modalities of operations. The written word in the public has become a tool through which the state continuously shapes national identity by constructing symbols that feed the imagined community and through a process called *banal nationalism*.[10] The written word in the public, put forth by the state through its agents, crystallizes the sense of national identity by capturing the citizens' subconsciousness. The names of the streets and the written word accompanying monuments, public buildings, parks, and other public structures have become influential mnemonic devices for the nation. The nation also remembers itself through the written word in its public space. As such, signage put out by the state in public constitutes an example of a top-down linguistic landscape.[11]

As noted in chapter 2, Cabo Verde's national identity has historically not been consensual. Some have constructed it in European identity; others have rejected this perspective and maintained that Cabo Verde is essentially African. Finally, the third school of thought, though a minority, considers Cabo Verde's national identity neither European nor African.[12] The public space, as dominated by the state, has become an arena of debate on national identity. In the first postcolonial regime (1975–1991), the city's toponymy and other areas emphasized African links and identity. In the city of Praia, the country's capital, street names honored men like Patrice Lumumba, Kwame Nkrumah, and other known pan-Africanists. In the 1990s, with regime change, African names were dropped, and, in many cases, the old colonial names were brought back. Thus, for instance, the Kwame Nkrumah Neighborhood was renamed its colonial name, Craveiro Lopes Neighborhood (Francisco Craveiro Lopes was the president of Portugal from 1951 to 1958, during the regime of ultranationalist Estado Novo). Toponymy, from street to building names, including any short narratives that typically accompany public monuments, is exclusively written in Portuguese. Maintaining Portuguese as the written language in the toponymy is part of a strategy of social control and dominance by the state and its elites.

A critical examination of the Cabo Verdean linguistic landscape makes it clear that it is an arena of durable yet subtle sociopolitical conflict. There are two dominant conflicts, namely intra-elite and inter-class, over the production of the linguistic landscape. Different elite segments with diverse material and ideological interests conflict with each other regarding how the space is linguistically manipulated. For instance, local elites from the island of São Vicente are more likely to use the etymological alphabet when the Cabo Verdean language is used. For example, the branding of the island, which is widely accepted by most, refutes the basic rule of the Cabo Verdean alphabet as codified in the mid-1990s. *Soncent*, commonly used in the public arena, particularly in social media, would be written as *Sonsent* if the Cabo Verdean Alphabet were used.

The other dimension of the conflict over the linguistic landscape is between different strata of society. As discussed later in the chapter, lower socioeconomic classes are increasingly appropriating their own space to redefine the linguistic landscape of their neighborhoods. In this situation, the construction of the neighborhood linguistic landscape is delinked from the interests of the elites. Portuguese is rarely used, and the Cabo Verdean language is dominant. Moreover, the conflict manifests in other ways, particularly in the choice of the medium through which the message is displayed to the public. Thus, the message can be disseminated in Portuguese or Cabo Verdean. When the latter is chosen, the actor constructing the signage can either adhere to the rules described in the Cabo Verdean Alphabet or, as is common, base the writing according to the etymological system. The manipulation of the written word in public can lead to many political consequences, including national and social identity, diglossia, monolingualism or bilingualism, marginalization and political exclusion, construction of zones of power, and language policy and practice.[13]

In linguistic terms, the participation of the agencies and departments of the state in the construction of the linguistic landscape is not consistent. First, the institutional boundary that frames the state decision-makers' linguistic choices is not codified. No law explicitly defines what languages can be used to produce signage. Instead, institutional practice, informed by how things were done in the past, has guided state linguistic choices. Thus, Portuguese is the only language used for certain types of signage (street names, for instance). However, with Cabo Verdean *Kriolu* making inroads in different realms of public life, different state departments use different languages to announce their information. In today's Cabo Verde, signage put out by the state and its agents can be in Portuguese, Cabo Verdean, or bilingual (with information in both languages, usually complementing each other). When Cabo Verdean is used as part of signage, there is no full adherence to the Cabo Verdean Alphabet's rules. As such, there is state-mandated signage that mostly follows the etymological orthographic system, in which the spelling of words is identical to Portuguese.

Top-down signage in the Cabo Verdean language has become relatively common—though not at the same level as those in Portuguese. The message of these signages tends to be short and straightforward and often is part of a state-led campaign regarding youth, public health, or other issues about the general welfare. Despite the current legislation that supports the use of the Cabo Verdean Alphabet (formerly known as the ALUPEC), many of the state-sanctioned signage in the mother tongue does not adhere to the rules of that writing system. Through in-person and online observations, particularly by following social media posts of key state departments and agencies, the lack of uniformity in writing the Cabo Verdean language became apparent. Yet, most state-sanctioned billboards and flyers tend to be in Portuguese. Regarding the written domain, the state heavily relies on Portuguese.

It is commonplace to find billboards all around major cities in Cabo Verde. Though private companies use these billboards for advertising their products to boost revenues, central and local governments rent them through various agencies and departments to pass on different messages. There is an implicit political objective in giving information to citizens: it is a means through which the state elites hint to their citizens that they are working for the common good—and, thus, hoping to maintain loyalty in the next electoral cycle. These billboards are used to disseminate information about public health, significant infrastructural development, and social campaigns carried out by state agencies. These billboards are perhaps the most conspicuous arenas displaying the written word.

THE ELECTORAL LINGUISTIC LANDSCAPE

Studies of linguistic landscape focus on the space per se, with *time* given less or no attention. However, specific dates and periods alter the city's life and can affect the linguistic landscape of the area. Religious holidays and festivities, which occur cyclically and last for given periods, change how the city is presented. New signages and other semiotic elements are added, periodically creating a new layer of the linguistic landscape. Similarly, periods of elections have a tremendous effect on the social life of the city, including its linguistic landscape. Despite numerous studies on the topic, the literature has yet to analyze how election periods change the semiotics of the space. In other words, to study to what extent electoral campaigns shape and re-imagine the space, with the written word, assisted by other semiotic elements, playing an important role. To this end, I critically analyze the electoral linguistic landscape and propose the concept of electoral linguistic landscape as part of a strategy to understand how the space is modified in a specific (i.e., electoral) period.

The electoral linguistic landscape is an arena of fluid contestation and (re)negotiation. By its very nature, multiparty electoral politics is basically about argumentative contestation. Opposition parties and candidates occupy the space with messages on the necessity of change. At the same time, the incumbents' communications keep the government—and, thus, the policy lines—unchanged. While major candidates and political parties are the main actors and agents in the definition of the field of electoral linguistic landscape, other less visible actors negotiate, however subtly, their actions to impact the linguistic landscape. The electoral linguistic landscape results from actions by social and political actors that transform the space into a noticeable political space. That is to say, the space becomes a medium through which political messages and communication, in general, are carried out. It becomes a sort of no man's land where different actors with different agendas and strategies confront each other to reshape it according to their political interests. The electoral linguistic landscape thus becomes an open marketplace filled with political ideas and ideals.

The concept of electoral linguistic landscape is here understood as the manipulation of the space through the written word (along with other semiotic elements, such as colors, typeface, and size) with clear political objectives, namely the conquest of voters and votes. The term denotes persuasive discourse; their ultimate goal is to persuade citizens that voting for a given candidate or party—or, the opposite, rejecting an appeal from another party/candidate—is their best choice. While the written word is the essence of the electoral linguistic landscape, other semiotic elements, ranging from colors, font type, size, and imagery to other metalinguistic elements, are also important.

As a subset of the linguistic landscape, an electoral linguistic landscape accomplishes informational and symbolic functions. Regarding the former, the electoral linguistic landscape provides information about the candidate or the party, its policy proposals, and often about the opponents—including resorting to negative ads. These form political advertising discourse since they are designed to promote a given political good. Through the careful display of electoral signage, candidates and political parties seek to nurture a charismatic and programmatic rapport with the electorate. Electoral signages also fulfill a symbolic function as they index socially relevant questions, such as language policy, language imperialism, marginalization, and discrimination. Put differently, electoral signages index a "larger discourse"; therefore, a lot can be learned by focusing on the public display of electoral paraphernalia. Since elections are generally understood as the competition among different political worldviews and ways of governing the community, the electoral linguistic landscape can help us understand how linguistically cohesive—or divisive—the elites are. Do they adhere to the same writing standards, or, on the contrary, do they rely on competing forms?

The introduction of multiparty electoral democracy in Cabo Verde in 1991 radically changed politics in the country. Electoral democracy translates into a competitive political market as different political parties and candidates develop strategies to attract support from citizens at the polls. Periods of elections, chiefly the times of electoral campaigns, have made significant changes in the language and politics nexus. As such, electoral politics is weaved with the politics of language in two different ways. On the one hand, political parties and candidates running from main offices are expected to develop—or at least to have concrete ideas—Cabo Verdean language policy. The question of the officialization of the Cabo Verdean language, its functions and roles in society and state, and the status of the Portuguese language are integral to the electoral agenda. In each significant election (legislative and presidential), top candidates are expected to discuss the question of language, share their views, and come up with a policy proposal—though these proposals have not translated into actual policies.

The other aspect of electoral politics is grounded on language use. Perhaps in no other sphere of politics is the Cabo Verdean language more widely used than the domain of electoral politics. Even though the Cabo Verdean language is overwhelmingly used, Portuguese is still the dominant language in various aspects of electoral politics. For instance, candidates' and political parties' platforms, that is, their comprehensive statements on government and policies, are written exclusively in Portuguese. Thus, though it is common to hear political candidates praise and celebrate the mother tongue, the Cabo Verdean language is yet to be used in such a function (as the medium to detail and explain policy proposals of the candidates or parties).

Contemporary Cabo Verdean electoral politics is dominated by two political parties: the PAICV and the MpD. While there are a handful of other parties, they lack the critical elements of party relevance: the ability to enter into a governing coalition and the capacity to blackmail other political parties into accepting their views and interests.[14] Third parties typically get three to four seats (out of seventy-two) in the National Assembly, a number that does not guarantee them any real power. Thus, Cabo Verde is essentially a two-party system, with MpD and PAICV behaving as *cartel parties*, parties that calculatedly use state resources to maintain their dominance in the electoral political game.[15] Given the amount of financial and otherwise resources, these two parties truly dominate the construction of the Cabo Verdean electoral linguistic landscape.

Electoral politics consists of several domains and aspects, such as electoral slogans, door-to-door canvassing, party/candidate platforms, televised political debates, social media posts, and electoral rallies. In certain domains and aspects of electoral politics in Cabo Verde, as in the cases of electoral slogans and mottos, both Cabo Verdean and Portuguese are used with high intensity. Candidates' electoral slogans and mottos are constructed in either of the two languages—and sometimes in those two languages. The candidates' electoral slogan/motto is their identity seal that is widely disseminated. In the 2021 presidential elections, six candidates ran for office—though, in effect, the electoral combat was between the former prime ministers José Maria Neves and Carlos Veiga, supported by the PAICV and MpD, respectively. The dominant electoral slogan of the two presidential candidates was in different languages. José Maria Neves opted for Cabo Verdean, written according to the rules of the Cabo Verdean Alphabet (formerly known as the ALUPEC): "Djunta Mon Kabesa y Kurason" (unite hand, head, and heart). Carlos Veiga, on the other hand, preferred to base its electoral message under a Portuguese banner "Unir para Avançar" (uniting to advance).

In the realm of orality, Cabo Verdean Creole is quite conspicuous during electoral campaign periods. Direct, face-to-face communication between party activists, leaders, and candidates tends to be almost exclusively in Cabo Verdean. Very few candidates use the Portuguese language when interacting with potential voters. One possible exception is the case of the Social Democratic Party leader João Além, who relies almost exclusively on Portuguese for his party's political communications. The use of Portuguese in the oral domain tends to happen during formal settings, such as debates or interviews with individual candidates conducted by the media—such as radio or television. It is not uncommon for candidates to code-switch between Cabo Verdean and Portuguese during televised debates.

The two languages are widely used in different domains and aspects of electoral politics in Cabo Verde. Some of these domains, such as door-to-door canvassing, are intensively on the mother tongue. Direct oral contact between candidates, their proxies, and citizens as part of electioneering is almost exclusively in the Cabo Verdean language. Other domains, such as electoral slogans/mottos, make intensive use of Cabo Verdean *Kriolu* and Portuguese. Finally, domains such as the party's electoral platforms are exclusively Portuguese (table 7.1).

Electoral paraphernalia is quintessentially political discourse insofar as they are concerned with conquering and/or maintaining political power—through persuasion and other methods designed to sway voters either to one's favor or at least against the opponents. They are discourse since they are cohesive statements put forth by social actors. In the months or weeks preceding the elections, the space goes through radical changes as the electoral paraphernalia, both mobile and immovable, becomes exposed in major cities and towns. The electoral political advertisement can be found on fixed (such as

Table 7.1 Domains and Aspects of Electoral Politics and Language Use

	Cabo Verdean Kriolu	*Portuguese*
Electoral slogans/mottos	High intensity	High intensity
Door-to-door canvassing	High intensity	Low intensity
Party/candidate platforms	Low intensity	High intensity
Televised political debates	Low intensity	High intensity
Social media posts	Low intensity	High intensity
Electoral rallies	High intensity	Low intensity

Source: Created by author.

signage, posters, and billboards) or mobile media (leaflets, flyers, drawings, and/or posters glued to circulating vehicles). Political parties and candidates intentionally occupy the public space to disseminate their images and policy proposals. Urban areas, given their high concentrations of voters of different demographics, are the primary targets for political actors. Candidates map the city for areas where their message can impact the most. Placing a candidate's billboard is calculated in terms of its visibility to voters. Electoral paraphernalia alters and modifies the public space. With the criterion of mobility in mind, electoral paraphernalia can be classified into two main groups: the first group forms static signages. These include billboards, paintings, and drawings with a political message, posters glued in the public arena, and so on. One should note that this first type of electoral signage tends to outlast the electoral cycle. Glued posters, t-shirts, party/candidate slogans, and watchwords painted in the public arena tend to last past the end of the elections. It is possible to encounter these electoral paraphernalia years after the end of the electoral cycle. Field observations in Riba Praia and other neighborhoods of the city of Praia, conducted in the summer of 2022 and previous years, found several examples of signage from past electoral cycles, including a few paintings, though fading, that date back to the 2001 presidential elections.

The second group constitutes the moving/movable signages, particularly vehicles with political messages. This temporary signage tends to disappear from public places with the end of the electoral cycle. Billboards are an excellent example of this temporary signage. Candidates and political parties buy these spaces for a short period—typically to coincide with the end of the electoral cycle. Once the elections are over, other (nonpolitical and commercial) agents often buy these billboards to advertise their products.

A careful analysis of the electoral linguistic landscape allows the researcher—or any curious mind—to see the most visible political actors in a given community. It should be emphasized that constructing the electoral linguistic landscape is, above all, a financial endeavor. Renting spaces to display a message and buying posters and other electoral materials to be displayed in public requires significant investment on the part of the candidate. Therefore, a quick overview of the local linguistic landscape allows one to discern and distinguish big political parties, conspicuous and ubiquitous in major urban areas and rural towns, from small and powerless ones. Strong candidates and political parties seek even to redesign the foreign linguistic landscape of communities with significant Cabo Verdean citizens. Cities like Boston, chiefly around the Dorchester neighborhood, where a significant number of voting citizens reside, or Amadora, in Portugal, are relatively inundated with electoral paraphernalia during election cycles.[16] Therefore, a study of the electoral linguistic landscape in Cabo Verde can offer insights into the role of money in politics in a small island state.

However, the electoral linguistic landscape is not simply about political parties and candidates' appropriation of the space for political purposes. Of their own volition, ordinary men and women participate in the redefinition of the electoral linguistic landscape. In this sense, the electoral linguistic landscape "belongs to all." The study of the electoral linguistic landscape is more than asking about authorship. Signs are not only made; they are also remade. While ordinary voters and citizens, in general, may not participate in producing electoral texts, they are active in its (re)packaging and dissemination. The candidate can make a t-shirt with their slogan and electoral appeal, but how the t-shirt is worn—and redesigned in many ways—clearly indicates the agency of ordinary voters. The redesigning of the t-shirt, as done by regular folks, is linked to languaging, that is, "the multiple ways of representation that are not limited to words but rather include additional ways of expression consisting of a variety of creative devices of expression such as languaging through music, clothes, gesture, visuals, food, tears and laughter."[17] Clothing—mainly when the agent remakes it—constitutes "a powerful form of languaging used to communicate and transmit messages."[18] Redesigning the t-shirts given by the parties or candidates constitutes a form of communicating one's party/candidate as fashionable, chic, and trendy. In some ways, the ordinary voter is not simply a target of electioneering; they become an agent of electioneering, and through their agency, chiefly regarding languaging, transmit specific messages about their candidates. The electoral linguistic landscape helps us understand the extent of political participation; the idea that electioneering is entirely conducted from the party headquarters by party bosses and consultants may not be supported by what happens on the ground. Party leaders usually decide on the main aspects of the electoral strategy. Still, one cannot discount the tactics employed by party rank-and-file and sympathizers in advancing their party/candidate's appeal. Increasingly, parties and candidates are also taking advantage of the new insights advanced in commercial advertising. New and innovative forms of advertising are being used to deepen the image of the candidate or the party in the collective subconsciousness. These include what the subfield of business studies calls transit advertising.[19]

As it is constructed, the electoral linguistic landscape provides subsidies for the ongoing ideological debate regarding writing the Cabo Verdean language. In the mid-1990s, a writing system called the Cabo Verdean Alphabet was designed to properly graphize the language. In chapter 2, I discuss how the writing system has yet to be fully adopted by society, and many who are for the promotion of the mother tongue still oppose the state-sanctioned writing system (the Cabo Verdean Alphabet). The construction of the electoral linguistic landscape is another dynamic process of the linguistic ideological debate, with sociopolitical actors either affirming or rejecting the norms of the Cabo Verdean Alphabet.

If Cabo Verdean is adopted, different dialectal forms are adopted in different circumstances to avoid alienating elements from other islands. Take, for instance, the slogan *mesti muda* (it needs to change) as put forth by Carlos Veiga as he was competing for prime minister in 2011. The motto was graphized differently in different parts of the country to emphasize dialectal differences. In Santiago, it was written as *mesti muda*, but it was *mestê mudá* in São Vicente.[20] Decision-makers within the MpD were aware of how controversial language politics is in Cabo Verde, particularly among the local elites of São Vicente. They have accused Santiago, the major island, of centralizing resources and opportunities. The motto *mesti muda* is in accordance with the dialect of Santiago. If it had been used in São Vicente as expressed in Santiago, it would have caused disastrous political consequences for the MpD. Therefore, the same slogan was re-graphized to represent the dialect of São Vicente better and avoid any political costs.

Another illustrative example of how candidates approach the Cabo Verdean language is the case of the 2016 local government elections. The two major political parties had two well-known candidates for the mayor of Praia, the capital city. The MpD had Oscar Santos, the second man in the city's previous administration, and the PAICV had Cristina Fontes. She had been a member of the central government for fifteen years (2001–2016) and had led several portfolios. These two candidates centered their political campaign on the Cabo Verdean language, which provided the central mottos for their electoral battle. The PAICV had as its slogan *Praia mutu midjor* (Praia much better), while the MpD based its campaign on *Na equipa qui ta ganha ca ta mexedu* (a winning team cannot be changed). Despite using the mother tongue, the chief difference is how the mother tongue was displayed. While the PAICV adhered to the rules of the Cabo Verdean Alphabet, the MpD, on the other hand, had a more laissez-faire approach, writing the language more according to the etymology of the words.[21] Regarding the position of these two parties vis-à-vis the writing of the Cabo Verdean language, the PAICV has often placed itself more in favor of the Cabo Verdean Alphabet. In contrast, the position of the MpD has been more flexible and less rigid regarding the system adopted by the state (see chapter 2).

Electoral periods tend to change the linguistic order. As noted in chapter 2, the sociolinguistic profile of Cabo Verde, like most other Creole island states in Africa and the Caribbean, is that of diglossia. This means that the official language of the state, often inherited through colonialism, is used for the formal business of the state (public administration, justice, education, media). In contrast, the mother tongue is relegated to informality and private life. During the electoral cycles, political actors rely extensively on the mother tongue for many reasons, including constructing a solid rapport with voters. One of this situation's consequences is the use of Cabo Verdean for most electoral functions. For instance, political rallies are conducted almost exclusively in Cabo Verdean—though some political actors still use only Portuguese for their electioneering activities. Political life seems to happen in the vernacular during the weeks and months before and after the elections.

POLITICAL LINGUISTIC LANDSCAPE
IN POOR NEIGHBORHOODS

Peripheral neighborhoods of modern cities in Africa are socially and politically relevant. Most urban dwellers live in those neighborhoods, providing these areas with significant demographic weight. The tendency is for these slums to grow, a clear indication that there is a problem with inclusive urbanization and politics in the continent.[22] There is increased interest in understanding politics in these "marginalized" communities. A new body of literature, often described as slum politics, has thus developed in the past two decades.[23] Though slums were often perceived as the space of anarchy and antidemocratic forces, a new generation of scholars is now approaching this area as a harbinger of true democracy in urban Africa.[24] Despite the vibrancy of the slum politics literature in Africa and elsewhere, there is a telling scarcity of studies on how local citizens in these marginalized areas construct their political linguistic landscape as a form of community empowerment and resistance against oppressive practices from the state and its elites. This is the approach taken in this section, in which I critically examine the instrumental use of the written word in poor neighborhoods of the city of Praia.

In the summer of 2022 (June/July), I spent three weeks in the city of Praia, conducting final field research for this book project. I visited many "peripheral" city neighborhoods, including Brazil, Paiol, Txadinha, and Vila Nova. In all these neighborhoods, graffiti dominates the linguistic landscape, whether painted or chalked. In many so-called *bairros periféricos* (peripheral neighborhoods) inhabited mainly by lower socioeconomic citizens, the physical space has become one of the primary vehicles through which locals, chiefly youngsters, voice their views, frustrations, and expectations. In these neighborhoods, the state is minimal or nonexistent; the essential public goods, particularly public safety, provided by the state are also minimal or nonexistent. The absence of the state has resulted in subversion against the state and its authority; illegal construction and use of utilities, chiefly electricity, are widespread. The absence of a formal and state-sanctioned linguistic landscape is evident; at the core of these communities, the written word put out by the state is absent. In some of the marginalized communities, the local government has intervened, and it is possible to note the Portuguese-based toponymy. Most urban voters live in these communities; political parties and candidates understand this reality. Against this backdrop, these communities are reformatted during electoral months: the semiotic landscape is radically changed, and the community becomes colorful as the colors typically associated with parties and candidates are displayed in the public space. Political elites seeking votes understand that colonization of the linguistic landscape of these communities is an essential pathway to power. In the period of electoral campaigns, these communities are inundated with electoral paraphernalia, mainly posters, stickers, and t-shirts brandishing party and candidates' pictures and slogans. Months after the end of the electoral campaign, it is still possible to find relics of the past electoral season—mainly stickers, posters, and sometimes graffiti.

Before analyzing the political linguistic landscape of these neighborhoods, a word is needed regarding the language-politics nexus. Given the low socioeconomic status of the majority of the population, the mother tongue dominates social life among their residents. Portuguese enters these community through the vehicles of power, chiefly the media (of which radio and television are the most common). Despite low socioeconomic status, these neighborhoods have become veritable factories of linguistic innovation, as youngsters from these areas constantly develop new phrases, lexica, and other linguistic devices to capture their social life. Many expressions that eventually become part of mainstream speech in Cabo Verdean find their origins in those communities. As can be imagined, political actors often negotiate with these communities and appropriate these linguistic innovations for their objectives. During electoral campaigns, major candidates and political parties import lexicon and expressions from these communities as part of a *strategy of condescension*, "the very act of negating symbolically the objective relation of power between two languages which co-exist in [the] market."[25] In other words, actors in higher sociopolitical status adopt and use language and linguistic expression from lower socioeconomic classes to negate the power relationship between the two languages (or variants of languages) and, therefore, of speakers. As such, it is not uncommon to find candidates employing expressions, phrases, and words that constitute the sociolect of these marginalized communities. Once borrowed by political agents, these neologisms and other novel linguistic devices are returned to these communities as part of the political linguistic landscape.

The manipulation of the space by the local agents is particularly conspicuous at the level of the written word in the public space. These areas are dominated by bottom-up transgressive discourses, signs "which violate (intentionally or accidentally) the conventional semiotics at that place such as a discarded snack food wrapper or graffiti."[26] Graffiti is quite noticeable and has become a dominant mode of communication among youngsters from these neighborhoods. The locals are reshaping the space, transforming it into a powerful vehicle through which their messages, political and otherwise, are disseminated. These signs are bottom-up insofar as the agents have full autonomy regarding the composition and display.[27]

However, non-mainstream political actors also work to shape, construct, and reconstruct the electoral landscape. It is possible to encounter transgressive electoral discourse, that is, written words by marginalized groups and social classes that are used to demonstrate their dissatisfaction with the current state of affairs.

Transgressive signages are more likely to rely on the subordinated language than on the dominant language. First, the social actors who engage in this type of social construction of the space lack mastery in the dominant language; many of these actors did not receive an adequate formal education, the sine qua non, to master Portuguese properly. Second, transgressive discourse is a form of in-group communication, and, as such, it is based on the idea of directness and reduction of translation costs. Messages are short in the mother tongue; those with minimal reading skills can easily capture that. Third, as an important marker of social identity, displaying the written words in the mother tongue constitutes a form of demonstrating their character.

One visible public transgressive discourse in these neighborhoods is the written word by street gangs and other petty criminals from these communities. It is not the scope of this section to discuss crime in these neighborhoods. It suffices to note that semi-organized gangs who operate in the city are most likely to come from many of these poor communities.[28] Graffiti is a tool used by these groups with different objectives, ranging from territorial demarcation to identity building. During my observations in various marginalized neighborhoods, a constant theme in the transgressive linguistic landscape is the name of gangs and their members. For instance, in the neighborhood of Txadinha, on the road that leads to the countryside, I have noticed several graffiti with "GDR." In one of the graffiti, GDR is spelled out as "Gangue de Rua" (Street Gang). What is striking is that one of the graffiti stated "GDR Soudja," in which the *Soudja* is the creolized pronunciation of English "soldier." The introduction of English words and expressions is not uncommon. Instead, these groups often colonize the public space with writings that combine the Cabo Verdean language with expressions and phrases from English (particularly swearwords). It can be argued that using these English expressions relates to the construction of globalized identity. In other words, youngsters from marginalized communities make instrumental use of the English language as they populate the linguistic community of their respective areas to reclaim their cosmopolitanism and symbolic connectedness with global youth culture.

Moreover, it can be suggested that using expressions and lexicon from English is part of a strategy against imposed social and political exclusion.

As noted in chapter 5, one of the main mechanisms of political strategy is through the illegibility of the state, which occurs almost exclusively in Portuguese. Given the lack of mastery of the Portuguese language in marginalized neighborhoods, expressions, and words in English, a global language with supposedly greater prestige than Portuguese, compensate for this deficiency. As noted in previous chapters, language hierarchy has been historically constructed and reproduced in countries like Cabo Verde. Ideologies, institutions, and resources have placed Portuguese over the mother tongue, a conspicuous phenomenon in contemporary Cabo Verde. Youngsters and other social actors understand that the English language maintains the status of a global lingua franca; as such, this language mobilizes far greater symbolic resources than Portuguese. Consequently, there is a tactical alliance with the English language, which is marshaled to resist—if not deconstruct—symbolically the linguistic hegemony of Portuguese.

Another illustrative example of youngsters using transgressive discourse to enhance their visibility—at least in their neighborhood—can be seen in the neighborhood of Txada Grande (figure 7.2). The wall of the FENACOOP (Federação Nacional Das Cooperativas De Consumo, National Federation of Consumer Cooperatives) is now filled with graffiti indicating the local gang. The name of the group, presumably given by its members, is quite interesting: Young Power (in English, in original). The graffiti indicates the members' names along with the group's name. Besides the fact that English is used, it is interesting to note the location of this graffiti. Not only is the display of the written word in a well-known institution, but the building itself is on the neighborhood's main street. Moreover, the building sits across from a soccer stadium that local youngsters use.

Youngsters are not the only visible players in constructing the linguistic landscape in these marginalized communities. Community organization is typical throughout the country, though some neighborhoods are better organized and led than others. These community-based organizations engage in myriad political activities, of which shaping the neighborhood's linguistic landscape concerns this chapter the most. I want to use an illustrative example from the neighborhood of Txadinha to illustrate how a community organization uses written language in the local space to accomplish political objectives. The local organization of the neighborhood of Txadinha has reshaped the semiotic landscape of the area through murals that send a positive message to the community and visitors. These murals ultimately serve to boost community self-esteem.

The community organization painted a mural on the neighborhood's main street (figure 7.3). Besides combining different semiotic materials, such as colors, font type and size, and drawings of flowers, plants, and children, the mural includes two quotes transcribed in Cabo Verdean, according to the

Figure 7.2 Txada Grandi, Street Graffiti. *Source*: Photo taken by author.

rules mandated by the Cabo Verdean alphabet. The first quote, painted as if it comes from a child's mind, states, "ami n tem un sonhu." The sentence is directly translated from Martin Luther King Jr.'s famous quote "I have a dream." On the other side of the same mural, another child is carrying a vase with a flower, while on top of it is the statement, "Kriansa é [image of a flower] di Revoluson." This quote was taken from Amílcar Cabral, the Cabo Verdean and Bissau-Guinean independence leader, who noted that "the children are the flowers of our revolution."

The choice of the Cabo Verdean language accomplishes several political objectives. First and foremost, it links the community with the nation through language. As the Cabo Verdean language is the central and defining characteristic of the nation, its use by local authors constitutes actions to reinforce and entrench the notion of collective identity.[29] Because the written words adhere strictly to the rules mandated by the Cabo Verdean alphabet, it can be argued that the authors of the mural made it very clear where they stand in the context of the debate regarding how the Cabo Verdean language is to be written. Furthermore, there is a functional element that explains the use of Cabo Verdean in these murals. Not only can these quotes be better understood as they are in the mother tongue, but they can also be better stored in the minds of those passing by this mural. Finally, the use of Cabo Verdean is, in itself, part of community strategies of resistance and empowerment. Given that the state operates almost exclusively in Portuguese, the use of the Cabo Verdean language in disseminating positive messages counters the Portuguese linguistic hegemony.

Figure 7.3   Txadinha, Message from and to the Community. *Source*: Photo taken by author.

The linguistic landscape of these communities is a significant element in understanding political participation. Traditional approaches to studying political participation often neglect aspects such as transgressive discourses from marginalized populations. Yet, these artifacts provide a powerful testament that these communities, particularly the youngsters, are far from being passive reactors of politics. By constructing their community's linguistic landscape, they negotiate with their community and the elites, indicating their autonomy and snubbing dominating culture and language. In other words, their written words constitute forms of political participation as they are repositories of critiques of the dominant political system and, as such, a manifest for collective action. Two languages dominate the transgressive discourse that constitutes the bulk of the linguistic landscape of these communities, namely Cabo Verdean and English. The Portuguese language is either minimally used or not used at all. When youngsters use Portuguese, there is no adherence to the strict rules of standard Portuguese—unless what is being written is a formulaic statement.

CONCLUSION

This chapter focuses on an important dimension of the language-politics nexus, namely the manipulation of the space through the written word, a sociolinguistic phenomenon called linguistic landscape. After noting the vibrancy of the new linguistic landscape subfield, I argue that this particular aspect needs to be studied—the political linguistic landscape. Though any signage and other written materials in public are political as they relate to the issue of choice of language or language variety, I developed a sensu stricto understanding of the political linguistic landscape. To this end, I focus on key political actors and how they manipulate the written language to maintain or redefine power relations.

One crucial actor who significantly shapes Cabo Verdean's linguistic landscape is the state itself. As the authoritative institution, the state possesses material, human, and other types of resources that allow it to manipulate the space as it seeks to accomplish its objective. However, the state's perspective as a single monolithic political entity is to be cast aside, particularly regarding constructing the linguistic landscape. I note that different agencies and departments of the state make autonomous decisions regarding what language (Portuguese or Cabo Verdean) or what Cabo Verdean writing system to use as they put out signage and other materials in the public space.

To further the understanding of Cabo Verde's political linguistic landscape, I centered my analysis on electoral campaigns. I argue that these periods of intense political debate shape and inform the development of a specific linguistic landscape; that is, they form the electoral linguistic landscape. Electoral cycles translate into a total alteration of the urban linguistic space, with electoral materials, ranging from posters, stickers, and t-shirts, among other paraphernalia occupying the public space. In the weeks or months preceding and after the election day, the public space represents the electoral dynamics, with words, expressions, colors, and other semiotic devices put out by political parties and candidates crowding out other non-electoral elements. I also argue that the electoral linguistic landscape tends to boost the mother tongue, as candidates rely increasingly on Cabo Verdean to develop a strong rapport with voters. Consequently, whether constructed according to the rules of the Cabo Verdean alphabet or not, slogans in Cabo Verdean abound during periods of electoral campaigns.

Finally, this chapter discusses the political linguistic landscape in the slum, that is, the poor and marginalized neighborhoods of the city. I discuss two types of social actors and how their actions help to shape the neighborhood linguistic landscape. One of the social groups is petty crime groups or gangs. As is common in many urban areas in the developing world, poor neighborhoods have become a reservoir of petty criminals. I note that these groups' manipulation of the space through language is carried out basically in Cabo Verdean, sprinkled with words or expressions from English. The use of the English language may constitute a political statement insofar as it demonstrates links with the global world. At the same time, it is the low socioeconomic classes' response against the Portuguese linguistic hegemony. Finally, I discuss community-based organizations' role in reshaping their neighborhoods' semiotic landscape, centering on passing positive images and messages to the community. To shorten the distance between reading and understanding, these groups center their use of the written word on Cabo Verdean.

NOTES

1. Rodrigue Landry and Richard Y. Bourhis, "Linguistic Landscape and Ethnolinguistic Vitality: An Empirical Study," *Journal of Language and Social Psychology* 16, no. 1 (1997): 23–49.

2. Florian Coulmas, "Linguistic Landscaping and the Seed of the Public Sphere," in *Linguistic Landscape: Expanding the Scenery*, ed. Elana Shohamy and Durk Gorter (New York: Routledge, 2009), 15.

3. Bethan Benwell and Elizabeth Stokoe, *Discourse and Identity* (Edinburgh: Edinburgh University Press, 2014); Rani Rubdy, "Conflict, Exclusion and Dissent in the Linguistic Landscape," in *Conflict and Exclusion: The Linguistic Landscape as an Arena of Contestation*, ed. Rani Rubdy and Selim Ben Said (London: Palgrave Macmillan, 2015), 1–24.

4. John Edwards, *Language and Iidentity: An Introduction* (Cambridge: Cambridge University Press, 2013).

5. Coulmas, "Linguistic Landscaping and the Seed of the Public Sphere," 14.

6. Annabelle Mooney and Betsy E. Evans, *Language, Society and Power: An Introduction* (London: Routledge, 2019).

7. Jasone Cenoz and Durk Gorter, "Linguistic Landscape and Minority Languages," *International Journal of Multilingualism* 3, no. 1 (2006): 67.

8. Rubdy, "Conflict, Exclusion and Dissent in the Linguistic Landscape."

9. Evans, Rueschemeyer, and Skocpol, *Bringing the State Back In*.

10. Michael Billig, *Banal Nationalism* (London: Sage, 1995); Anderson, *Imagined Communities*.

11. Elana Shohamy and Durk Gorter, "Introduction," in *Linguistic Landscape: Expanding the Scenery*, ed. Elana Shohamy and Durk Gorter (New York: Routledge, 2009), 3; Mooney and Evans, *Language, Society and Power: An Introduction*.

12. Fernandes, *A Diluição da África*; Lopes da Silva, *Cabo Verde visto por Gilberto Freyre*; Amilcar Cabral, *Cabo verde reflexoes e mensagens* (Praia: Fundacao Amilcar Cabral, 2015); Ferreira, *A Aventura Crioula*.

13. Kerry Jane Taylor-Leech, "Language Choice as an Index of Identity: Linguistic Landscape in Dili, Timor-Leste," *International Journal of Multilingualism* 9, no. 1 (2012): 15–34; Landry and Bourhis, "Linguistic Landscape and Ethnolinguistic Vitality"; Shohamy, *Language Policy*; Hirut Woldemariam and Elizabeth Lanza, "Language Contact, Agency and Power in the Linguistic Landscape of Two Regional Capitals of Ethiopia," *International Journal of the Sociology of Language* 228 (2014): 79–103.

14. Giovanni Sartori, *Parties and Party Systems* (Cambridge: Cambridge University Press, 1976).

15. Katz and Mair, "Changing Models of Party Organization and Party Democracy"; Detterbeck, "Cartel Parties in Western Europe?"

16. Kimze Brito, "Cartazes Da Campanha Eleitoral Em Cabo Verde Retirados Pela Junta de Freguesia de Agualva e Mira-Sintra," April 15, 2021, https://mindelinsite.com/atualidade/cartazes-da-campanha-eleitoral-em-cabo-verde-retirados-pela-junta-de-freguesia-de-agualva-e-mira-sintra/.

17. Shohamy, *Language Policy*, 16.

18. Shohamy, 17.

19. Cleopatra Veloutsou and Claire O'Donnell, "Exploring the Effectiveness of Taxis as an Advertising Medium," *International Journal of Advertising* 24, no. 2 (2005): 217.

20. MpD, "Manifesto Eleitoral MpD São Vicente," 2011, https://issuu.com/antaochantre/docs/menisfestoeleitoralmpd.

21. Abel Djassi Amado, "Languages of Power and Cabo Verde's 2016 Elections," September 20, 2016, https://politicalmatter.org/2016/09/20/languages-of-power-and-cabo-verdes-2016-elections-by-abel-djassi-amado/.

22. Jacqueline M. Klopp and Jeffrey W. Paller, "Slum Politics in Africa," in *Oxford Research Encyclopedia. Politics*, ed. William R. Thompson (Oxford: Oxford University Press, 2020), https://doi.org/10.1093/acrefore/9780190228637.013.985.

23. Klopp and Paller; Michael Hooper and Leonard Ortolano, "Motivations for Slum Dweller Social Movement Participation in Urban Africa: A Study of Mobilization in Kurasini, Dar Es Salaam," *Environment and Urbanization* 24, no. 1 (2012): 99–114; Paul Stacey and Christian Lund, "In a State of Slum: Governance in an Informal Urban Settlement in Ghana," *Journal of Modern African Studies* 54, no. 4 (2016): 591–615; Paul Stacey, *State of Slum: Precarity and Informal Governance at the Margins in Accra* (London: Zed Book, 2019).

24. Amaka Anku and Tochi Eni-Kalu, "Africa's Slums Aren't Harbingers of Anarchy—They're Engines of Democracy The Upside of Rapid Urbanization," *Foreign Affairs*, December 16, 2019, https://www.foreignaffairs.com/africa/africas-slums-arent-harbingers-anarchy-theyre-engines-democracy; Klopp and Paller, "Slum Politics in Africa."

25. Bourdieu, *Language and Symbolic Power*, 81.

26. Ronald Scollon and Suzanne Wong Scollon, *Discourses in Place: Languages in the Material World* (London: Routledge, 2003), 217.

27. Mooney and Evans, *Language, Society and Power: An Introduction*.

28. Redy Wilson Lima, "Diagnóstico Safende 2020" (Praia, Cabo Verde: Associação Comunitária Amigos de Safende, August 2020).

29. Carmen Fought, *Language and Ethnicity* (Cambridge: Cambridge University Press, 2012); William Safran, "Nationalism," in *Handbook of Language and Ethnic Identity*, ed. Joshua A. Fishman (New York: Oxford University Press, 1999), 77–93.

Conclusion

Cabo Verde is an interesting case for the study of the language-politics nexus. Though the mother tongue is widely used in everyday interaction, the Cabo Verdean language, or *Kriolu* as its speakers call it, has yet to attain de jure official language status. Political actors and members of civil society from different political and ideological backgrounds emphasize language as an essential component of the Cabo Verdean identity. Nonetheless, more than three decades after the democratic transition in the islands and with different parties in power, the role of the Cabo Verdean language is far from fully official. While making Cabo Verdean the official language does not equate to the end of the language problems in the country, it is nonetheless an important political and symbolic step toward linguistic parity with the dominant language, Portuguese. Throughout the book, I demonstrate three things: first, there have been inroads of the Cabo Verdean language into different domains that until quite recently were sealed off to this language; second, despite the language spread of Cabo Verdean into different domains, the political authorities have not planned, Portuguese still maintains a definite linguistic hegemony; and, finally, the political consequences of the Portuguese linguistic community are particularly observable in the overall quality of democracy and ordinary citizens' political participation in the affairs of the polity.

CABO VERDEAN LANGUAGE SPREAD

In the early nineteenth century, Cabo Verdean was the dominant language in Cabo Verde. The language was used by local elites in their interactions, including political schemes, and those who moved to the islands, chiefly Portuguese, knew that their social success and acceptance meant performing well in the local language. Various reports on the islands indicate this situation.[1] This sociolinguistic situation drastically changed in the mid- to late-nineteenth century as the colonial state underwent significant political and institutional changes designed to help it become a modern political institution, free from competition from social actors.[2] In linguistic terms, the construction of the contemporary state in Cabo Verdean meant two interrelated social forces, namely the retreat of Cabo Verdean and the subsequent Portuguese linguistic hegemony. Through a combination of stick and carrot, the colonial state radically changed the sociolinguistic situation of the early nineteenth century.

The dynamics of constructing Portuguese linguistic hegemony were further escalated during the late colonial state under the Estado Novo (1933–1974). Informed and influenced by imperial mysticism and the discourses of "Portugal is not a small country," "pluri-continental and pluri-racial nation," "Portugal from Minho [the northernmost province in continental Portugal] to Timor [today's East Timor]," and the ideology of lusotropicalism, the Portuguese colonial state developed many policies and institutions that ultimately resulted in the sociopolitical predominance of Portuguese throughout the empire.[3]

The prevalence of the colonial discourse and institutions regarding the language question was to such a level that they went unchallenged by anticolonial nationalists of the 1960s and 1970s. In other words, while many organizations were formed to challenge the colonial political order, anticolonialism in Cabo Verde, as in other former Portuguese colonies in Africa, was based more on territorial and civic nationalism than on linguistic notions. While significant proponents of indigenous culture as the primary source of the national liberation struggle, anticolonial leaders such as Amílcar Cabral did not see any contradiction in maintaining the Portuguese language. Cabral, like many others, accepted the instrumentalist perspective on language. Portuguese was taken to be a tool and, as such, ideologically neutral. Therefore, Cabral's position clashes with that of Franz Fanon, who argued in terms of linguistic relativism: language modifies behavior.[4] Guinean and Cabo Verdean Creoles, two distinct and mutually intelligible Portuguese-based Creole languages, played critical roles in anticolonial mobilization and underwent significant lexical and morphosyntactic changes. These changes allowed those two languages to be used as a medium of modern politics.[5] Nonetheless, anticolonial organizations did not construct institutions or discourses to support the social primacy of local languages.

The robustness of the colonial language policy, sustained by prevailing language ideology, did not result in a radical change with independence. Despite the regime instituted in Cabo Verde—as in other former Portuguese colonies—being radical and socialist-leaning, a conservative outlook informed and shaped postcolonial language policy. Consequently, political expediency and practice strengthened the position of the Portuguese language.

Nonetheless, national independence in Cabo Verde has helped the mother tongue gain some ground and, little by little, infiltrate many domains. The advent of multiparty electoral democracy has also assisted in spreading the Cabo Verdean language in different domains of political activity. It is now common to hear the Cabo Verdean language in state-society direct relations, parliamentary debates, electioneering, and other political activities deemed to constitute the realm of formality.

The Cabo Verdean language spread in the past three decades has been unplanned and unmanaged by the state authorities. Some agencies within the state, chiefly the Ministry of Culture and Creative Industries, have worked with Cabo Verdean language corpus and status planning. Nonetheless, the spread of the Cabo Verdean language has yet to be regulated and entirely accepted by public authorities. The process of officialization of the Cabo Verdean language has long ago reached a stalemate.

PORTUGUESE LINGUISTIC HEGEMONY

One of its key theorists, Antonio Gramsci, understands hegemony means domination by consensus. Linguistic hegemony entails the general acceptance, as something natural, of the sociopolitical preponderance of a language or a variety of a language. In the case of Cabo Verde, there is Portuguese linguistic hegemony despite the inroads made by the mother tongue. Throughout the book, I argue that Portuguese linguistic hegemony derives from a combination of different sociopolitical forces. At the domestic level, it derives from language ideologies that sustain its predominance, whose origins can be traced back to colonial times, which went unchallenged by anticolonial nationalists. One of the widely used language ideologies is that Portuguese allows and facilitates international communication. While this is undoubtedly the case, Cabo Verdeans can and have used many languages for transnational and international contacts, including the Cabo Verdean language.

Language practice and choices by the elites also support Portuguese linguistic hegemony. Portuguese is not simply a communication tool in Cabo Verde; it symbolizes social distinction. To use it in public is to make a sociopolitical statement. In other words, the use of Portuguese in public, and the confining of Cabo Verdean chiefly to private, informal settings, constitutes a strategy for constructing a social hierarchy in which the Portuguese speaker assumes the dominant position. I argue that Portuguese is often used as a strategy for silencing its non-speakers.

Finally, the institution of the state, which relies almost exclusively on the Portuguese language, maintains such a hegemony. In this book, I argue that the state in Cabo Verde is illegible, as its primary medium of carrying out its functions is Portuguese, a language that most either can't grasp or understand on a rudimentary level. Nonetheless, through its rules, operations, procedures, and processes, the state facilitates Portuguese linguistic hegemony at the expense of monoglossic citizens.

International politics, chiefly interactions among states with Portuguese as the official language, is another dimension through which Portuguese linguistic hegemony is reconstructed and maintained. Multilateral language-promoting intergovernmental organizations, such as the Community of Po rtuguese Language Countries (CPLP) and International Institute of the Port uguese Language (IILP), have now become powerhouses of material and ideological resources to preserve the predominance of the Portuguese language. One of the most influential sociopolitical ideologies is that of *lusofonia*, the notion that speakers of Portuguese, whether first or second language, form an organic community. The CPLP and IILP behave as if they are the organized wing of lusofonia. This ideology serves the interests of major states such as Portugal and Brazil, which have used the language to wield soft power.

Bilateral relations are another important mechanism through which Portuguese linguistic hegemony is reconstructed and upheld. Portugal—and to a lesser extent Brazil—has developed Portuguese language-spread policies that target its former colonies in Africa, with the deployment of institutions such as the Instituto Camões and its network of Portuguese Cultural Centers and state-owned news companies such as RTP-Africa and RDP-Africa. Moreover, Portuguese linguistic hegemony is further endorsed through strengthening relations between Portugal and Cabo Verde. Iteration, the repetition of interactions, and linkage, interlocking different policy areas, have formed a fertile ground for maintaining Portuguese linguistic hegemony.

Portuguese linguistic hegemony does not go unchallenged; social actors from different backgrounds have used various sociolinguistic and political strategies to resist the imposition of Portuguese. This book has focused on two main dimensions: the political linguistic landscape and sociolinguistic remittances. In chapter 7, I argue that citizens from peripheral neighborhoods demonstrate agency as they construct their areas' linguistic landscape. The occupation of the space with the written word is part of a strategy directed against linguistic domination by the elites. Youngsters, in particular, use Cabo Verdean, often sprinkled with words from English, as transgressive discourses in the public space.

The second dimension of linguistic resistance is the diaspora's sociolinguistic remittance. Cabo Verdean diaspora around the world maintains organic links with the homeland. The contacts made with the homeland are significant mediums through which language expressions, ideas, ideals, and ideologies, in general, are transferred. This sociolinguistic transference forms a resistance strategy against Portuguese linguistic hegemony.

DECREASED QUALITY OF DEMOCRACY

This study has entered into close dialogue with the literature on democracy and has argued that a new approach needs to be developed to adequately capture ordinary people's participation or lack thereof. The move toward electoral democracy, at the global level, during the last quarter of the twentieth century—a phenomenon aptly called the third wave of democratization—has given new impetus to studying democracy. Scholars began to note the vast diversity of the proclaimed democratic regimes around the globe.[6] Liberal Democracy had become a key element in political discourse (though often not in practice).[7] Careful scholars began to note severe problems with the new democracies. From a global comparative perspective, scholars pointed out that the dichotomy of "democratic" versus "nondemocratic" does not hold. Instead, a regime continuum exists in which the two extremes are authoritarian/totalitarian and fully democratic regimes.[8] Therefore, assuming a minimal definition of democracy, scholars now talk about different degrees of democracy.

This book brings language policy considerations into discussions of the quality of democracy. A particular dimension examined in this book is the notion of diglossic language policy, the combination of language ideologies, practices, and institutions that construct and maintain a hierarchy of languages in a given society. Democracy is often hailed as the best regime to protect and even strengthen the catalog of human rights. Current scholarship points to the fact that one of the pillars of these human rights, the linguistic pillar, often goes unprotected. Linguistic human rights are "the right to learn the mother tongue, including at least basic education through the medium of the mother tongue and the rights to use in many of the (official) contexts."[9] The keyword of the definition is "mother tongue," the language that one acquires without going through the formal education process. These rights are highlighted to significantly impact the process of changing the current language policy by calling attention to some languages that, while they serve as the primary communicative means to many, are not part of the set of formal and official functions and roles. A lack of linguistic human rights negatively affects the overall quality of democracy. Deprivation in linguistic human rights ultimately results in a considerable reduction in the enjoyment of other human rights, such as fair trial and fair political representation.[10]

There is also another way of looking at the paths through which diglossic language policy negatively impacts the quality of democracy. This book points out that the diglossic language policy creates an artificial linguistic hierarchy in which the mother tongues are placed at the bottom. Despite being the primary linguistic device for everyday interactions, the mother tongue is seldom used in formal and official roles and functions. Postcolonial thinkers and critics have pointed out the damaging impact of postcolonial language policies on citizens' psychology, which facilitates their increasing depoliticization. As mentioned above, radical thinkers, such as Franz Fanon and Ngugi wa Thiong'o, are very critical of the post-colonial reliance on the language of the former colonial power.[11] To these writers, decolonization without its linguistic component invites neo-colonialism, a novel but common and pernicious form of external domination.

Moreover, continuous reliance on a foreign language reinforces the alien culture as the primary reference and standard, against which all must be compared. Indigenous political institutions cannot gain tangible political and social value, for they are constructed and disseminated in the local languages. A language policy that maintains and even emphasizes the continuous and sole reliance on a foreign language, such as English, French, or Portuguese, is equivalent to a Trojan horse within the post-colonial society. This state of affairs, as such, perpetuates the condition of exploitation and domination through cultural neo-colonial links. Following the insights of these radical thinkers, Donaldo Macedo writes that, concerning Cabo Verde, the use of the Portuguese language as the only medium of education in the post-colonial era brings the "danger of creating a distorted consciousness."[12] Politics can be best exercised in the vernacular, for the psychological costs are kept at a minimum.

This book additionally discussed the impact of diglossic language policy on political participation. Contemporary democratic institutions nurture their representative component, often at the expense of the participatory elements. Political representation, the mechanism through which the many supposedly find a voice in a few, ultimately works against the many. Some political theorists have long called attention to the inherent flaws of representation. Jean Jacques Rousseau, for instance, writing centuries ago, claimed that sovereignty, popular in nature, cannot be delegated.[13] Two centuries later, Robert Michaels contends that according to the "iron law of oligarchy," the representatives tend to promote their interests at the expense of the represented.[14] Contemporary scholars like Nadia Urbinati and Mark E. Warren consider political representation in modern democracies to have been clouded by the "growing complexity of issues, which increasingly strains the power of representative agents, and thus their capacity to stand for and act on the interests of those they represent."[15] Given the new social and political reality, the value and effectiveness of political representation have fallen drastically. I noted in the introduction of this book that ordinary citizens have increased feelings of distrust toward their representatives. Representative democracy is failing in its most basic, essential, and fundamental feature: representation.

Present-day democratic institutions overemphasize representation. Representative democracy in Cabo Verde focuses on voting. Citizens are called to choose who gets to form the government every four years. The voter is expected to leave the political representatives alone between elections. The representatives know what is best for the citizens. Thus, in the process of public policymaking and implementation, the citizens are not to interfere, for they have already delegated power. Because of these, citizens are made into passive recipients of policy. They do not effectively take part in the policy debate.

One of the main arguments this book has developed is that diglossic language policy fundamentally sustains the system of representative democracy while simultaneously limiting the extension of participatory elements. Diglossic language policy, as noted throughout this book, creates a linguistic hierarchy between a dominant language and other languages. In the case of Cabo Verde, the case study of this book, such a language policy has effectively maintained the predominance of the Portuguese language at the expense of the local language, the Cabo Verdean language—even though the population widely uses this language. Diglossic language policy fundamentally limits two primary forms of political participation: initiatory and surveillatory.

The state, inherited from colonialism, was founded on and developed through the medium of the colonial power's language and not in the mother tongue of the subject population. This means that the state, colonial and its post-colonial offspring, is fundamentally encrypted: the language of political communication used within and by the state is not entirely grasped by ordinary citizens. Such a state of affairs provides a competitive advantage to the post-colonial elite, who have become the linguistic decoder of the state. Language policy, as noted above, has become a means to "elite closure."[16]

Diglossic language policy curtails citizens' surveillatory participation. As described in chapter 6, this form of political participation is fundamentally about supervision and demands of accountability to the state and its agents. State literacy, understanding how the state should and does act, is a significant precondition for active involvement in the surveillance of the state, its institutions, and its personnel. This should not be taken as if those without knowledge of the state do not participate in politics. One of the key points of this book is that certain forms of political participation may be difficult for a subsection of the population, given their lack of state literacy. Political participation is multidimensional. The focus of the thesis is on non-contentious forms of political participation. These include participation in the public debate, whether in person or in writing, contacting the political and state officials at the local and central levels to resolve a political problem, and demanding accountability for the actions (and lack thereof) of those in positions of authority.

Political debate within the elite and among the elite and the general population is essential to a democratic regime. After all, political debate is directly correlated to one of the most fundamental rights and principles of democracy: freedom of speech and rule by consensus. It is possible to reach a policy consensus that serves the interests of all—or a sizeable majority through public debate. Deliberation, discussion, debate, and argumentation are the fundamental mechanisms through which consensus is manufactured, and actions are taken. In this aspect, Jürgen Habermas talks about communicative action to describe how political actions may be the outcome of the communicative process of the interested.[17]

The elite uses many linguistic strategies to avoid, control, manipulate, or even terminate a political debate with the general population. Strategies may include upward code-switching (from Cabo Verdean to Portuguese) and the employment of esoteric language and metaphors. Opinion articles written in the local newspapers are self-referential and crafted for a limited audience: the cultural and sociopolitical elite. This form of political communication is not about conveying an idea that many readers can quickly grasp—fostering further debate on the subject—but rather an opportunity for the author to show their mastery of esoteric Portuguese. There is a fixation on less common vocabulary ("difficult words," as put by one of my informants), as the evaluation by the writer's peers is often on the form instead of the content of the message.

One way to limit the number of participants in the public debate is to start and maintain public debate in high language, a medium in which most citizens lack complete competence. This situation results from two main aims: first, to keep some people from even attempting to enter the debate, as they do not possess the necessary linguistic skills to understand the content of the debate. Second, while others may understand some or even most of the content of the debate, they may find it intimidating to participate when faced with those who are perceived to have mastered the dominant language. There is, as such, a psychological mechanism of withdrawal.

Public political debate is limited through the application of a strategy of code-switching. Code-switching is the alteration of the linguistic medium used by a given agent. Code-switching may be downward, from the dominant language to a subaltern one. I mentioned earlier that the political elite sometimes uses this strategy to emphasize their purported belonging to the masses. As mentioned earlier, this refers to Bourdieu's concept of the *strategy of condescension*, the use of the vernacular as a populist tool by the political elite.[18]

The other side of the code-switching strategy, which has far more political consequences, is the upward switch from the low to the dominant language. This strategy is a powerful weapon employed by the elite to silence the general masses. It creates and sustains a linguistic fortress whose entrance is limited to those proficient in the superstrate language. Upward code-switching is essentially about conveying political symbolism, namely that of social authority. By switching to a language of prestige and authority, the dominant social position of the speaker is emphasized—for the high language is, in itself, a mark of social distinction and status. The emphasis on social authority can thus be a means of silencing the audience or the other debating party, who may not be proficient in the high language. When conducted in the dominant language, public political debate is not extensive to a large part of the population, alienated and silenced.

Social practices, attitudes, beliefs, and behaviors (language practices and ideology) inform and often determine who gets to speak. The legitimacy to speak—and to be heard—is often linked to the language used as the means. The use of low language to participate in politics may result in the speaker being "inaudible"—not in the sense that the audience may not discern the words coming out of their mouth, but in the sense that the audience may not find the message pertinent, for the carrier is socially perceived as irrelevant. The subaltern thus can't speak. Their voice is not heard, neither in the official domain nor in the sphere of the mass media—except perhaps for brief periods.

Like its colonial counterparts, the post-colonial state in Cabo Verde (as in sub-Saharan Africa generally) has focused on establishing authority. Language policy—and linguistic practices carried out by the elite—constitutes viable mechanisms of authority enforcement. For this reason, one can extend to Cabo Verde Bourdieu's argument that post-revolutionary France's policy of linguistic unification was fundamentally about the imposition of authority and less about communication.[19]

I have chosen Cabo Verde as the case study for my analysis of the quality of democracy because of the amount of praise the country gets from international media, policy circles, foreign diplomats, and politicians. I have indicated throughout the book that, according to the scores provided by the index developed by the Freedom House, or even European and North American policymakers, the country is doing exceptionally well regarding the quality of democracy. A profound analysis of the political institutions and modes of political behavior—with a clear focus on active and engaging political participation beyond voting—indicates that things are not as rosy as they seem. Effective and real democracy is about citizens' participation in all aspects of political life, from selecting officials to making and implementing policies. A political regime that limits—or even hinders—its citizens' ability and willingness to participate in the political debate and/ or adequately supervise the actions taken on their behalf is far from being a participatory democracy. The institutions may seem democratic because robust mechanisms of checks and balances exist. Yet, these institutions are not a guarantee of participatory democracy because the checks and balances are internal and performed horizontally by other institutions, not the people. Most of the general population may not participate in the state's surveillance process.

Ordinary Cabo Verdeans do not fully exercise initiatory and surveillatory participation. Despite the inroads of the Cabo Verdean language into the public sphere, the Portuguese language still enjoys the predominant status. Political—and fundamentally public policy—life is far from being in the vernacular. Data from several rounds of Afrobarometer surveys indicate such a trend. Whether nominated or elected, state officials rarely engage in political contact with ordinary citizens. The contact between the two is limited to two main events: mass meetings during electoral periods and inaugurating ceremonials of public works. In these two cases, communication is one-sided, from the officials to the citizens. This form of engagement does not allow for questioning on the part of the ordinary citizen.

At the same time, the Afrobarometer surveys indicate that a sizeable portion of the society, chiefly in the rural areas, are not interested in politics nor engaged in debates or discussions within their circles of friends, family, and neighbors. Information about the state and its agents is disseminated mainly through written vehicles in Portuguese. Robert Dahl argues that an enlightened understanding of politics is a significant precondition to effective and engaging citizenship. Not having sufficient knowledge about operations, procedures, and power processes limits the participants, public debate, and discussion content.

The last point I want to emphasize and criticize is the direct correlation between size and democracy. Several thinkers and scholars have argued that small states tend to be democratic or, at least, experience more democracy than large states. This argument can be found in the writings of classical and modern thinkers, including Aristotle, Plato, Montesquieu, and Rousseau, and among contemporary empirical social scientists such as Larry Diamond and Dag Anckar.[20] Diamond's 1999 study found that small states are more likely to be democratic than larger countries. According to this line of argument, small states foster democratic practices because smallness

enhances the opportunities for participation in and control of the government . . . made it possible for every citizen to know every other, to estimate his qualities, to understand his problems, to develop friendly feelings towards him, to analyze and discuss with comprehension the problems facing the polity.[21]

These scholars and thinkers have neglected a decisive variable, namely language policy. Classical and modern thinkers did not need to bother with the language policy question as they focused on small, ethnically, and linguistically homogenous territories. Contemporary empirical scholars, whose studies follow the large-N comparative approach, frequently neglect that many micro-states are post-colonial states, where a linguistic hierarchy has been fostered since colonial times. Where geography works toward approximation and shortening distance between social and political actors, language effectively creates a social divide that hinders full and engaging political participation by speakers of the socially devalued languages. In terms of political participation, size may not be as significant as the language policy implemented in a given state, either de facto or de jure. The case of Cabo Verde, as analyzed throughout this book, indicates that despite its smallness, a linguistic wall divides the elite and the ordinary citizens, leading to an increased de-politicization of the latter. Effective, real, and participatory democracy can become a fact when politics, in its different phases, is in the vernacular.

TOWARD EFFECTIVE DEMOCRACY

There is an analytical and actual value in thinking about a democratic continuum. The notion that states and polities, in general, can be classified into two major camps, democratic and nondemocratic, is problematic as this classification tends to overlook subtle and understated processes that minimize and curtail ordinary citizens' political participation. Moreover, such a classification methodologically would eventually result in the "conceptual stretching problem," as Giovanni Sartori noted.[22]

Democracy is better thought of in terms of "gradation."[23] The democratic continuum implies using a referential against empirical cases to be compared and contrasted.[24] The democratic referential need not be an actual and existing regime. Instead, it is a mental construction, an ideal type in the Weberian sense, the main characteristic of which is the complete application of the word's etymology: the unlimited and unconstrained rule of the people in all aspects. The closer the regime approximates this democratic referential, the higher its quality.

While the Schumpeterian model of democracy permits and encourages great political enthusiasm at the top, it dictates de-participation during nonelectoral periods.[25] This model of democracy is problematic for the following reasons. First, it creates what can be called "policy paternalism," in which citizens can only indirectly choose the policies to be made and implemented. The choice is made through the election of those who would form the government. Accordingly, a vote for Candidate A or Party A is for the candidate's policy proposals. This political model may ultimately create a the-political-elite-know-better culture nurtured by the elites and the general population.

Second, there is an internal contradiction in the Schumpeterian model. The ordinary citizens are not to participate in the supposedly complex and challenging process of policymaking and implementation and yet are called to discern from several policy packages which best serve the polity's needs. How can they judge policies and be kept out of the loop during their making and implementation?

There is another issue with Schumpeterian democracy: the conditions of the electoral period may not be constant. The candidate party may bring forth a policy package in light of their analysis of the sociopolitical conditions. The policy package that is "voted" by the people may be put aside, radically or minimally changed, and transformed, in time, as a consequence of new conditions. Since these changes occur between electoral periods, citizens are not asked to intervene or provide feedback.

Effective democracy is one in which ordinary citizens genuinely engage in all aspects of political business. Linguistic democratization is the starting point for effective democracy. Ali A. Mazrui and Michael Tidy somehow developed this point. They argued that the diglossic language policy in post-colonial African states ultimately resulted in the political marginalization of the general citizens.[26] Linguistic democratization facilitates political partici-pation by leveling the playing field: minimizing—or, better, eliminating—the practice of reserving influence, power, and authority for a single language at the expense of all other languages spoken by the people. For one, it does matter in what language political participation is.

The leap from a Schumpeterian democracy into a more participatory democracy must include not only institutional reforms but also a remark-able transformation in the linguistic field. Diglossia must be deleted at the level of the state and society if the goal of generalized autonomous political participation is to be attained. Reforming political institutions alone may not necessarily lead to greater political participation. For instance, the introduc-tion of mechanisms of direct democracy, such as public hearings or town hall meetings, would not stir participation in the debates if those reforms were not accompanied by a new way of thinking and acting upon the languages used in the community. One can only imagine how the non-speakers of the high language would feel in a public discussion where the primary vehicle is that high language.

A quality democracy implies that the state-citizen relation is a direct one. This relationship, to be straightforward, must eliminate obstacles that invite the intervention of a third party. A diglossic language policy, which creates a linguistic hiatus between the political and social domains, is an example of such an obstacle. Legibility of the state means the state's political and bureaucratic communication should be in a language that the common man and woman easily understand.

The idea of making the state legible—that is, to foster the understanding of its policies, operations, procedures, and processes—is gaining wide acceptance among policymakers and the intellectual community. It is important to note two examples. Legal scholars across the globe have created an international nongovernmental organization (Clarity International) whose main objective is the replacement of legalese with "plain language."[27] On October 13, 2010, US president Obama signed the Plain Writing Act of 2010. The main objective of this law is to make the state and its agencies easily readable to its citizens. The law requires that federal agencies use *"clear Government communication that the public can understand and use."*[28] To be a state literate—capable of minimally understanding its procedures, processes, and operations—is an invitation to participate in its supervision.

There is a political value in fostering ordinary citizens' political participation. Tom Lodge points out four main advantages of participatory democracy over other political regimes. First, he notes that it brings more efficient government; then, he notes that more participation by the citizens is translated into a law-abiding citizenry, for there is a stronger inclination to respect the decisions that one has somehow taken part in making; third, more participation, as it brings more knowledge about the system, brings far more "sophisticated and knowledgeable decisions." Lastly, political participation has a psychological value insofar as it increases one's self-esteem and the perception of political worthiness.[29] Citizens' engagement and involvement in politics bring in double developments at the individual and societal levels. From the point of view of the individual, more participation can be translated into accumulated knowledge and practice of partaking in community political affairs. The more individuals know about the operations and procedures of political agents and institutions, the more they are inclined to use different mechanisms of political participation. More participation, therefore, breeds further participation. A case can be made that the more individuals autonomously partake in the polity's political affairs, the more they will be inclined to use and take advantage of other mechanisms and instruments of political participation.

To conclude, the heart of democracy is the ordinary citizens' political participation in different aspects and levels. Their "occupation" of the public sphere and political institutions ultimately makes the regime more efficient and more responsive to their demands and of higher quality. Since politics is rarely a silent activity, language is generally the core of political participation. Social and political importance given to one language eventually impacts its speakers.

BEYOND CABO VERDE: LANGUAGE-POLITICS
NEXUS IN THE CREOLE ISLAND STATES

This book has critically analyzed the language-politics nexus in Cabo Verde. Many Creole island states in Africa and the Caribbean have similar sociolinguistic situations as Cabo Verde. In most of these sovereign Creole island states, there is a growing sociopolitical movement to make their respective Creole the official language. Like Cabo Verde, these Creole island states face similar challenges, mainly linguistic hegemony from a European language (French in Haiti, English in Jamaica). In contrast, the Creole language, though used throughout the polity, has suffered since colonial times from debasement and disparagement. To this day, it is not uncommon to read op-ed articles in newspapers in places like Jamaica, Haiti, or any other Creole island state that argue against the promotion of the Creole languages in areas of formality, such as public administration or school, as we saw in the case of Cabo Verde.[30] Common views that can still be heard and read include notions that the Creole language is not a language but a broken language—a non-language derivative of English, French, or Portuguese.[31]

Like in the case of Cabo Verde, anti-Creole bias is part of these societies. With few exceptions, de jure and de facto language policy in Creole island states tend to reproduce old colonial inequalities and social injustice. Through its operations, procedures, and processes, the state is illegible to a significant percentage of the population, who can't reasonably perform in high languages, such as French or English. The state's daily re-constitution through its institutional memory occurs through the medium of these languages inherited from colonialism. Competence in these languages derives almost exclusively from years of formal schooling, a condition many families cannot meet. At the same time, knowledge of the Creole language is still informed by the idea of constituting a problem, inhibiting its speakers from grasping the dominant language properly.[32]

Across the creolophone world, a new orientation in language planning seems to be developing, language-as-right, championed by language scholars and intellectuals. Creolists from the Caribbean have played historical roles in defending, promoting, and eliminating anti-Creole language ideologies.[33] Informed by the new approach to the minority language, many are pushing for Creole linguistic human rights, that is, an inherent right to the individual to use this language in every aspect of social life, including, and perhaps more importantly, formal schooling. In many ways, this orientation (language as a right) opposes the orientation of language as a problem, which has a long history dating back to the colonial period. The constitutions of Creole island states have been relatively shy regarding Creole language rights, with these supreme laws supporting the linguistic hegemony of lexifiers such as English, French, or Portuguese.

As in the case of Cabo Verde, Creole speakers in the Creole island state are relegated to a position of second-class citizenship. National debates, including public policymaking, happen in the dominant language, which excludes these citizens. The inability to speak the dominant language becomes a forced exit from politics.[34] Where electoral democracy exists, these citizens are sometimes invited to cast votes, but the extent of political participation is reduced to this activity. In between elections, creolophone speakers are unlikely to shape or form the contours of politics in their homeland.

NOTES

1. Chelmicki and Varnhagen, *Corografia Cabo-Verdiana.*

2. Carreira, *Cabo Verde.*

3. Castelo, *O modo portugues.*

4. Abel Djassi Amado, "Língua, Modernidade e Libertação: A Linguística Política de Amílcar Cabral," *Desafios* (2014): 85–109; Fanon, *Black Skin, White Masks.*

5. Almada, *Bilinguismo ou diglossia?*

6. Guillermo O'Donnell, "Delegative Democracy," *Journal of Democracy* 5, no. 1 (1994): 55–69; Fareed Zakaria, *The Future of Freedom: Illiberal Democracy at Home and Abroad* (New York: W.W. Norton & Co., 2004); Adrian Leftwich, "Governance, Democracy and Development in the Third World," *Third World Quarterly* 14 (1993): 605–24; Guillermo A. O'Donnell and Philippe C. Schmitter, *Transitions from Authoritarian Rule. Tentative Conclusions about Uncertain Democracies* (Baltimore: Johns Hopkins University Press, 2013); David Collier and Steven Levitsky, "Research Note: Democracy with Adjectives: Conceptual Innovation in Comparative Research | WorldCat.Org," *World Politics* 49, no. 3 (1997): 430–51.

7. World Bank, *Sub-Saharan Africa: From Crisis to Sustainable Growth: Along-Term Perspective Study | WorldCat.Org* (Washington, DC: World Bank, 1989), https://www.worldcat.org/title/Sub-Saharan-Africa-:-from-crisis-to-sustainable-growth-:-along-term-perspective-study/oclc/654858099.

8. Juan J. Linz and Alfred C. Stepan, *Problems of Democratic Transition and Consolidation: Southern Europe, South America, and Post-Communist Europe* (Baltimore: Johns Hopkins University Press, 1996), 38.

9. Tove Skutnabb-Kangas, Robert Phillipson, and Mart Rannut, "Introduction," in *Linguistic Human Rights: Overcoming Linguistic Discrimination*, ed. ove Skutnabb-Kangas, Robert Phillipson, and Mart Rannut (Berlin: Mouton de Gruyter, 1994), 2.

10. Skutnabb-Kangas, Phillipson, and Rannut.

11. Fanon, *Black Skin, White Masks*; Ngugi wa Thiong'o, *Decolonizing the Mind: The Politics of Language in Africa* (London: J. Currey, 1986).

12. Macedo, "Cape Verdean Language Project: Final Report," 114.

13. Nadia Urbinati and Mark E. Warren, "The Concept of Representation in Contemporary Democratic Theory," *Annual Review of Political Science* 11, no. 1 (June 1, 2008): 391.

14. Seymour Martin Lipset, *Revolution and Counter-Revolution: The United States and Canada*, Comparative/International Series, Reprint No. 193 (Berkely, CA: University of California, Insititute of International Studies, 1966).

15. Urbinati and Warren, "The Concept of Representation in Contemporary Democratic Theory," 390.

16. Myers-Scotton, "Elite Closure."

17. Habermas and McCarthy, *The Theory of Communicative Action.*

18. Bourdieu, *Language and Symbolic Power*, 68.

19. Bourdieu, 45–49.

20. Dahl and Tufte, *Size and Democracy*; Larry Jay Diamond, *Developing Democracy: Toward Consolidation* (Baltimore: Johns Hopkins University Press, 1999); Dag Anckar, "Why Are Small Island States Democracies?," *The Round Table* 91, no. 365 (July 2002): 375–90, https://doi.org/10.1080/0035853022000010344; Carsten Anckar, "Size, Islandness, and Democracy: A Global Comparison," *International Political Science Review / Revue Internationale de Science Politique* 29 (2008): 433–59.

21. Robert Dahl and Edward Tufte cited in Henry Srebrnik, "Small Island Nations and Democratic Values," *World Development* 32, no. 2 (2004): 329 (italics added).

22. Giovanni Sartori, "Concept Misformation in Comparative Politics," *The American Political Science Review* 64, no. 4 (n.d.): 1033–53; Collier and Levitsky, "Research Note."

23. Zachary Elkins, "Gradations of Democracy? Empirical Tests of Alternative Conceptualizations," *American Journal of Political Science* 44, no. 2 (2000): 293–300.

24. Dahl, *Polyarchy.*

25. Schumpteter and Swedberg, *Capitalism, Socialism and Democracy*; Huntington, *The Third Wave*; Adam Przeworski, *Democracy and Development: Political Institutions and Well-Being in the World, 1950–1990*, Cambridge Studies in the Theory of Democracy (Cambridge: Cambridge University Press, 2000).

26. Ali Al'Amin Mazrui and Michael Tidy, *Nationalism and New States in Africa from about 1935 to the Present* (Nairobi: Heinemann, 1985), 299 ff.

27. Clarity, accessed July 22, 2022, https://www.clarity-international.org/plain-legal-language/.

28. "Plain Writing Act, Law 111-274" (2010), http://www.gpo.gov/fdsys/pkg/PLAW-111publ274/pdf/PLAW-111publ274.pdf.

29. Tom Lodge, *South Africa: Democracy and Political Participation: A Discussion Paper* (Newlands, South Africa: Open Society Foundation for South Africa, 2006), 64; Macartan Humphreys, William A. Masters, and Martin E. Sandbu, "The Role of Leaders in Democratic Deliberations: Results from a Field Experiment in São Tomé and Príncipe," *World Politics* 58 (2006): 583–622.

30. Celia Brown-Blake, "The Right to Linguistic Non-Discrimination and Creole Language Situations: The Case of Jamaica," *Journal of Pidgin and Creole Languages* 23, no. 1 (April 25, 2008): 32–73, https://doi.org/10.1075/jpcl.23.1.03bro; Beverley Bryan, "Language and Literacy in a Creole-Speaking Environment: A Study of Primary Schools in Jamaica," *Language, Culture and Curriculum* 17, no. 2 (June 2004): 87–96, https://doi.org/10.1080/07908310408666685; Benjamin Hebblethwaite, "French and Underdevelopment, Haitian Creole and Development: Educational Language Policy Problems and Solutions in Haiti," *Journal of Pidgin and Creole Languages* 27, no. 2 (August 28, 2012): 255–302, https://doi.org/10.1075/jpcl.27.2.03heb.

31. Silvia Kouwenberg et al., "Linguistics in the Caribbean: Empowerment through Creole Language Awareness," *Journal of Pidgin and Creole Languages* 26, no. 2 (August 16, 2011): 387–403, https://doi.org/10.1075/jpcl.26.2.06kou; Arthur K. Spears, "Introduction: The Haitian Creole Language," in *The Haitian Creole Language: History, Structure, Use, and Education*, ed. Arthur K. Spears and Carole M. Berotte Joseph (Lanham, MD: Lexington Books, 2010).

32. Richard Ruiz, "Orientations in Language Planning," *NABE: The Journal for the National Association for Bilingual Education* 8, no. 2 (1984): 15–34.

33. Devonish, *Language and Liberation*.

34. Hirschman, *Exit, Voice, and Loyalty*.

Bibliography

Abdenur, Adriana Erthal. "Brazil-Africa Relations: From Boom to Bust?" In *Africa and the World: Bilateral and Multilateral International Diplomacy*, edited by Dawn Nagar and Charles Mutasa, 189–208. London: Palgrave Macmillan, 2018.

"A Distinção Entre Língua e Díalecto Tem Uma Base Política." *Voz de Povo*. May 13, 1976.

Afrobarometer. "Cabo Verde Round 8 Resumo Dos Resultados, 2019." 2021. https://www.afrobarometer.org/publication/cabo-verde-round-8-resumo-dos-resultados/.

Almada, José Luis Hopffer. "Ainda Sobre o Crioulo e Os Seus Apaixonados." *Voz Di Povo*, May 7, 1986.

Almada, Maria Dulce de. *Bilinguismo ou Diglossia? As Relações de Força entre o Crioulo e o Português na Sociedade Cabo-Verdiana: Ensaios*. Praia, Cabo Verde: Spleen, 1998.

Almeida, Raymond A. *Cape Verdeans in America: Our Story*. Boston, MA: The American Committee for Cape Verde, 1978.

Amado, Abel Djassi. "Languages of Power and Cabo Verde's 2016 Elections." September 20, 2016. https://politicalmatter.org/2016/09/20/languages-of-power-and-cabo-verdes-2016-elections-by-abel-djassi-amado/.

———. "Língua, Modernidade e Libertação: A Linguística Política de Amílcar Cabral." *Desafios* (2014): 85–109.

———. "Parliamentary Elections Under Covid-19: The Case of Cabo Verde Case Study." October 26, 2021. http://democracyinafrica.org/elections-in-a-pandemic-the-case-of-cabo-verde/.

———. "Whose Independence? Cabo Verdean-Americans and the Politics of National Independence of Cabo Verde (1972–1976)." *Journal of Cape Verdean Studies* 5, no. 1 (2020): 36–53.

Ammon, Ulrich. "Language-Spread Policy." *Language Problems and Language Planning* 21, no. 1 (1997): 51–57.

Anckar, Carsten. "Size, Islandness, and Democracy: A Global Comparison." *International Political Science Review / Revue Internationale de Science Politique* 29 (n.d.): 433.

Anckar, Dag. "Small Is Democratic, But Who Is Small?" *Arts and Social Sciences Journal* 1, no. 1 (2013): 1–10.

———. "Why Are Small Island States Democracies?" *The Round Table* 91, no. 365 (July 2002): 375–90. https://doi.org/10.1080/0035853022000010344.

Anderson, Benedict. *Imagined Communities: Reflections on the Origin and Spread of Nationalism*. New York: Verso, 1991.

Animashaun, M. A. "State Failure, Crisis of Governance and Disengagement from the State in Africa." *Africa Development* 34, no. 3–4 (2009): 47–63.

Anjos, Jose Carlos Gomes dos. *Intelectuais, Literatura e Poder em Cabo Verde: Lutas de Definiçao da Identidade Nacional*. Porto Alegre: UFRGS Editora, 2006.

Anku, Amaka, and Tochi Eni-Kalu. "Africa's Slums Aren't Harbingers of Anarchy— They're Engines of Democracy: The Upside of Rapid Urbanization." *Foreign Affairs*, December 16, 2019. https://www.foreignaffairs.com/africa/africas-slums -arent-harbingers-anarchy-theyre-engines-democracy.

Anteby-Yemini, Lisa, and William Berthomière. "Diaspora: A Look Back on a Concept." *Bulletin Du Centre de Recherche Français à Jérusalem* 16 (2005): 262–70.

Arenas, Fernando. *Lusophone Africa: Beyond Independence*. Minneapolis, MN: University of Minnesota Press, 2011.

Armelle Enders. "Le Lusotropicalisme, Théorie d'exportation: Gilberto Freyre En Son Pays." *Lusotopie* (1997): 201–10.

A Semana, "Donaldo Macedo: 'A Nossa Língua é Viável Como Instrumento Pedagogico.'" December 10, 2005. http://www.asemana.publ.cv/spip.php?article14036 &var_recherche=Procurar&ak=1.

A Semana, "Novo Ministro Cultura Aposta No Crioulo." Outubro 2004.

A Semana. "Oficializar o Crioulo? Porque a Pressa?" April 24, 2009.

Ashcroft, Bill, Gareth Griffiths, and Helen Tiffin. *Postcolonial Studies: The Key Concepts*. London: Routledge, 2013.

Assembleia Nacional de Cabo Verde. "Atas Da Assembleia Nacional de Cabo Verde." July 20, 1999.

Austin, Gareth. "National Poverty and the 'Vampire State' in Ghana: A Review Article." *Journal of International Development: Policy, Economics and International Relations* 8, no. 4 (1996): 553–73.

Azarya, Victor. "Reordering State-Society Relations: Incorporation and Disengagement." In *The Precarious Balance: State and Society in Africa*, edited by Donald Rothchild and Naomi Chazan. New York: Routledge, 1988.

Baker, Bruce. "Cape Verde: Marketing Good Governance." *Afrika Spectrum* 44, no. 2 (2009): 135–47.

———. "Cape Verde: The Most Democratic Nation in Africa?" *Journal of Modern African Studies* 44, no. 4 (2006): 493–511.

Bamgbose, Ayo. *Language and Exclusion: The Consequences of Language Policies in Africa*. Piscataway, NJ: Transaction Publishers, 2000.

Baptista, Marlyse. *The Syntax of Cape Verdean Creole: The Sotavento Varieties*. Linguistik Aktuell. Amsterdam: John Benjamins Pub., 2002.

Baptista, Marlyse, Inês Brito, and Saídu Bangura. "Cape Verdean Creole in Education: A Linguistic and Human Right." In *Creoles and Education*, edited by Bettina Migge, Isabelle Léglise, and Angela Bartens, 273–96. Amsterdam/Philadelphia: John Benjamins Pub., 2010.

Baptista, Marlyse, Manuel Veiga, Sérgio Costa, and Lígia Herbert Robalo. "Language Contact in Cape Verdean Creole: A Study of Bidirectional Influences in Two Contact Settings." In *Oxford Handbook of Language Contact*, edited by Anthony Grant, 713–40. Oxford: Oxford University Press, 2019.

Barber, Benjamin R. *Strong Democracy: Participatory Politics for a New Age.* Berkeley: University of California Press, 2009.

Batalha, Luís, and Jørgen Carling, eds. *Transnational Archipelago: Perspectives on Cape Verdean Migration and Diaspora.* Amsterdam: Amsterdam University Press, 2008.

Baxter, Alan N. "Portuguese as a Pluricentric Language." In *Pluricentric Languages: Differing Norms in Different Nations*, edited by Michael Clyne, 11–44. Berlin: Mouton de Gruyter, 1992.

Bayart, Jean-François. "Africa in the World: A History of Extraversion." *African Affairs* 99, no. 395 (2000): 217–67.

———. *The State in Africa: The Politics of the Belly.* Cambridge: Polity, 2009.

Bayart, Jean-François, Stephen Ellis, and Béatrice Hibou. *The Criminalization of the State in Africa.* Oxford: James Currey, 2001.

Benoni, Daniel. "O Crioulo, Língua Oficial Porque? Par Que?" *Voz Di Povo*, 1986.

Benwell, Bethan, and Elizabeth Stokoe. *Discourse and Identity.* Edinburgh: Edinburgh University Press, 2014.

Bermel, Neil. *Linguistic Authority, Language Ideology, and Metaphor: The Czech Orthography Wars.* New York: Mouton de Gruyter, 2007.

Bherer, Laurence, Pascale Dufour, and Françoise Montambeault. "The Participatory Democracy Turn: An Introduction." In *The Participatory Democracy Turn*, edited by Laurence Bherer, Pascale Dufour, and Francoise Montambeault, 1–6. London: Routledge, 2018.

Bickerton, Derek. *Dynamics of a Creole System.* London: Cambridge University Press, 1975.

Billig, Michael. *Banal Nationalism.* London: Sage, 1995.

Blommaert, Jan. *Language Ideological Debates.* New York: Mouton de Gruyter, 1999.

Blouet, Olwyn M. *The Contemporary Caribbean: History, Life and Culture Since 1945.* London: Reaktion, 2007.

Bondoso, António. *Lusofonia e CPLP: desafios na globalização : "ângulos e vértices" ou "defeitos & virtudes" de um processo intemporal.* Moimenta da Beira: Edições Esgotadas, 2013.

Borges, Sónia Vaz. *Militant Education, Liberation Struggle, Consciousness: The PAIGC Education in Guinea Bissau 1963–1978.* New York: Peter Lang, 2019.

Bourdieu, Pierre. *Language and Symbolic Power.* Cambridge: Polity Press, 2011.

Brann, Conrad M. B. "The National Language Question: Concepts and Terminologies." *Logos. Anales Del Seminario de Metafísica* 14 (1994): 125–34.

Bratton, Michael, and N. Van de Walle. "Neopatrimonial Regimes and Political Transitions in Africa." *World Politics (Print)* 46, no. 4 (1994): 453–89.

Brito, Kimze. "Cartazes Da Campanha Eleitoral Em Cabo Verde Retirados Pela Junta de Freguesia de Agualva e Mira-Sintra." April 15, 2021. https://mindelinsite.com/atualidade/cartazes-da-campanha-eleitoral-em-cabo-verde-retirados-pela-junta-de-freguesia-de-agualva-e-mira-sintra/.

Brooks, Georges E. *Western Africa and Cabo Verde, 1790s–1830s: Symbiosis of Slave and Legitimate Trades.* Bloomington, IN: Authorhouse, 2010.

Brown-Blake, Celia. "The Right to Linguistic Non-Discrimination and Creole Language Situations: The Case of Jamaica." *Journal of Pidgin and Creole Languages* 23, no. 1 (April 25, 2008): 32–73. https://doi.org/10.1075/jpcl.23.1.03bro.

Bruthiaux, Paul. "Language Rights in Historical and Contemporary Perspective." *Journal of Multilingual and Multicultural Development* 30, no. 1 (2009): 73–85.

Brutt-Griffler, Janina. *World English: A Study of Its Development.* Clevedon: Multilingual Matters, 2004.

Bryan, Beverley. "Language and Literacy in a Creole-Speaking Environment: A Study of Primary Schools in Jamaica." *Language, Culture and Curriculum* 17, no. 2 (June 2004): 87–96. https://doi.org/10.1080/07908310408666685.

Cabral, Amílcar. *Analise De Alguns Tipos De Resistencia.* Lisboa: Seara Nova, 1975.

———. *Cabo verde reflexoes e mensagens.* Praia: Fundação Amílcar Cabral, 2015.

———. *Our People Are Our Mountains: Amilcar Cabral on the Guinean Revolution.* London: Committee for Freedom in Mozambique, Angola and Guiné, 1973.

Caetano, Marcelo. *Tradiçoes, Principios e Métodos da Colonização Portuguesa.* Lisboa: Agencia Geral do Ultramar, 1951.

Calvet, Louis-Jean. "Géopolitique Des Langues Romanes." *Hermès, La Revue* 75, no. 2 (2016): 25–33.

———. *Linguistique et Colonialisme: Petit Traité de Glottophagie.* Paris: Payot, 1974.

———. *Towards an Ecology of World Languages.* Cambridge: Polity, 2006.

Cameron, Deborah. "Ideology and Language." *Journal of Political Ideologies* 11, no. 2 (2006): 141–52.

Camões, I. P. "Acordo Cultural Entre Portugal e Cabo Verde – Acordo Geral de Cooperação e Amizade of January 27, 1976." Https://www.instituto-camoes.pt/component/content/article?id=14690:acordo-cabo-verde, n.d.

———. "Estatísticas Da Ajuda Pública Ao Desenvolvimento (APD)." Accessed August 1, 2022. https://www.instituto-camoes.pt/activity/o-que-fazemos/cooperacao/atuacao/reportamos/reportamos-2.

Capeverdean Creole Institute. "CAPEVERDEAN CREOLE INSTITUTE." *Capeverdean Creole Institute* (blog). Accessed July 5, 2022. http://www.capeverdeancreoleinstitute.org/.

Capoccia, Giovanni, and R. Daniel Kelemen. "The Study of Critical Junctures: Theory, Narrative, and Counterfactuals in Historical Institutionalism." *World Politics* 59, no. 3 (2007): 341–69.

Cardoso, Ana Josefa. "As Interferências Linguísticas Do Caboverdiano No Processo de Aprendizagem Do Português." Masters Thesis, Universidade Aberta, 2005.

———. "Falar Cabo-Verdiano e Português: A Educação Bilingue Em Cabo Verde e Na Diáspora." *Iberografias: Revista de Estudos Ibericos* 15 (2019): 41–52.

Cardoso, Eduardo. "Contribuição Para o Debate Sobre o Estatuto Do Crioulo." *Voz Di Povo*, 1986.

Cardoso, Pedro Monteiro. *Folclore Caboverdiano*. Paris: Solidariedade Caboverdiana, 1983.

Carling, Jørgen, and Lisa Åkesson. "Mobility at the Heart of a Nation: Patterns and Meanings of Cape Verdean Migration." *International Migration* 47, no. 1 (2009): 123–55.

Carneiro, Alan Silvio Ribeiro. "O Programa Leitorado Do Governo Brasileiro: Ideologias Linguísticas e Práticas de Ensino Em Um Contexto Situado." *Línguas e Instrumentos Linguísticos* 43 (June 2019): 259–89. https://doi.org/10.20396/lil .v0i43.8658373.

Carreira, António. *Cabo Verde: Formação e Extinção de Uma Sociedade Escravocrata (1460–1878)*. Lisboa: A. Carreira, 1983.

———. *O Crioulo de Cabo Verde: Surto e Expansão*. Lisboa: Gráfica Europam, 1984.

———. *The People of the Cape Verde Islands: Exploitation and Emigration*. London; Hamden, CT: C. Hurst; Archon Books, 1983.

Carter, Katherine, and Judy Aulette. *Cape Verdean Women and Globalization: The Politics of Gender, Culture, and Resistance*. New York, NY: Palgrave Macmillan, 2009.

Carvalho, Clara. "Africa and Portugal." In *Africa and the World: Bilateral and Multilateral International Diplomacy*, edited by Dawn Nagar and Charles Mutasa, 143–66. London: Palgrave Macmillan, 2018.

Castelo, Claudia. *"O modo portugues de estar no mundo": o luso-tropicalismo e a ideologia colonial portuguesa (1933–1961)*. Porto: Edicoes Afrontamento, 2011.

Cenoz, Jasone, and Durk Gorter. "Linguistic Landscape and Minority Languages." *International Journal of Multilingualism* 3, no. 1 (2006): 67–80.

Chabal, Patrick. *Amílcar Cabral: Revolutionary Leadership and People's War*. Trenton, NJ: Africa World Press, 2003.

Chantre, Ercie. "Artigo 9º: A Situação Linguística Em Cabo Verde." YouTube video, 42:26, February 21, 2022. https://www.youtube.com/watch?v=pevjwn2cbp4&t =1s.

Chelmicki, José Conrado Carlos de, and Francisco Adolfe de Varnhagen. *Corografía Cabo-Verdiana, Ou, Descripção Geographico-Historica Da Provincia Das Ilhas de Cabo-Verde e Guiné*. Lisbon: Typ. de L.C. da Cunha, 1841.

Chilcote, Ronald H. *Emerging Nationalism in Portuguese Africa: A Bibliography of Documentary Ephemera through 1965*. Stanford, CA: Hoover institution on war, revolution and peace Stanford University, 1969.

Chimbutane, Feliciano. "Can Sociocultural Gains Sustain Bilingual Education Programs in Postcolonial Contexts? The Case of Mozambique." In *Bilingual*

Education and Language Policy in the Global South, edited by Jo Arthur Shoba and Feliciano Chimbutane, 167–83. New York: Routledge, 2013.

Cillia, Rudolf de, and Brigitta Busch. "Language Policies: Policies on Language in Europe." In *Encyclopedia of Language and Linguistics*, edited by Keith Brown, 575–83. Amsterdam: Elsevier, 2006.

Citrin, Jack, Amy Lerman, Michael Murakami, and Kathryn Pearson. "Testing Huntington: Is Hispanic Immigration a Threat to American Identity?" *Perspectives on Politics* 5, no. 1 (2007): 31–48.

Clarence-Smith, Gervase. *The Third Portuguese Empire, 1825–1975: A Study in Economic Imperialism*. Manchester: University Press, 1985.

Clarity. "Https://Www.Clarity-International.Org/Plain-Legal-Language/." Accessed July 22, 2022. https://www.clarity-international.org/plain-legal-language/.

Clyne, Michael G. *Pluricentric Languages: Differing Norms in Different Nations*. Berlin: Mouton de Gruyter, 1992. https://www.worldcat.org/title/Pluricentric-languages-:-differing-norms-in-different-nations/oclc/858282330.

Cohen, Ronald Lee. *Global Diasporas: An Introduction*. Seattle, WA: University of Washington Press, 1997.

Collier, David, and Steven Levitsky. "Research Note: Democracy with Adjectives: Conceptual Innovation in Comparative Research | WorldCat.Org." *World Politics* 49, no. 3 (1997): 430–51.

Collier, Ruth Berins, and David Collier. *Shaping the Political Arena: Critical Junctures, the Labor Movement, and Regime Dynamics in Latin America*. Notre Dame: University of Notre Dame Press, 2009.

"Combate Ao Analfabetismo Exigência Do Nosso Partido." *Voz de Povo*. August 14, 1975.

"Comemorações Do 10 de Junho Começam No Domingo Em Portalegre e Terminam Em Cabo Verde." *Observador*. June 8, 2019. https://observador.pt/2019/06/08/comemoracoes-do-10-de-junho-comecam-no-domingo-em-portalegre-e-terminam-em-cabo-verde/.

"Comentário Discurso Do Presidente Aristides Pereira Na ANP." *Voz di Povo*. December 31, 1987.

Conklin, Alice L. *A Mission to Civilize: The Republican Idea of Empire in France and West Africa, 1895–1930*. Stanford, CA: Stanford University Press, 1997.

Cooper, Robert L. *Language Planning and Social Change*. Cambridge: Cambridge University Press, 1990.

———. *Language Spread: Studies in Diffusion and Social Change*. Bloomington, Washington, DC: Indiana University Press ; Center for Applied Linguistics, 1982.

Cooperação portuguesa: uma leitura dos últimos quinze anos de cooperação para o desenvolvimento, 1996–2010. Lisboa: IPAD, 2011.

"Costumes Supersticiosos Nas Ilhas de Cabo Verde." *O Panorama, Jornal Litterario e Instructivo*, 1840.

Coulmas, Florian. "Linguistic Landscaping and the Seed of the Public Sphere." In *Linguistic Landscape: Expanding the Scenery*, edited by Elana Shohamy and Durk Gorter, 13–24. New York: Routledge, 2009.

————. *Writing Systems: An Introduction to Their Linguistic Analysis.* Cambridge Textbooks in Linguistics. Cambridge: Cambridge University Press, 2003. https:// doi.org/10.1017/CBO9781139164597.

CPLP. "ESTATUTOS Dʋ IILP." Accessed August 31, 2022. https://www.cplp.org/ Admin/Public/DWSDownload.aspx?File=%2FFiles%2FFiler%2Fcplp%2FCMNE %2FX_CMNE%2FESTATUTOS_do_IILP.pdf.

————. "Plano Operacional Para a Promoção e Difusão Da Língua Portuguesa (2021–2026)." 2021. https://www.cplp.org/Files/Filer/1_CPLP/Lingua/Livro -Plano-Operacional-Lingua-Portuguesa-vfinal.pdf.

Cruz, Eutrópio Lima da. "No Limiar Do Bilinguismo." In *Cabo Verde 30 Anos de Cultura,* edited by Filinto Correia e Silva, 70–76. Praia: Intituto da Biblioteca Nacional e do Livro, 2005.

Cunliffe, Daniel. "Minority Languages and Social Media." In *The Palgrave Handbook of Minority Languages and Communities,* edited by Gabrielle Hogan-Brun and Bernadette O'Rourke, 451–80. London: Palgrave Macmillian, 2019.

Curran, James. *Media and Democracy.* Communication and Society. Oxford: Routledge, 2011.

Curtain, Gregory G., Michael H. Sommer, and Veronika Vis-Sommer. *The World of E-Government.* New York, NY: Haworth Press, 2004.

Dahl, Robert A. *On Democracy.* New Haven: Yale University Press, 2020.

————. *Polyarchy: Participation and Opposition.* New Haven, CN: Yale University Press, 1978.

————. "The Behavioral Approach in Political Science: Epitaph for a Monument to a Successful Protest." *The American Political Science Review* 55, no. 4 (1961): 763–72.

Dahl, Robert Alan, and Edward Roef Tufte. *Size and Democracy.* Stanford, CA: Stanford University Press, 1975.

Dambarà, Kaoberdiano. *Noti.* Guinea: Edição do Departamento da Informação e Propaganda do Comite Central de Parido Africano da Independência da Guiné e Cabo Verde, 1965.

Delgado, Carlos Alberto. *Crioulos de Base Lexical Portuguesa como Factores de Identidades em África: O Caso de Cabo Verde, Subsídios para uma Abordagem Metodológica.* Praia: Instituto da Biblioteca Nacional e do Livro, 2009.

Delgado, José Pina, Odair Barros Varela, and Suzano Costa, eds. *As Relações Externas de Cabo Verde: (Re)Leituras Contemporâneas.* Praia: Edições ISCJS, 2014.

DeSipio, Louis. "Making Citizens or Good Citizens? Naturalization As a Predictor of Organizational and Electoral Behavior Among Latino Immigrants." *Hispanic Journal of Behavioral Sciences* 18, no. 2 (1996): 194–213.

Detterbeck, Klaus. "Cartel Parties in Western Europe?" *Party Politics* 11, no. 2 (2005): 173–91.

Devonish, Hubert. *Language and Liberation: Creole Language Politics in the Caribbean.* London: Karia Press, 1986.

Dhada, Mustafah. *Warriors at Work: How Guinea Was Really Set Free.* Niwot, CO: University Press of Colorado, 1993.

Diamond, Larry Jay. *Developing Democracy: Toward Consolidation*. Baltimore: Johns Hopkins University Press, 1999. http://www.gbv.de/dms/sub-hamburg /249103761.pdf.

Diamond, Larry, Juan J. Linz, and Seymour Martin Lipset. "Introduction: Comparing Experiences with Democracy." In *Politics in Developing Countries: Comparing Experiences with Democracy*, edited by Larry Diamond, Juan J. Linz, and Seymour Martin Lipset, 1–35. Boulder, CO: L. Rienner Publishers, 1990.

Djité, Paulin G. *The Sociolinguistics of Development in Africa*. Clevedon: Multilingual Matters, 2008.

Do You... Papia Kriolu ? "RENATO SANCHES Ku NELSON SEMEDO TA DA KEL KRIOLU de CABO VERDE." May 15, 2016. https://fb.watch/f2DTjVK49n/.

Dubois, Laurent. *Avengers of the New World: The Story of the Haitian Revolution*. Cambridge, MA: Harvard University Press, 2005.

Duncan, Thomas Bentley, and University of Chicago. *Atlantic Islands; Madeira, the Azores, and the Cape Verdes in Seventeenth-Century Commerce and Navigation*. Chicago: University of Chicago Press, 1972.

Duverger, Maurice. *Political Parties: Their Organization and Activity in the Modern State*. New York: Science Editions, 1993.

Edwards, John. *Language and Identity: An Introduction*. Cambridge: Cambridge University Press, 2013.

Ekeh, Peter P. "Colonialism and the Two Publics in Africa: A Theoretical Statement." *Comparative Studies in Society and History* 17, no. 1 (1975): 91–112.

Elkins, Zachary. "Gradations of Democracy? Empirical Tests of Alternative Conceptualizations." *American Journal of Political Science* 44, no. 2 (2000): 293–300.

Ellis, Andrew, Alan Wall, International Institute for Democracy and Electoral Assistance, and Instituto Federal Electoral (Mexico). *Voting from Abroad: The International IDEA Handbook*. Stockholm: International Institute for Democracy and Electoral Assistance: Instituto Federal Electoral, 2007.

Englebert, Pierre. "The Contemporary African State: Neither African nor State." *Third World Quarterly* 18, no. 4 (1997): 767–75.

Eugénio Tavares: pelos jornais ... 2a Edição. Coleção Os clássicos. Praia, Cabo Verde: Biblioteca Nacional de Cabo Verde, 2017.

Evans, Peter B., Dietrich Rueschemeyer, and Theda Skocpol. *Bringing the State Back In*. New York: Cambridge University Press, 2002.

Évora, Roselma. *Cabo Verde: A Abertura Política e a Transiçao para a Democracia*. Praia: Spleen Edições, 2004.

Faingold, Eduardo D. "Language Rights and Language Justice in the Constitutions of the World." *Language Problems and Language Planning* 28, no. 1 (2004): 11–24.

Fanon, Frantz. *Black Skin, White Masks*. New York: Grove Press, 2017.

———. *The Wretched of the Earth*. New York: Grove Press, 2021.

Faraco, Carlos Alberto. "A Lusofonia: Impasses e Perspectivas." *Sociolinguistic Studies* 5, no. 3 (October 21, 2012): 399–421. https://doi.org/10.1558/sols.v5i3 .399.

Fereira, Manuel. "Comentarios Em Torno Do Bilinguismo Cabo-Verdiano." In *Coloquios Cabo-Verdianos*, 51–80. Lisbon: Junta de Investigações do Ultramar, 1959.

Ferguson, Charles A. "Diglossia." *Word* 15 (1959): 325–40.

Fernandes, Gabriel. *A Diluição da África: Uma Interpretação da Saga Identitária Cabo-verdiana no Panorama Político (Pós)colonial*. Florianópolis: Editora da UFSC, 2002.

Ferreira, Eduardo de Sousa. *Portuguese Colonialism in Africa, the End of an Era ; The Effects of Portuguese Colonialism on Education, Science, Culture and Information*. Paris: Unesco Press, 1974.

Ferreira, Manuel. *A Aventura Crioula*. Lisboa: Plátano, 1985.

Ferreira, Ondina. "Crioulês – o Novo Veículo de Comunicação Dos Quadros." *Expresso Das Ilhas*, 2006.

———. "O Acordo Ortografico Do Nosso Desacordo?" *Expresso Das Ilhas*, April 25, 2008.

Firmino, Gregorio. "Diversidade Linguistica e Nacao-Estado Em Africa: O Caso de Mocambique." *Platô* 1, no. 1 (2012): 43–55.

Firmino, Gregório Domingos. "Ascensão de Uma Norma Endógena Do Português Em Moçambique: Desafios e Perspectivas." *Gragoatá* 26, no. 54 (2021): 163–92. https://doi.org/10.22409/gragoata.v26i54.46324.

Fishman, Joshua A. "Bilingualism with and Without Diglossia; Diglossia with and Without Bilingualism." *Journal of Social Issues* 23 (1967): 29–38.

———. *Language and Nationalism: Two Integrative Essays*. Rowley, MA: Newbury House Publishers, 1996.

Fought, Carmen. *Language and Ethnicity*. Cambridge: Cambridge University Press, 2012.

Fukuyama, Francis. *The End of History and the Last Man*. New York, NY: Free Press, 2006.

Gal, Susan, and Kathryn A. Woolard. "Constructing Languages and Publics Authority and Representation." *Pragmatics* 5, no. 2 (1995): 129–38.

Garcia, Eugênio V. "De Como o Brasil Quase Se Tornou Membro Permanente Do Conselho de Segurança Da ONU Em 1945." *Revista Brasileira de Politica Internacional* 54, no. 1 (2011): 159–77.

Garcia, Eugenio V., and Natalia B. R. Coelho. "A Seat at the Top? A Historical Appraisal of Brazil's Case for the UN Security Council." *SAGE Open*. Accessed August 25, 2022. doi:10.1177/2158244018801098.

García, Ofelia. "Language Spread and Its Study in the 21st Century." In *Oxford Handbook of Applied Linguistics*, edited by Robert Kaplan, 398–411. Oxford: Oxford University Press, 2011.

Geertz, Clifford. *The Interpretation of Cultures: Selected Essays*. New York: Basic Books, 1973.

Gellner, Ernest. *Nationalism*. Washington Square, NY: New York University Press, 1997.

Gerring, John. *Case Study Research: Principles and Practices*. Cambridge: Cambridge University Press, 2019.

Gerschenkron, Alexander. *Economic Backwardness in Historical Perspective: A Book of Essays*. Cambridge, MA: Belknap Press of Harvard University Press, 1966.

Gourevitch, Peter. "The Second Image Reversed: The International Sources of Domestic Politics." *International Organization* 32, no. 4 (1978): 881–912.

Governo de Cabo Verde. "Programa Do Governo. IX Legislatura." Governo de Cabo Verde, 2016.

Grillo, R. D. *Dominant Languages: Language and Hierarchy in Britain and France.* Cambridge: Cambridge University Press, 2009.

Grupo para a Padronização do Alfabeto. *Proposta de Bases do Alfabeto Unificado para a Escrita do Cabo-Verdiano.* Praia: Instituto da Investigação e do Património Culturais (IIPC), 2006.

Grupo Parlamentar do Partido Africano da Independência de Cabo Verde. "Projecto de Lei de Revisão Constitucional." n.d. http://www.parlamento.cv/downloads /projectos%20de%20revisao%20consticioanal/Projectos%20dos%20Deputados %20do%20PAICV.pdf.

Guimarães, José Marques. *A Difusão Do Nativismo Em África Cabo Verde e Angola Séculos XIX e XX.* Lisbon: África Debate, 2006.

Habermas, Jürgen, and Thomas McCarthy. *The Theory of Communicative Action.* Cambridge: Polity, 2007.

Halter, Marilyn. "Cape Verdeans in the U.S." In *Transnational Archipelago: Perspectives on Cape Verdean Migration and Diaspora,* edited by Luís Batalha and Jørgen Carling, 35–46. Amsterdam: Amsterdam University Press, 2008.

Hamilton, Russell. "Cape Verdean Poetry and the PAIGC." In *Critical Perspectives on Lusophone African Literature,* edited by Donald Burness, 143–57. Washington, DC: Three Continents, 1981.

Hammond, R. J. *Portugal and Africa: A Study in Uneconomic Imperialism 1815–1910.* Stanford, CA: Stanford University Press, 1996.

Harris, Cheryl I. "Whiteness as Property." *Harvard Law Review* 106, no. 8 (1993): 1707–91.

Haugen, Einar. *Language Conflict and Language Planning: The Case of Modern Norwegian.* Cambridge, MA: Harvard University Press, 1966.

———. *The Ecology of Language.* Stanford, CA: Stanford University Press, 1972.

———. "The Implementation of Corpus Planning: Theory and Practice." In *Progress in Language Planning: International Perspectives,* edited by J. Cobarrubias and J. A. Fishman, 269–89. Berlin: Mouton, 1983.

Hay, Colin. "Constructivist Institutionalism." In *The Oxford Handbook of Political Institutions,* edited by R. A. W. Rhodes, Sarah A. Binder, and Bert A. Rockman, 56–74. Oxford: Oxford University Press, 2006.

Hebblethwaite, Benjamin. "French and Underdevelopment, Haitian Creole and Development: Educational Language Policy Problems and Solutions in Haiti." *Journal of Pidgin and Creole Languages* 27, no. 2 (August 28, 2012): 255–302. https://doi.org/10.1075/jpcl.27.2.03heb.

Hirschman, Albert O. *Exit, Voice, and Loyalty: Responses to Decline in Firms, Organizations, and States.* Cambridge, MA: Harvard University Press, 2007.

Hobsbawm, Eric J. *Nations and Nationalism Since 1780: Pogramme, Myth, Reality.* Cambridge: Cambridge University Press, 2012.

Holm, John A. *An Introduction to Pidgins and Creoles*. Cambridge: Cambridge University Press, 2000.

Hooper, Michael, and Leonard Ortolano. "Motivations for Slum Dweller Social Movement Participation in Urban Africa: A Study of Mobilization in Kurasini, Dar Es Salaam." *Environment and Urbanization* 24, no. 1 (2012): 99–114.

Hopffer Almada, Jose. "O Bilinguismo Oficial Caboverdiano – Bilinguismo, Diglossia e Problemáticas Relativas Às Políticas de (Co)Oficialização Da Língua Caboverdiana." *Santiago Magazine*, March 27, 2019. https://santiagomagazine.cv/cultura/o-bilinguismo-oficial-caboverdiano-bilinguismo-diglossia-e-problematicas-relativas-as-politicas-de-cooficializacao-da-lingua-caboverdiana.

Humphreys, Macartan, William A. Masters, and Martin E. Sandbu. "The Role of Leaders in Democratic Deliberations: Results from a Field Experiment in São Tomé and Príncipe." *World Politics* 58 (2006): 583.

Huntington, Samuel P. *The Third Wave: Democratization in the Late Twentieth Century*. Norman, OK: University of Oklahoma Press, 1993.

———. *Who Are We?: The Challenges to America's National Identity*. New York: Simon & Schuster, 2005.

Hupe, Peter L., Michael Hill, and Aurélien Buffat, eds. *Understanding Street-Level Bureaucracy*. Bristol: Policy Press, 2015. http://site.ebrary.com/id/11084104.

IILP. "CABO VERDE: PORTUGUÊS PASSA A SER ENSINADO COMO LÍNGUA ESTRANGEIRA." *IILP* (blog), December 8, 2016. https://iilp.wordpress.com/2016/12/08/cabo-verde-portugues-passa-a-ser-ensinado-como-lingua-estrangeira/.

———. "Por Uma Educação Bilíngue Competente." February 27, 2017. https://iilp.wordpress.com/2017/02/27/por-uma-educacao-bilingue-competente/.

IPC. "Conselho de Ministros Aprova Elevação Da Língua Cabo-Verdiana e Da Tabanca a Património Cultural e Imaterial." July 29, 2019. https://www.facebook.com/patrimoniocultural.caboverde/posts/pfbid02BuKPpPNtqnKcSVDzpJAiNqaXsqsVUDBtsFein15E1FkE45B6XJKtpR1jLJN4ZgH4l.

Ives, Peter. *Language and Hegemony in Gramsci*. London: Pluto Press, 2004.

James, Carl. *Errors in Language Learning and Use*. London: Routledge, 2014.

Jernudd, Bjorn, and Jyotirindra Das Gupta. "Towards a Theory of Language Planning." In *Can Language Be Planned?: Sociolinguistic Theory and Practice for Developing Nations*, edited by Joan Rubin and Björn H. Jernudd, 185–204. Honolulu: University Press of Hawaii, 1971.

Johnson, David Cassels. *Language Policy*. Basingstoke: Palgrave Macmillan, 2013.

Johnson, Sally A. *Spelling Trouble?: Language, Ideology and the Reform of German Orthography*. Clevedon: Multilingual Matters, 2005.

Jones, Elin Haf Gruffydd, and Enrique Uribe-Jongbloed, eds. *Social Media and Minority Languages: Convergence and the Creative Industries*. Multilingual Matters (Series). Bristol: Multilingual Matters, 2013.

Jourdan, C. "Pidgins and Creoles: The Blurring of Categories." *Annual Review of Anthropology* 20 (1991): 187–209.

Kachru, Braj. "Standards, Codification and Sociolinguistic Realism: English Language in the Outer Circle." In *English in the World: Teaching and Learning the*

Language AndLliteratures, edited by R. Quirk and H. Widowson, 11–36. Cambridge: Cambridge University Press, 1985.

Kalu, Kenneth. "State-Society Relations, Institutional Transformation and Economic Development in Sub-Saharan Africa." *DPR Development Policy Review* 35 (2017): O234–45.

Kamwangamalu, Nkonko. *Language Policy and Economics: The Language Question in Africa*. London: Palgrave Macmillan, 2016. https://doi.org/10.1057/978-1-137-31623-3.

Kapur, Devesh. "Ideas and Economic Reforms in India: The Role of International Migration and the Indian Diaspora." *India Review* 3, no. 4 (2004): 364–84.

Katz, Richard S., and Peter Mair. "Changing Models of Party Organization and Party Democracy: The Emergence of the Cartel Party." *Party Politics* 1, no. 1 (1995): 5–28.

Kemp, R. "Planning, Public Hearings, and the Politics of Discourse." In *Critical Theory and Public Life*, edited by John Forester, 177–201. Cambridge, MA: MIT Press, 1985.

King, Charles, and Neil Melvin. "Diaspora Politics: Ethnic Linkages, Foreign Policy, and Security in Eurasia." *International Security* 243 (1999): 108–38.

Klopp, Jacqueline M., and Jeffrey W Paller. "Slum Politics in Africa." In *Oxford Research Encyclopedia. Politics*, edited by William R. Thompson. Oxford: Oxford University Press, 2020. https://doi.org/10.1093/acrefore/9780190228637.013.985.

Kouwenberg, Silvia, Winnie Anderson-Brown, Terri-Ann Barrett, Shyrel-Ann Dean, Tamirand De Lisser, Havenol Douglas, Marsha Forbes, et al. "Linguistics in the Caribbean: Empowerment through Creole Language Awareness." *Journal of Pidgin and Creole Languages* 26, no. 2 (August 16, 2011): 387–403. https://doi.org/10.1075/jpcl.26.2.06kou.

Kroskrity, Paul V. "Regimenting Languages: Language Ideological Perspectives." In *Regimes of Language: Ideologies, Polities, and Identity*, edited by Paul V. Kroskrity, 1–34. Sante Fe, New Mexico: School of American Research Press, 2000.

Kymlicka, Will. *Politics in the Vernacular: Nationalism, Multiculturalism and Citizenship*. Oxford: Oxford University Press, 2000.

Kymlicka, Will, and University of Oxford. *Politics in the Vernacular: Nationalism, Multiculturalism and Citizenship*. Oxford: Oxford University Press, 2001.

Laban, Michel. *Angola: encontro com escritores*. Porto, Portugal: Fundação Eng. António de Almeida, 1991.

———. *Cabo Verde: encontro com escritores*. Porto, Portugal: Fundação Eng. António de Almeida, 1992.

———. *Moçambique: encontro com escritores*. Porto, Portugal: Fundação Eng. António de Almeida, 1998.

Laguerre, Michel S. *Diaspora, Politics, and Globalization*. New York: Palgrave Macmillan, 2006.

———. *Parliament and Diaspora in Europe*. New York: Palgrave Macmillan, 2015.

Laitin, David D. *Language Repertoires and State Construction in Africa*. Cambridge: Cambridge University Press, 2006.

————. *Politics, Language, and Thought: The Somali Experience.* Chicago: University of Chicago Press, 1977.

Landman, Todd. *Issues and Methods in Comparative Politics: An Introduction.* London: Routledge, 2003.

Landry, Rodrigue, and Richard Y. Bourhis. "Linguistic Landscape and Ethnolinguistic Vitality: An Empirical Study." *Journal of Language and Social Psychology* 16, no. 1 (1997): 23–49.

Leftwich, Adrian. "Governance, Democracy and Development in the Third World." *Third World Quarterly* 14 (1993): 605–24.

Leitão da Graça, José André. *Golpe de estado em Portugal ... : traída a descolonização de Cabo Verde!* Praia: José André Leitão da Graça, 2004.

Leite, David. "ALUPEC, Um Alfabeto Nos Ku Nos. E Os Nossos Emigrantes?" *A Semana*, September 19, 2009. https://www.asemana.publ.cv/spip.php?page=article&id_article=45529&ak=1#ancre_comm.

————. "Tubarões Azuis, a Diáspora e a Caboverdeanidade." *A Semana*, November 2, 2013. http://asemana.publ.cv/spip.php?article93309&ak=1.

Leonard, Yves. "As Ligações a África e Ao Brasil." In *História Da Expansão Portuguesa*, edited by Francisco Bethencourt and Kirty Chaudhiri, V:421–41. Lisbon: Círculo de Leitores, 1998.

Levitt, Peggy. "Social Remittances: Migration Driven, Local-Level Forms of Cultural Diffusion." *The International Migration Review : IMR* 32, no. 4 (1998): 926.

Levitt, Peggy, and Deepak Lamba-Nieves. "Social Remittances Revisited." *Journal of Ethnic and Migration Studies* 37, no. 1 (2011): 1–22.

Lima, Adriano Miranda. "Diálogo Sobre a Questão Da 'Língua Cabo-Verdiana': II Parte." *Notícias Do Norte*, March 10, 2015. https://noticiasdonorte.publ.cv/31751/dialogo-sobre-a-questao-da-lingua-cabo-verdiana-ii-parte/.

Lima, Redy Wilson. "Diagnóstico Safende 2020." Praia, Cabo Verde: Associação Comunitária Amigos de Safende, August 2020.

Expresso. "Língua: Português Deve Ser Ensinado Em Cabo Verde Como Língua Estrangeira, Defende Germano de Almeida." (Portugal), March 27, 2010." March 27, 2010. http://expresso.sapo.pt/lingua-portugues-deve-ser-ensinado-em-cabo-verde-como-lingua-estrangeira-defende-germano-de-almeida=f573370.

Linz, Juan J., and Alfred C. Stepan. *Problems of Democratic Transition and Consolidation : Southern Europe, South America, and Post-Communist Europe.* Baltimore: Johns Hopkins University Press, 1996.

Lipset, Seymour Martin. *Revolution and Counter-Revolution: The United States and Canada.* Comparative/International Series, Reprint No. 193. Berkely, CA: University of California, Insititute of International Studies, 1966.

Lobban, Richard. *Cape Verve: Crioulo Colony to Independent Nation.* Boulder, CO: Westview, 1995.

Lobo, Andréa de Souza. "Bambinos and Kassu Bodi: Comments on Linguistic Appropriations in Cape Verde Islands." In *Creolization and Pidginization in Contexts of Postcolonial Diversity: Language, Culture, Identity*, edited by Jacqueline Knörr and Wilson Trajano Filho, 272–87. Boston, MA: Brill, 2018.

Lodge, Tom. *South Africa: Democracy and Political Participation : A Discussion Paper*. Newlands, South Africa: Open Society Foundation for South Africa, 2006. http://www.afrimap.org/english/images/report/AfriMAP_SApolpart_discdoc.pdf.

Lopes, Amália Maria Vera-Cruz de Melo |. "Língua Cabo-Verdiana: Desconstruindo Mitos-Mito 12/12." *Santiago Magazine*, September 24, 2020. https://santiagomagazine.cv/cultura/lingua-cabo-verdiana-desconstruindo-mitos-mito-1212.

Lopes da Silva, Baltasar. *Cabo Verde visto por Gilberto Freyre: Apontamentos lidos aoMicrofone de Rádio Barlavento*. Praia: Impremsa Nacional, 1956.

———. *Chiquinho: romance*. Lisboa: Livros Cotovia, Lda., 2008.

———. *O Dialecto Crioulo de Cabo Verde*. Lisboa: Junta de investigações do Ultramar, 1957.

———. "'As Ilhas Adjacentes de Cabo Verde.'" *Notícias de Cabo Verde*, 1931.

Lührmann, Anna, and Staffan I. Lindberg. "A Third Wave of Autocratization Is Here: What Is New about It?" *Democratization* 26, no. 7 (October 3, 2019): 1095–113. https://doi.org/10.1080/13510347.2019.1582029.

Lumsdaine, David. "The Intertwining of International and Domestic Politics." *Polity* 29, no. 2 (1996): 293–98.

Macedo, Donaldo. "A Língua Caboverdiana Na Educação Bilingue." In *Issues in Portuguese Bilingual Education*, edited by Donaldo Macedo, 183–200. Cambridge, MA: National Assessment and Dissemination Center for Bilingual/Bicultural Education, 1980.

Macedo, Donaldo P. "A Linguistic Approach to the Capeverdean Language." PhD Thesis, Boston University, 1979.

———. "Cape Verdean Language Project: Final Report." Washington, DC: Department of Education, 1985.

Majumdar, Margaret A. "'Une Francophonie à l'offensive'? Recent Developments in Francophonie." *Modern & Contemporary France* 20 (2012): 1–20.

Mallinson, Christine. "Language and Its Everyday Revolutionary Potential: Feminist Linguistic Activism in the U.S." In *The Oxford Handbook of U.S. Women's Social Movement Activism*, edited by Holly J. McCammon, Jo Reger, Rachel L. Einwohner, and Verta Taylor, 419–39. Oxford: Oxford University Press, 2017.

Mamdani, Mahmood. *Citizen and Subject: Contemporary Africa and the Legacy of late Colonialism*. Princeton: University Press, 2003.

Marshall, Judith. *Literacy, Power and Democracy in Mozambique: The Governance of Learning from Colonization to the Present*. New York: Routledge, 2018.

Martins, Moisés de Lemos. "A Lusofonia Como Promessa e o Seu Equivoco Lusocentrico." In *Comunicação e Lusofonia. Para Uma Abordagem Crítica Da Cultura e Dos Media*, edited by Moisés de Lemos Martins, Helena Sousa, and Rosa Cabecinhas, 79–90. Porto: Campo das Letras, 2006.

Martins, Moisés de Lemos, Helena Sousa, and Rosa Cabecinhas, eds. *Comunicação e Lusofonia: Para uma Abordagem Crítica da Cultura e dos Media*. 2a edição. Ribeirão: Húmus, 2018.

Mass.Gov. "Informason Sobri COVID-19 (COVID-19 Information in Cape Verdean Creole)." Accessed August 16, 2022. https://www.mass.gov/info-details/informason-sobri-covid-19-covid-19-information-in-cape-verdean-creole.

Mazrui, Alamin M. *English in Africa: After the Cold War.* Clevedon; Toronto: Multilingual Matters, 2004.

Mazrui, Ali A. "The Afro-Saxons." *Society* 12, no. 2 (February 1975): 14–21.

———. *The Political Sociology of the English Language: An African Perspective.* The Hague: Mouton, 1975.

Mazrui, Ali Al'Amin, and Alamin M Mazrui. *The Power of Babel: Language & Governance in the African Experience.* Oxford: Currey, 1998.

Mazrui, Ali Al'Amin, and Michael Tidy. *Nationalism and New States in Africa from About 1935 to the Present.* Nairobi: Heinemann, 1985.

Meintel, Deirdre. "Cape Verdean Transnationalism, Old and New." *Anthropologica* 44, no. 1 (2002): 25.

Melo, Victor Andrade de, and Rafael Fortes. "Identidade Em Transição: Cabo Verde e a Taça Amílcar Cabral." *Afro-Ásia*, no. 50 (December 2014): 11–44. https://doi.org/10.1590/0002-05912014v50vic11.

"Memorando de Entendimento Entre o MPD e o PAICV Sobre Matérias. Essenciais Para a Segunda Revisão Ordinária Da Constituição." In *As Constituições de Cabo Verde e Textos Históricos de Direito Constitucional Cabo-Verdiano*, edited by Mário Ramos Pereira Silva, 497–502. Praia: Edições ISCJS, 2014.

Mesquita, Bruce Bueno de. "Domestic Politics and International Relations." *International Studies Quarterly* 46 (2002): 1–9.

Meyns, Peter. "Cape Verde: An African Exception." *Journal of Democracy* 13, no. 3 (2002): 153–65.

Migdal, Joel Samuel. *Strong Societies and Weak States: State Society Relations and State Capabilities in the Third World.* Princeton: Princeton University Press, 1988.

Migge, Bettina, and Isabelle Léglise. "Language and Colonialism. Applied Linguistics in the Context of Creole Communities." In *Language and Communication : Diversity and Change. Handbook of Applied Linguistics*, edited by Marlis Hellinger and Anne Pauwels, 297–338. Berlin: Mouton de Gruyter, 2007.

Milbrath, Lester W., and Maden Lal Goel. *Political Participation: How and Why Do People Get Involved in Politics?* Lanham, MD: University Press of America, 1982.

Miller, Robert L. *The Linguistic Relativity Principles and Humboldtian Ethnolinguistics: A Historical and Appraisal.* The Hague: Mouton, 1968.

Milner, Helen V. *Interests, Institutions, and Information : Domestic Politics and International Relations.* Princeton, NJ: Princeton University Press, 1997.

Monteiro, Arcádio. "De Perguntas a Respostas. Um Terceiro Atingido No 'Directo' Benoni/Veiga." *Voz Di Povo*, September 10, 1986.

Monteiro, Felix. "A Margem de Uma Agenda." *Cabo Verde: Boletim Documental e de Cultura*, 3, no. 26 (1951): 5–7.

Mooney, Annabelle, and Betsy E. Evans. *Language, Society and Power: An Introduction.* London: Routledge, 2019.

Moreira, Adriano. *O Novíssimo Príncipe: Análise da Revolução.* Braga: Intervenção, 1977.

Morgenthau, Ruth S. *Political Parties in French-speaking West Africa.* Oxford: Clarendon Press, 1967.

MpD. "Manifesto Eleitoral MpD São Vicente." 2011. https://issuu.com/antaochantre /docs/menisfestoeleitoralmpd.

Murdoch, Zuzana, Magali Gravier, and Stefan Gänzle. "International Public Administration on the Tip of the Tongue: Language as a Feature of Representative Bureaucracy in the Economic Community of West African States." *International Review of Administrative Sciences* (2021): 1–19. https://doi.org/10.1177 /0020852320986230.

Murphy, Craig N. "Cape Verde." In *The Political Economy of Foreign Policy in ECOWAS*, edited by Timothy M. Shaw and Julius Emeka Okolo, 17–31. London: St Martin Press, 1994.

Muysken, Pieter, and Norval Smith. "The Study of Pidgin and Creole Languages." In *Pidgins and Creoles: An Introduction*, Jacques Arends, Pieter Muysken, and Norval Smith, 3–14. Amsterdam/Philadelphia: John Benjamins Pub. Co, 1994.

Myers-Scotton, Carol. "Elite Closure as a Powerful Language Strategy: The African Case." *International Journal of the Sociology of Language* 103, no. 1 (1993): 149–64.

Nelson, Joan M., and Samuel P. Huntington. *No Easy Choice: Political Participation in Developing Countries.* Cambridge, MA: Harvard University Press, 1976.

Nkrumah, Kwame. *Neo-Colonialism: The Last Stage of Imperialism.* London: Panaf, 1970.

Notícias do Norte. "Os Recados de Onésimo Silveira Para Mário Lúcio e JMN." April 30, 2014. https://noticiasdonorte.publ.cv/990/os-recados-de-onesimo-silveira-para -mario-lucio-e-jmn/.

Nye, Joseph S. "Soft Power." *Foreign Policy* 80 (Fall 1990): 153–71.

———. "Soft Power: The Evolution of a Concept." *Journal of Political Power* 14 (2021): 196–208.

Nylen, William R. *Participatory Democracy versus Elitist Democracy: Lessons from Brazil.* 1st ed. New York: Palgrave Macmillan, 2003. http://site.ebrary.com/id /10135680.

"O Impacto Social e Económica Da Pesca." *Converça Em Dia.* Praia, Cabo Verde: Televisão de Cabo Verde, October 13, 2011. http://www.rtc.cv/index.php?paginas =47&id_cod=12881&nome_programa=Conversa%20em%20Dia&data=2011-10 -13&codigo=ced.

"'O Problema Do Bilinguismo'. Nota Oficiosa Do Ministério Da Educação e Cultura." *Voz de Povo.* November 5, 1977.

O'Donnell, Guillermo A. "Delegative Democracy." *Journal of Democracy* 5, no. 1 (1994): 55–69.

O'Donnell, Guillermo A., and Philippe C. Schmitter. *Transitions from Authoritarian Rule. Tentative Conclusions about Uncertain Democracies.* Baltimore: Johns Hopkins University Press, 2013.

Oliveira, Gilvan Müller de. "O Instituto Internacional Da Língua Portuguesa e a Gestão Multilateral Da Língua Portuguesa No Âmbito Da CPLP." *Revista Internacional de Lingüística Iberoamericana* 13 (2015): 19–34.

Onda Kriolu. "Conjunto 'Os Tubarões' Recorri a Empréstimo Bancário Pa Salva Totinho Di Bai Cadeia." Facebook Post, January 16, 2016. https://www.facebook

.com/onda.kriolu/photos/conjunto-os-tubar%C3%B5es-recorri-a-empr%C3 %A9stimo-banc%C3%A1rio-pa-salva-totinho-di-bai-cadei/1147313268614046/.

"Ondina Ferreira Diz Que Língua Portuguesa Tem Sido Votada Ao Desprezo Na Sua Oralidade e No Seu Uso Quotidiano Em Cabo Verde." Inforpress, May 9, 2019. https://inforpress.cv/ondinaferreira-diz-que-lingua-portuguesa-tem-sido-votada-ao -desprezo-na-sua-oralidade-e-no-seu-uso-quotidiano-em-cabo-verde/.

Paffey, Darren. "Policing the Spanish Language Debate: Verbal Hygiene and the Spanish Language Academy (Real Academia Española)." *Language Policy* 6, nos. 3–4 (2007): 313–32.

"PAICV Quer Oficialização Já, Do Crioulo." *A Semana*. July 9, 1999.

Partido Africano da Independência de Cabo Verde. *III Congresso, 25–30 de Novembro de 1988: Resoluções, Moções, Discurso de Encerramento Do Secretário Geral*. Praia: O Partido, 1988.

Pateman, Carole. *Participation and Democratic Theory*. Cambridge: Cambridge University Press, 2014.

Paul, David M., and Rachel Anderson Paul. *Ethnic Lobbies and US Foreign Policy*. Boulder, CO: Lynne Rienner Publishers, 2009.

Paul Stacey. *State of Slum: Precarity and Informal Governance at the Margins in Accra*. London: Zed Book, 2019.

Pauwels, Anne. "Linguistic Sexism and Feminist Linguistic Activism." In *The Handbook of Language and Gender*, edited by Janet Holmes and Miriam Meyerhoff, 550–70. Malden, MA: Blackwell Pub., 2003. https://doi.org/10.1002 /9780470756942.ch24.

Péclard, Didier. "Savoir Colonial, Missions, Chrétiennes et Nationalisme En Angola." *Genèses* 4, no. 45 (2001): 114–33.

Pennycook, Alastair. "Language, Ideology and Hindsight: Lessons from Colonial Language Policies." In *Ideology, Politics, and Language Policies: Focus on English*, edited by Thomas Ricento, 49–66. Amsterdam: John Benjamins Pub., 2000.

Pereira, Dulce. "Aprender a Ser Bilingue." In *Múltiplos Olhares Sobre o Bilinguismo: Transversalidades II*, edited by Cristina Flores, 15–43. Húmus: Universidade do Minho, 2011.

Pereira, Eduardo Adilson Camilo. *Política e Cultura: As Revoltas, Engenhos (1822), Achada Falcão (1841), Ribeirão Manuel (1910)*. Praia: Imprensa Nacional de Cabo Verde, 2015.

Phillipson, Robert. *Linguistic Imperialism*. Oxford: Oxford University Press, 2012.

Piétri, Claudia. "Les Trois Espaces Linguistiques: Quel Parcours et Quelles Synergies Développer ?" *Hermès* 75, no. 2 (2016): 147–53. https://doi.org/10.3917/herm.075 .0147.

Pina, Arsénio Fermino de, José Fortes Lopes, and Adriano Miranda Lima. *Na Encruzilhada da Regionalização: Rumo à Descentralização*. Mindelo: Movimento para a Regionalização de Cabo Verde, Grupo de Reflexão da Diáspora, 2017.

Pinto, Antonio Costa. *Salazar's Dictatorship and European Fascism: The Problems of Interpretation*. Boulder, CO: Columbia University Press, 1995.

Pinto, José Filipe. *Estratégias da ou para a Lusofonia?: o futuro da língua portuguesa*. Lisboa: Prefácio, 2009.

Pires, Virgilio. "'O "Crioulo Reinventado."'" *Novo Jornal Cabo Verde*, September 5, 1974.

Plain Writing Act, Law 111-274 (2010). http://www.gpo.gov/fdsys/pkg/PLAW-111publ274/pdf/PLAW-111publ274.pdf.

Przeworski, Adam. *Democracy and Development: Political Institutions and Well-Being in the World, 1950–1990.* Cambridge Studies in the Theory of Democracy. Cambridge: Cambridge University Press, 2000.

Quint, Nicolas. "Les Apontamentos de António de Paula Brito (1887) ou laNaissance d'une Tradition Grammaticale Capverdienne Autochtone." *Histoire Épistémologie Langage* 30, no. 1 (2008): 127–53.

———. "O Cabo-Verdiano: Uma Língua Mundial." *Revista de Estudos Cabo-Verdianos* 3 (2009): 129–44.

Raimundo, Mariano Verdeano. "O Crioulo e o Português No Futuro de Cabo Verde." *Voz de Povo*, June 26, 1976.

Rego, Márcia. *The Dialogic Nation of Cape Verde: Slavery, Language, and Ideology.* Lanham, MD: Lexington Books, 2015. http://site.ebrary.com/id/11047976.

Resende-Santos, João. "Cape Verde and Its Diaspora: Economic Transnationalism and Homeland Development." *Journal of Cape Verdean Studies* 2, no. 1 (2015): 69–107.

Ricento, Thomas. "Ideology, Politics and Language Policies: Introduction." In *Ideology, Politics and Language Policies: Focus on English*, edited by Thomas Ricento, 1–8. Amsterdam: Benjamin, 2000.

Romano, Luis. "Luta de Nôs Letrad." *Voz de Povo*, May 3, 1976.

Ronneberg, Espen. "Small Islands and the Big Issue: Climate Change and the Role of the Alliance of Small Island States." In *The Oxford Handbook of International Climate Change Law*, edited by Kevin R. Gray, Richard Tarasofsky, and Cinnamon P. Carlarne, 761–77. Oxford: Oxford University Press, 2016.

Rouvez, Alain, Michael Coco, and Jean-Paul Paddack. *Disconsolate Empires: French, British, and Belgian Military Involvement in Post-Colonial Sub-Saharan Africa.* Lanham, MD: University Press of America, 1994.

Rubdy, Rani. "Conflict, Exclusion and Dissent in the Linguistic Landscape." In *Conflict and Exclusion: The Linguistic Landscape as an Arena of Contestation*, edited by Rani Rubdy and Selim Ben Said, 1–24. London: Palgrave Macmillan, 2015.

Rudebeck, Lars. *Guinea-Bissau: A Study of Political Mobilization.* Uppsala: Scandinavian Institute of African Studies, 1974.

Ruiz, Richard. "Orientations in Language Planning." *NABE: The Journal for the National Association for Bilingual Education* 8, no. 2 (1984): 15–34.

Safran, William. "Nationalism." In *Handbook of Language and Ethnic Identity*, edited by Joshua A. Fishman, 77–93. New York: Oxford University Press, 1999.

Samarin, William J. "The Linguistic World of Field Colonialism." *Language in Society* 13, no. 4 (1984): 435–53.

Sanches, Edalina Rodrigues. "The Community of Portuguese Language Speaking Countries: The Role of Language in a Globalizing World." *CIDOB*, n.d.

Sanches, Rui. "Falando Português Ou Brutuguês?", YouTube. Online Video Clip, (a—." Video. *YouTube.* Accessed November 21, 2012. http://www.youtube.com/watch?v=YX8bqYplfjM.

Santos, Horácio. "Kiriolu?...Purtugues?...Kal d'es Dos?" *Voz Di Povo*, May 28, 1986, 9.

Santos, Theotonio Dos. "The Structure of Dependence." *The American Economic Review* 60 (May 1970): 231–36.

Sartori, Giovanni. "Concept Misformation in Comparative Politics." *The American Political Science Review* 64, no. 4 (n.d.): 1033–53.

———. *Parties and Party Systems*. Cambridge: Cambridge University Press, 1976.

Schieffelin, Bambi B., and Rachelle Charlier Doucet. "The 'Real' Haitian Creole: Ideology, Metalinguistics, and Orthographic Choice." *American Ethnologist* 21 (1994): 176–200.

Schmidt, Vivien A. "Discursive Institutionalism: The Explanatory Power of Ideas and Discourse." *Annual Review of Political Science* 11, no. 1 (2008): 303–26.

Schmitter, Philippe. "The 'Régime d'Exception' That Became the Rule: Forty-Eight Years of Authoritarian Domination in Portugal." In *Contemporary Portugal: The Revolution and Its Antecedents*, edited by Lawrence S. Graham and Harry M. Makler, 5–23. Austin: University of Texas Press, 1979.

Schumpteter, Joseph A., and Richard Swedberg. *Capitalism, Socialism and Democracy*. London: Routledge, 2005.

Scollon, Ronald, and Suzanne Wong Scollon. *Discourses in Place: Languages in the Material World*. London: Routledge, 2003.

Scott, James C. *Seeing like a State: How Certain Schemes to Improve the Human Condition Have Failed*. New Haven: Yale University Press, 2020.

"Sem Verbas Para Canil, CM de Santa Catarina de Santiago vê Como Única Solução Abater Cães Vadios." *Noticias*. RTC. Accessed November 21, 2012. http://rtc.cv/index.php?paginas=13&id_cod=16281.

Semedo, Manuel Brito. *A Construção da Identidade Nacional: Análise da Imprensa entre 1877 e 1975*. Praia: Instituto da Bibliotheca Nacional e do Livro, 2006.

Serapião, Luis B. "The Preaching of Portuguese Colonialism and the Protest of the White Fathers." *Issue: A Journal of Opinion* 2, no. 1 (1972): 34–41.

Shabaka, Lumumba Hamilcar. "Transformation of 'Old' Slavery into Atlantic Slavery: Cape Verde Islands, c. 1500–1879." PhD Thesis, Michigan State University, 2013.

Sheffer, Gabriel. *Diaspora Politics: At Home Abroad*. New York: Cambridge University Press, 2010.

———. *Modern Diasporas in International Politics*. London: Croom Helm, 1986.

Shohamy, Elana. *Language Policy: Hidden Agendas and New Approaches*. New York: Routledge, 2006.

Shohamy, Elana, and Durk Gorter. "Introduction." In *Linguistic Landscape: Expanding the Scenery*, edited by Elana Shohamy and Durk Gorter, 1–10. New York: Routledge, 2009.

Silverstein, Michael. "Language Structure and Linguistic Ideology." In *The Elements*, edited by P. Clyne, W. Hanks, and C. Hofbauer, 193–248. Chicago: Chicago Linguistic Society, 1979.

Skaaning, Svend-Erik. "Waves of Autocratization and Democratization: A Critical Note on Conceptualization and Measurement." *Democratization* 27, no. 8 (2020): 1533–42. https://doi.org/10.1080/13510347.2020.1799194.

Skutnabb-Kangas, T. "Multilingualism and the Education of Minority Children." In *Minority Education: From Shame to Struggle*, edited by T. Skutnabb-Kangas and J. Cummins, 9–44. Clevedon: Multilingual Matters, 1988.

Skutnabb-Kangas, Tove. "Human Rights and Language Wrongs: A Future for Diversity?" *Language Sciences* 20, no. 1 (1998): 5–27.

———. *Linguistic Genocide in Education, or, Worldwide Diversity and Human Rights?* New York: Routledge, 2000.

Skutnabb-Kangas, Tove, and Robert Phillipson. "Human Rights: Perspective on Language Ecology." In *Encyclopedia of Language and Education*, edited by Angela Creese, Peter Martin, and Nancy Hornberger, 3–14. New York: Springer, 2008.

———. "'Mother Tongue': The Theoretical and Sociopolitical Construction of a Concept." In *Status and Function of Languages and Language Varieties*, edited by Ulrich Ammon, 450–77. Berlin: de Gruyter, 1989.

Skutnabb-Kangas, Tove, Robert Phillipson, and Mart Rannut. "Introduction." In *Linguistic Human Rights: Overcoming Linguistic Discrimination*, edited by Ove Skutnabb-Kangas, Robert Phillipson, and Mart Rannut, 1–22. Berlin: Mouton de Gruyter, 1994.

Smith, Anthony David. *Nationalism and Modernism: A Critical Survey of Recent Theories of Nations and Nationalism*. London: Routledge, 2017.

———. *Theories of Nationalism*. New York: Holmes & Meier Publishers, 1983.

Spears, Arthur K. "Introduction: The Haitian Creole Language." In *The Haitian Creole Language: History, Structure, Use, and Education*, edited by Arthur K. Spears and Carole M. Berotte Joseph, 1–22. Lanham, MD: Lexington Books, 2010.

Spolsky, Bernard. *Language Policy*. Cambridge: Cambridge University Press, 2004.

———. *The Languages of Diaspora and Return*. Boston, MA: Brill, 2016.

Srebrnik, Henry. "Small Island Nations and Democratic Values." *World Development* 32, no. 2 (2004): 329–41.

Stacey, Paul, and Christian Lund. "In a State of Slum: Governance in an Informal Urban Settlement in Ghana." *Journal of Modern African Studies* 54, no. 4 (2016): 591–615.

Stepan, Alfred C. *The State and Society: Peru in Comparative Perspective*. Princeton: Princeton University Press, 2015.

Stroud, Christopher. "Portuguese as Ideology and Politics in Mozambique: Semiotic (Re)Constructions of Post Colony." In *Language Ideological Debates*, edited by J. Blommaaert, 343. Berlin: Mouton de Gruyter, 1999.

Suarez, Debra. "The Paradox of Linguistic Hegemony and the Maintenance of Spanish as a Heritage Language in the United States." *Journal of Multilingual and Multicultural Development* 23, no. 6 (December 2002): 512–30. https://doi.org/10.1080/01434630208666483.

Taylor-Leech, Kerry Jane. "Language Choice as an Index of Identity: Linguistic Landscape in Dili, Timor-Leste." *International Journal of Multilingualism* 9, no. 1 (2012): 15–34.

Thiong'o, Ngugi wa. *Decolonizing the Mind: The Politics of Language in Africa*. London: J. Currey, 1986.

Tollefson, James W. *Planning Language, Planning Inequality: Language Policy in the Community*. London: Longman, 1996.

Tollison, Robert D. "Rent Seeking." In *The Encyclopedia of Public Choice*, edited by C. K. Rowley and F. Schneider. Boston, MA: Springer, 2004. https://doi.org/10 .1007/978-0-306-47828-4_179.

Trask, Robert Lawrence. *The Key Concepts in Language and Linguistics*. London: Routledge, 2005.

Urbinati, Nadia, and Mark E. Warren. "The Concept of Representation in Contemporary Democratic Theory." *Annual Review of Political Science* 11, no. 1 (June 1, 2008): 387–412. https://doi.org/10.1146/annurev.polisci.11.053006.190533.

Uriarte, Miren, Nicole Lavan, Nicole Agusti, Mandira Kala, Faye Karp, Peter Nienchu Kiang, Lusa Lo, Rosann Tung, and Cassandra Villari. "English Learners in Boston Public Schools: Enrollment, Engagement and Academic Outcomes of Native Speakers of Cape Verdean Creole, Chinese Dialects, Haitian Creole, Spanish, and Vietnamese." Gastón Institute Publications. 130. Gastón Institute. UMass Boston, 2009. https://scholarworks.umb.edu/gaston_pubs/130.

Valdman, Albert. "Diglossia and Language Conflict in Haiti." *International Journal of the Sociology of Language* 1988, no. 71 (1988): 67–80.

———. "Language Standardization in a Diglossia Situation: Haiti." In *Language Problems of Developing Nations*, edited by Joshua A. Fishman, Charles A. Ferguson, and Jyotirindra Das Gupta, 313–26. New York: John Wiley and Sons, Inc., 1968.

Vallin, Victor-Manuel. "France as the Gendarme of Africa, 1960–2014: FRANCE AS THE GENDARME OF AFRICA." *Political Science Quarterly* 130, no. 1 (March 2015): 79–101. https://doi.org/10.1002/polq.12289.

Van den Berghe, Pierre Louis. "European Languages and Black Mandarins." *Transition: A Journal of the Arts, Culture and Society* 7, no. 34 (1968): 19–23.

Veiga, Manuel. "Ainda a Proposito Do Crioulo." *Voz Di Povo*, June 11, 1986.

———. "Introducao: O Primeiro Colóquio Linguístico, 21 Anos Depois." In *Primeiro Colóquio Linguístico Sobre o Crioulo de Cabo Verde*, edited by Manuel Veiga, 9–30. Praia: Instituto Nacional de Investigação Cultural, 2000.

———. "Kriolu: Dja Bu Grandi Dja." *A Semana*, May 14, 1999.

———. "O Diálogo de Surdos Não é Meu Estilo." *Voz Di Povo*, August 9, 1986.

———, ed. *Primeiro Colóquio Linguístico sobre o Crioulo de Cabo Verde*. Praia: Instituto Nacional de Investigação Cultural, 2000.

Veloutsou, Cleopatra, and Claire O'Donnell. "Exploring the Effectiveness of Taxis as an Advertising Medium." *International Journal of Advertising* 24, no. 2 (2005): 217.

Verba, Sidney, Henry E. Brady, and Kay Lehman Schlozman. "Beyond SES: A Resource Model of Political Participation." *American Political Science Review* 89, no. 2 (1995): 271–94.

———. *Voice and Equality: Civic Voluntarism in American Politics*. Cambridge, MA: Harvard University Press, 2002.

Verba, Sidney, and Norman H. Nie. *Participation in America: Political Democracy and Social Equality*. Chicago: The University of Chicago Press, 1991.

Vicente Lopes, José. *Cabo Verde: Os Bastidores da Independência*. Praia: Spleen, 2002.

Vieira, Artur. "A Questão Do 'Crioulo'—Uma Réplica de Artur Vieira." *Voz de Povo*, August 7, 1976.

Wallerstein, Immanuel Maurice. *World-Systems Analysis: An Introduction*. Durham: Duke University Press, 2004.

Waltz, Kenneth N. *Man, the State, and War: A Theoretical Analysis*. New York: Columbia University Press, 2010.

Webb, Vic. "Language Planning and Politics in South Africa." *International Journal of the Sociology of Language*, 1996, no. 118 (1996): 139–62.

Webb, Victor N. *Language in South Africa: The Role of Language in National Transformation, Reconstruction and Development*. Amsterdam: Benjamins, 2002.

Weber, Eugen Joseph. *Peasants into Frenchmen: The Modernization of Rural France, 1870–1914*. London: Chatto & Windus, 1979.

Weber, Max, Hans-Heinrich Gerth, and Charles Wright Mills. *From Max Weber: Essays in Sociology*. New York: Oxford University Press, 1972.

Weiner, Myron. "Political Participation: Crisis of the Political Process." In *Crises and Sequences in Political Development*, edited by Leonard Binder and Joseph LaPalombara, 159–204. Princeton, NJ: Princeton University Press, 1971.

Weinstein, Brian. *The Civic Tongue: Political Consequences of Language Choices*. New York: Longman, 1983.

Wilensky, Alfredo Héctor. *Trends in Portuguese Overseas Legislation for Africa*. Braga: Editora Pax, 1971.

Wiley, Terrence G. "Language Planning and Policy." In *Sociolinguistics and Language Teaching*, edited by S. L. McKay and N. H. Hornberger, 103–48. Cambridge: Cambridge University Press, 2000.

Wilson, James Q. *Bureaucracy: What Government Agencies Do and Why They Do It*. New York: Basic Books, 2000.

Woldemariam, Hirut, and Elizabeth Lanza. "Language Contact, Agency and Power in the Linguistic Landscape of Two Regional Capitals of Ethiopia." *International Journal of the Sociology of Language* 228 (2014): 79–103.

Woolard, Kathryn. "Introduction: Language Ideology as a Field of Inquiry." In *Language Ideologies: Practice and Theory*, edited by Bambi Schieffelin, Kathryn Woolard, and Paul Kroskrity, 3–50. New York: Oxford University Press, 1998.

Woolard, Kathryn A., and Bambi B. Schieffelin. "Language Ideology." *Annual Review of Anthropology* 23 (1994): 55–82.

World Bank. *Sub-Saharan Africa : From Crisis to Sustainable Growth: Along-Term Perspective Study | WorldCat.Org*. Washington, DC: World Bank, 1989.

Yang, Wenfen. "A Tentative Analysis of Errors in Language Learning and Use." *JLTR Journal of Language Teaching and Research* 1, no. 3 (2010): 266–68.

Zakaria, Fareed. *The Future of Freedom: Illiberal Democracy at Home and Abroad*. New York: W.W. Norton & Co., 2004.

Index

221

About the Author

Abel Djassi Amado is an assistant professor of Political Science and International Relations at Simmons University. He holds a Ph.D. in Political Science/African Studies from Boston University. Amado was the secretary of the board of the West African Research Association (WARA) and, from 2019 to 2022, presided over the board of the Lusophone African Studies Organization (LASO). Amado researches and has published articles and book chapters on the politics of language, the political history of national liberation in Africa, Amilcar Cabral's political biography, and Cabo Verde's foreign policy. His works have been published in *Lusotopie*, *Desafios*, *Journal of Cape Verdean Studies*, and *Portuguese Literary and Cultural Studies*.